Social Stress and the Family:
Advances and Developments in Family Stress Theory and Research

The *Marriage & Family Review* series:

- *Family Medicine: A New Approach to Health Care*, edited by Betty E. Cogswell and Marvin B. Sussman
- *Cults & the Family*, edited by Florence Kaslow and Marvin B. Sussman
- *Alternatives to Traditional Family Living*, edited by Harriet Gross and Marvin B. Sussman
- *Intermarriage in the United States*, edited by Gary A. Cretser and Joseph J. Leon
- *Family Systems and Inheritance Patterns*, edited by Judith N. Cates and Marvin B. Sussman
- *The Ties that Bind: Men's and Women's Social Networks*, edited by Laura Lein and Marvin B. Sussman
- *Social Stress and the Family: Advances and Developments in Family Stress Theory and Research*, edited by Hamilton I. McCubbin, Marvin B. Sussman, and Joan M. Patterson.

Social Stress and the Family:
Advances and Developments in Family Stress Theory and Research

Hamilton I. McCubbin, Marvin B. Sussman, and Joan M. Patterson
Editors

The Haworth Press
New York

Social Stress and the Family: Advances and Developments in Family Stress Theory and Research has also been published as *Marriage & Family Review*, Volume 6, Numbers 1/2, Spring/Summer 1983.

Copyright © 1983 by The Haworth Press, Inc. All rights reserved. Copies of articles in this publication may be reproduced noncommercially for the purpose of educational or scientific advancement. Otherwise, no part of this work may be reproduced or utilized in any form or by any means, electronic or mechanical, including photocopying, microfilm and recording, or by any information storage and retrieval system, without permission in writing from the publisher. Printed in the United States of America.

The Haworth Press, Inc., 28 East 22 Street, New York, NY 10010

Library of Congress Cataloging in Publication Data
Main entry under title:

Social stress and the family.

(Marriage & family review ; v. 6, no. 1/2)
Includes bibliographies.
1. Family—Addresses, essays, lectures. 2. Stress (Psychology)—Addresses, essays, lectures. I. McCubbin, Hamilton I. II. Sussman, Marvin B. III. Patterson, Joan M. IV. Series.
HQ734.S767   1983   306.8'5   83-190
ISBN 0-86656-163-3

Social Stress and the Family:
Advances and Developments in Family Stress Theory and Research

Marriage & Family Review
Volume 6, Numbers 1/2

CONTENTS

Acknowledgements	xi

Introduction
    Hamilton I. McCubbin
    Marvin B. Sussman
    Joan M. Patterson
	1

Chapter 1: The Family Stress Process: The Double ABCX Model of Adjustment and Adaptation
    Hamilton I. McCubbin
    Joan M. Patterson
	7

Chapter 2: Critical Transitions Over the Family Life Span: Theory and Research
    Helen Mederer
    Reuben Hill
	39

Chapter 3: Family Stress as Community Frame
    David Reiss
    Mary Ellen Oliveri
	61

Chapter 4: Family Problem Solving and Family Stress *David M. Klein*	85
Chapter 5: Individual Coping Efforts and Family Studies: Conceptual and Methodological Issues *Elizabeth G. Menaghan*	113

Chapter 6: Social Support and Family Stress 137
    Marc Pilisuk
    Susan Hillier Parks

Chapter 7: Contribution of Personality Research
   to an Understanding of Stress and Aging 157
    Paul T. Costa, Jr.
    Robert R. McCrae

Chapter 8: Family Divorce and Separation:
   Theory and Research 175
    Stephen W. White
    Kitty Mika

Chapter 9: Mundane Extreme Environmental Stress
   in Family Stress Theories: The Case of Black Families
   in White America 193
    Marie F. Peters
    Grace Massey

Chapter 10: Analytic Essay: Family Stress and Bereavement 219
    Kris Jeter

Chapter 11: Researching Family Stress 227
    Laura A. Shepard

EDITOR

MARVIN B. SUSSMAN, PhD, *Unidel Professor of Human Behavior, Department of Individual and Family Studies, College of Human Resources, University of Delaware, Newark, DE*

CO-EDITORS

HAMILTON I. McCUBBIN, *Professor and Chair, Department of Family Social Science, University of Minnesota, St. Paul, MN*
JOAN M. PATTERSON, *Research Associate, Department of Family Social Science, University of Minnesota, St. Paul, MN*

SPECIAL ISSUE ASSOCIATE EDITORS

CONSTANCE AHRONS
PAULINE G. BOSS
RONALD BURKE
A. ELIZABETH CAUBLE
WILLIAM DOHERTY
DAVID KLEIN
ANDREA S. LARSEN

HELEN MEDERER
RUDOLF MOOS
ROSALIE NOREM
SHARON PRICE-BONHAM
DAVID REISS
JOAN ROBERTSON
LYNDA HENLEY WALTERS

EDITORIAL BOARD

EDGAR F. BORGATTA, PhD, *University of Washington*
BETTYE M. CALDWELL, PhD, *University of Arkansas*
CATHERINE CHILMAN, PhD, *University of Wisconsin*
BETTY COGSWELL, PhD, *University of North Carolina, Chapel Hill*
ELYSE FLEMING, PhD, *Cleveland State University*
C. JACK FRIEDMAN, PhD, *Clinical Psychologist, Philadelphia*
EDITH GROTBERG, PhD, *Washington, DC*
TAMARA HAREVEN, PhD, *Clark University*
HOWARD HOFFMAN, MD, *Psychiatric Institute Foundation, Washington, DC*
JACQUELYNE J. JACKSON, PhD, *Howard University*
FLORENCE KASLOW, PhD, *Independent Practice, West Palm Beach, FL*
HOPE J. LEICHTER, PhD, *Teachers College, Columbia University*
HAROLD LIEF, MD, *University of Pennsylvania School of Medicine*
TERESA D. MARCIANO, PhD, *Fairleigh Dickinson University*
JOHN MOGEY, PhD, *Annapolis, MD*
KRISTIN ANDERSON MOORE, PhD, *The Urban Institute, Washington, DC*
E. T. PROTHRO, PhD, *American University of Beirut*
ROBERT N. RAPOPORT, PhD, *W. T. Grant Foundation, NY*
CLIFFORD J. SAGER, MD, *Jewish Family Service, New York, NY*
ROSE M. SOMERVILLE, PhD, *San Diego State University*
CAROL STACK, PhD, *Duke University*
FRED STRODBECK, PhD, *University of Chicago*

ANALYTIC ESSAY EDITOR

KRIS JETER, PhD

DEDICATION

To those special people who have encouraged us to pursue understanding of family strengths: Dr. Victor Howery, Dr. Eugene Craven, Dr. John Plag, Lt. General Maxwell Thurman, and Major General (Chaplain) Kermit Johnson.

Acknowledgements

Obviously, this anthology took a concerted effort on the part of numerous fine and devoted individuals who gave much of their time and of themselves to see that we prepared a valuable product. Specifically, we want to make special note of the wonderful contributions of our editor and friend, Catherine Davidson, who talked to all the authors, encouraged them, and made sure that we met our deadlines. Were it not for her kindness and gentle touch along with her editorial skills, this volume would not be in print.

Additionally we would like to thank Dean Keith McFarland, College of Home Economics, University of Minnesota, who offered us house and home to develop this publication. We thank Dr. Richard Sauer, Director, Agricultural Experiment Station, University of Minnesota, who saw the value of this work and provided us the funding to ensure its completion and success. Finally, we would like to acknowledge our fine staff at the University of Minnesota and the University of Delaware who contributed much to fine-tuning this integrated publication. We thank Susan Rains-Johnson, Jane Schwanke, and Gloria Lawrence, our secretaries, Kay Lapour, Lynne Shears, and Todd J. McCubbin, our research assistants; Kris Kahn, our artist-in-residence, and Emma Haugan, Dorothea Berggren, and Barbara Doughty of the Family Social Science Department.

Finally, we would like to thank the authors and scholars who gave much of themselves to share their thinking and perspectives so that others may benefit.

Hamilton I. McCubbin
Marvin B. Sussman
Joan M. Patterson

Introduction

Hamilton I. McCubbin
Marvin B. Sussman
Joan M. Patterson

Our major purpose in developing this volume evolved as we attempted to integrate and adapt various approaches to the systematic study of families faced with normative and non-normative family stressors and crises. As researchers, we were concerned that many of our colleagues were faced with the same dilemma, that is, attempting to conduct research, build theory and practice in a field that lacked integration and which appeared to be a hodgepodge of partial theories and perspectives on families under stress.

In organizing this anthology, we attempted to identify those critical arenas of family research and theory building which showed the most promise of promoting our knowledge of families under stress, of advancing efforts to integrate the psychological, social psychological, and sociological theories of stress and coping, and which would set the stage for future scientific inquiry in this domain. As we have become more familiar with the breadth of research in this area (McCubbin, Joy, Cauble, Comeau, Patterson & Needle, 1980), we have become increasingly cognizant of the most salient dimensions of family stress research which have in turn guided the development of this edited volume. We anticipate that these chapters will aid researchers, theoreticians, and practitioners in their efforts to develop more integrated and effective research strategies to understand families under stress.

Our review of the field has left us with some discomfort regarding the lack of recognition, on the conceptual and empirical levels, that stress can be productive in some instances. Researchers have tended to use a unidirectional, pathological model which implies that the recipient experiencing stress as a consequence of one or more stressors must adapt, reach a steady state, recover, or if not destroyed will function less than adequately afterwards. If this negative posture does not prevail or result from the approach of the

© 1983 by The Haworth Press, Inc. All rights reserved.

investigation to the stress issue, it remains that few workers can visualize stress in a more positive framework.

It can be postulated that creativity, effective communication in interpersonal relationships, motivation, and increased competence in brain, verbal and physical skills are outcomes of stress experience. There is neither time nor space to develop this thesis. The next development stage of theory and research should focus on the ways and conditions stress experience catalyzes and enhances the psychosocial, neurophysical development of family members.

The chapters in this volume present some of the emerging frameworks for the analysis and systematic study of families under stress: Family Adaptation, Family Critical Transitions, Family Paradigms, Family Problem-Solving, Social Support, and Coping.

The processes of family adjustment and adaptation are described in Chapter 1. Drawing from longitudinal observations on families faced with the chronically stressful condition of a husband/father missing and unaccounted for in military combat, McCubbin and Patterson describe the critical variables influencing family adjustment and adaptation and set forth the processes through which these variables interact during family efforts at resistance, restructuring and consolidation in the face of family demands and crisis. With research in progress on systematic measurement of these variables and processes (Olson, McCubbin, Barnes, Larsen, Muxen & Wilson, 1982; McCubbin & Patterson, 1981), we can anticipate additional refinements in concepts and propositions.

In Critical Transitions Over the Life Span (Chapter 2), Mederer and Hill shed light on what combination of circumstances precipitate a shift in families from one stage of structural equilibrium to the next. They explore two important questions: Why should families give up their scripted roles, rules, and procedures to regroup around a different allocation of roles and duties? How does the family transition occur and what are the phases of the transition process? This classic chapter sharpens our focus upon those important normative transitions over the life span, which are often overlooked in stress research, and sets the stage for future research on the processes of change over time.

Building upon their laboratory studies and theory construction efforts, Reiss and Oliveri (chapter 3) focus upon the family's definitional processes which shape family behavior. Not only do family definitional processes determine the magnitude of the experienced stress, but they also shape the nature of the family's coping response in recovering from the impact of that stress. The family's blueprint for responding to stress may be influenced by the community: "Our hypothesis is that all communities develop some consensus on events that happen within them and their potential impact on families."

Families respond to specific stressors and to associated hardships precipitated by these stressors. How families respond to these demands has been the subject of considerable research and theory building efforts. In Chapter 4, Klein summarizes two important lines of research, namely family problem solving and family stress, crisis, and coping. By examining the vocabularies, definitions, basic propositions, and the history of each of these arenas of theory building, Klein underscores the value of bridging both lines of research. Family problem solving is indeed an integral part of family stress studies but has not been given the attention it so richly deserves. This important chapter encourages and sets the stage for integrative research and theory building; "The hope expressed here is that the beginnings made in a relatively short period of time by problem solving scholars are not lost as work advances in the area of family stress-crisis-coping."

The central mechanism through which family stressors, demands, and strains are eliminated, managed, or adapted to appears to be coping. In Chapter 5, Menaghan examines the concept of coping and attempts to shed light upon its idiosyncracies and upon its complexity. By drawing from research on individual coping, Menaghan engages the reader in examining three sets of coping variables: resources, styles, and efforts. Through a careful and relatively thorough review of the salient research literature on coping, the author sets the stage for future research in noting: (a) the need for conceptual clarity and specific theoretical models, e.g., "should generalized coping strategies have a greater impact on specific coping efforts when the situation is ambiguous rather than clear?"; (b) the need to assess the interface between individual and family level coping; and (c) the need for improved research designs and analyses which would facilitate integrative theory building efforts.

The role of the community in shaping the course of family transitions, family definitions, family problem solving, and family adaptation takes on added importance in the social support propositions advanced by Pilisuk and Parks in Chapter 6. Two major hypotheses are advanced: First, the authors argue that individuals who are part of a socially supportive network of continuing interpersonal ties achieve a measure of protection or immunity from disorders. Second, while social support is an amorphous and multifaceted concept, it appears, nonetheless, to be the construct best able to bring order to a variety of studies showing the buffering effect against illness provided by marriage, church or organizational affiliation, community cohesiveness, or the presence of a confidant. We are challenged by this careful review and analysis of research on social support; we need to explore the nature of social support to the "family unit," the conditions under which various types of support are most effective and ineffective, and why.

In the final three chapters, attention is shifted from theory and methodology to the analysis of three important social and family stressors: aging, divorce and separation, and mundane stress in Black families. These chapters were commissioned to address some of the salient theoretical, methodological, and practice issues related to major social problems affecting family life in this decade. In Chapter 7, Costa and McCrae review the research on aging and family stress and discuss the implications of these studies for future investigations on these interrelated subjects. The importance of psychological variables of individual family members cannot be overstated:

> There is increasing recognition that stress cannot be understood without some consideration of the characteristics of the individuals under stress. Personality traits influence the stressful life events people encounter, the perception of them as stressful, the choice of coping mechanisms, and the outcomes of psychological distress and dissatisfaction.

These authors present a strong argument that personality disposition requires the attention of family stress scholars: "To the extent that studies of family stress remain studies of stress in family members, these facts make it necessary to control for individual differences in personality when interpreting data."

In Chapter 8 on family divorce and separation, White and Mika do more than draw our attention to the annual increase in the divorce rate and the rise in interest in the subject. They push the family scholar to identify and review the research approaches that have characterized recent investigations, to examine theoretical premises that provide the foundation for current research, and to advance the integration of theory and transitions in future research designs.

Specifically, the authors call attention to the paucity of research which attempts to measure and document the process of family adjustment:

> In order to assess the process of adjustment and how it relates to positive and negative outcomes, prospective research designs are necessary . . . . Our conceptualizations of adjustment may, therefore, have been limited by our research designs; progress may in turn, depend on the expansion of design parameters.

Theory to guide research on adjustment and consequences and family adaptation have been limited. However, the authors note that "theory, perhaps based on family stress and coping theory, may prove to be a viable bridge between generations of research into this common and seriously stressful event." Consistent with arguments in other chapters on family transitions, White and Mika underscore the importance of examining the total process of disruption to include the separation process among nontraditional families (e.g., unmarried cohabiting couples). Research on marital disruption is really research in family relationships and how they change.

In the final chapter on Black families, Peters and Massey point to the importance of understanding family behavior in response to stressful and oppressive social circumstances. Because of their cultural identity, Black families have had a negative status in American society, deterring their capability to provide for basic needs. The authors present a challenge to family scholars to evaluate the relevance and applicability of family stress theory to how these families define and respond to the stresses of everyday survival under such adverse circumstances. Blacks live in a mundane, extreme environment; that is, an environment where racism and subtle oppression are ubiquitous, constant, and continuing, as opposed to an occasional misfortune. They live in the reality of a devalued and depreciated status. Peters and Massey respond to their own challenge by building on existing family stress frameworks and noting the coping strategies Black families employ.

Bereavement, with its attendant grief, mourning, and often accompanied depression, is a process experienced by those who have lost a loved one by death. Such separation is a catalyst for adaptive and maladaptive stress responses. Kris Jeter, in Chapter 10, in an analytic essay, examines various bereavement conditions and situations and recommended procedures to deal with stress responses associated with the death of family members and intimates. She uses the writings of eight authors to relate family behavior to death, bereavement, and adaptation to stress.

Researching Family Stress, Chapter 11, provides the reader with the tools and sources all scholars require in order to research stress and families. It is intended to save the motivated investigator or interested person countless hours of precious time by directing the individual to the proper data source in the library with minimal expenditure of energy and funds.

It is our hope that the reader will gain an appreciation of the advances and developments in family stress theory and research, particularly in relationship to the stressors of aging, divorce and separation, and mundane stress. The reader will also note the existing gaps in both theory and methodology associated with our efforts to understand family behavior in response to stressful life events and family transitions. While we may have overlooked related and important theory building efforts and recent advances in measurement and research designs on family stress, coping, and social support, we can anticipate that this collection of readings will serve as a major set of references against which advances and progress can be measured. We hope that the readings can and will be used to guide future research and theory building efforts and will be viewed as reference points for family scholars, both novice and seasoned alike, in their search to understand and predict family behavior in response to the host of demands arising from stressful life events, normative transitions, and changing societal conditions confronting families across the life cycle.

REFERENCES

McCubbin, H. I., Joy, C., Cauble, A. E., Comeau, J. K., Patterson, J. M., & Needle, R. Family stress and coping: A decade review. *Journal of Marriage and the Family,* 1980, *42*(4), 855-870.

McCubbin, H. I., & Patterson, J. M. *Systematic assessment of family stress, resources and coping: Tools for research, education, and clinical intervention.* St. Paul, MN: Family Social Science, 1981.

Olson, D. H., McCubbin, H. I., Barnes, H., Larsen, A., Muxen, M., & Wilson, M. *Family Inventories.* St. Paul, MN: Family Social Science, 1982.

Chapter 1

The Family Stress Process: The Double ABCX Model of Adjustment and Adaptation

Hamilton I. McCubbin
Joan M. Patterson

In reviewing family stress research since the advent of Hill's AB-CX family crisis model (1949, 1958) and Burr's (1973) synthesis of family stress research (McCubbin, Joy, Cauble, Comeau, Patterson, & Needle, 1980; see Klein, Chapter 4), it would appear that family outcomes following the impact of a stressor and a crisis are the by-product of multiple factors in interaction with each other. This would suggest that one productive research and theory building strategy for studying family adaptation to normative and non-normative crises would be to employ a multivariate model where psychological, intra-familial, and social variables identified from prior family stress studies would be addressed simultaneously. By so doing, the individual and collective contributions of these variables could be ascertained. The central research questions for family stress investigations then become how much and what kinds of stressors; mediated by what personal, family, and community resources and by what family coping responses; and what family processes shape the course and ease of family adjustment and adaptation over time. This chapter addresses these issues by using longitudinal observations of families under stress to advance our understanding of the family stress process which includes the Dou-

---

Hamilton I. McCubbin is Professor and Head and Joan M. Patterson is a Research Associate, Department of Family Social Science, University of Minnesota, St. Paul.

This project was funded by a grant from the Agricultural Experiment Station. The authors would like to thank Dr. Richard Sauer, Director, Agricultural Experiment Station, for his support.

© 1983 by The Haworth Press, Inc. All rights reserved.

ble ABCX framework (McCubbin & Patterson, 1982; in press) and the family processes of adjustment and adaptation.

THE HILL ABCX MODEL REDEFINED

Family scholars have attempted to identify the variables which account for the observed differences among families in their positive adaptations to stressful situations. The earliest conceptual foundation for research to examine this variability has been the Hill (1949; 1958) ABCX family crisis model:

> A (the stressor event)—interacting with B (the family's crisis meeting resources)—interacting with C (the definition the family makes of the event)—produce X (the crisis).

Family Demands: Stressor and Hardships (a Factor)

In an effort to render clarity to the ABCX model and to establish a link to physiological (Selye, 1974) and psychological (Lazarus, 1966; Mikhail, 1981) concepts of stress, we define a *stressor* as a life event or transition impacting upon the family unit which produces, or has the potential of producing, change in the family social system. This change may be in various areas of family life such as its boundaries, goals, patterns of interaction, roles, or values. Family *hardships* are defined as those demands on the family unit specifically associated with the stressor event. An example of hardships would be the family's need to obtain more money or to rearrange family work and recreation plans to accommodate the increased medical expenses and the demand for home care of a handicapped member. Both the stressor and its hardships place demands on the family system which need to be managed.

Family Capabilities: Resistance Resources (b Factor)

The b factor, the family's resources for meeting the demands of a stressor and hardships, has been described as the family's ability to prevent an event of change in the family social system from creating a crisis or disruptiveness in the system (Burr, 1973). Resources, then, become part of the family's capabilities for resisting crisis. Angell (1936), one of the early theorists attempting to describe more specifically what constituted family resources, emphasized the value of family integration, that is, the thorough family life, of which common interests, affection, and a sense of economic inter-dependence are perhaps the most prominent; and family adaptability, that is, the family's capacity to meet obstacles and shift its course of action. Cavan and Ranck (1938) and Koos (1946) identified additional resources of family agreement about its role structure, subordination of personal ambitions to family goals, satisfactions within the family obtained because it is successfully meeting the physical and emotional needs of its members, and goals toward which the family is moving collectively. Hill (1958) summarized the b factor as "adequacy-inadequacy of family organization."

Family Definition: Focus on Stressor (c Factor)

The c factor in the ABCX Model is the definition the family makes of the seriousness of the experienced stressor. There are objective cultural definitions of the seriousness of life events and transitions which represent the collective judgment of the social system (see Reiss & Oliveri, Chapter 3), but the c factor is the family's subjective definition of the stressor and its hardships and how they are affected by them. This subjective meaning reflects the family's values and their previous experience in dealing with change and meeting crises. A family's outlook can vary from seeing life changes and transitions as challenges to be met to interpreting a stressor as uncontrollable and a prelude to the family's demise.

Family Tension: Stress and Distress

Stressor events and related hardships produce tension in the family which needs to be managed (Antonovsky, 1979). When this tension is not overcome, stress emerges. Family stress (as distinct from stressor) is defined as a state which arises from an actual or perceived demand-capability imbalance in the family's functioning and which is characterized by a multidimensional demand for adjustment or adaptive behavior. Stress, then, is not stereotypic, but rather varies depending upon the nature of the situation, the characteristics of the family unit, and the psychological and physical well-being of its members. Concomitantly, family distress is defined as an unpleasant or disorganized state which arises from an actual or perceived imbalance in family functioning and which is also characterized by a multidimensional demand for adjustment or adaptive behavior. In other words, stress becomes distress when it is subjectively defined as unpleasant or undesirable by the family unit.

Family Crisis: Demand for Change (x Factor)

These factors taken together: (a) the stressor event and hardships; (b) the family's resources for dealing with stressors and transitions; (c) the definition the family makes of this situation; and (d) the resulting stress or distress, all influence the family's resistance, that is, its ability to prevent the stressor event or transition from creating a crisis. Crisis (the x factor) has been conceptualized as a continuous variable denoting the amount of disruptiveness, disorganization, or incapacitatedness in the family social system (Burr, 1973). As distinct from stress, which is a demand-capability imbalance, crisis is characterized by the family's inability to restore stability and by the continuous pressure to make changes in the family structure and patterns of interaction. In other words, stress may never reach crisis proportions if the family is able to use existing resources and define the situation so as to resist systemic change and maintain family stability.

LONGITUDINAL OBSERVATIONS OF FAMILIES IN CRISIS: EMERGING CONCEPTS

The Hill ABCX framework was used initially to guide a longitudinal study of families which had a husband/father held captive or unaccounted for in the Vietnam War. Observations of the 216 families in crisis, precipitated by the prolonged absence (average 6.6 years) of fathers, revealed at least four additional factors which appeared to influence the course of family adaptation over time: (a) the pile-up of additional stressors and strains; (b) family efforts to activate, acquire, and utilize new resources from within the family and from the community; (c) modifications in the family definition of the situation with a different meaning attached to the family's predicament; and (d) family coping strategies designed to bring about changes in family structure in an effort to achieve positive adaptation. In addition, observations from this longitudinal study suggested that, over time, families go through phases of adjustment and adaptation characterized by different processes in which these factors interact.

In previous publications (McCubbin, Olson, & Patterson, in press; McCubbin & Patterson, 1982; in press), we have used these observations to advance a Double ABCX Model of family behavior (see Figure 1) which uses Hill's original ABCX model as its foundation and adds post-crisis variables in an effort to describe: (a) the additional life stressors and strains which shape the course of family adaptation; (b) the critical psychological, intra-familial, and social resources families acquire and employ over time in managing crisis situations; (c) the changes in definition and meaning families develop in an effort to make sense out of their predicament; (d) the coping strategies families employ; and (e) the range of outcomes of these family efforts.

In this chapter, we will describe the components of the Double ABCX Model with select observations from these 216 families which provide the inductive support for this line of theory building.

This description will be followed by an expansion of the Double ABCX Model which identifies, describes, and integrates the *process components* of family behavior in response to a stressor and to a family crisis. This family stress process is called the Family Adjustment and Adaptation Response—FAAR.

Family Demands: Pile-up (aA Factor)

Because family crises evolve and are resolved over a period of time, families seldom are dealing with a single stressor, but rather, our longitudinal data suggest they experience a pile-up of stressors and strains (i.e., demands), particularly in the aftermath of a major stressor, such as a death, a major role change for one member, or a natural disaster. This pile-up is referred to as the "aA" factor in the Double ABCX Model. These demands or changes may emerge from (a) individual family members, (b) the family system, and/or (c) the community of which the family and its members are a part.

There appear to be at least five broad types of stressors and strains contributing to a pile-up in the family system in a crisis situation: (a) the initial stressor and its hardships, (b) normative transitions, (c) prior strains, (d) the consequences of family efforts to cope; and (e) ambiguity, both intra-family and social.

Stressor and its hardships. Inherent in the occurrence of a stressful event such as a husband/father being reported as missing or a prisoner of war are hardships which increase and possibly intensify as the stressor situation persists or is unresolved. Wives in our longitudinal study, whose husbands were absent, were taxed with both the traditional and inherited responsibilities of the dual mother-

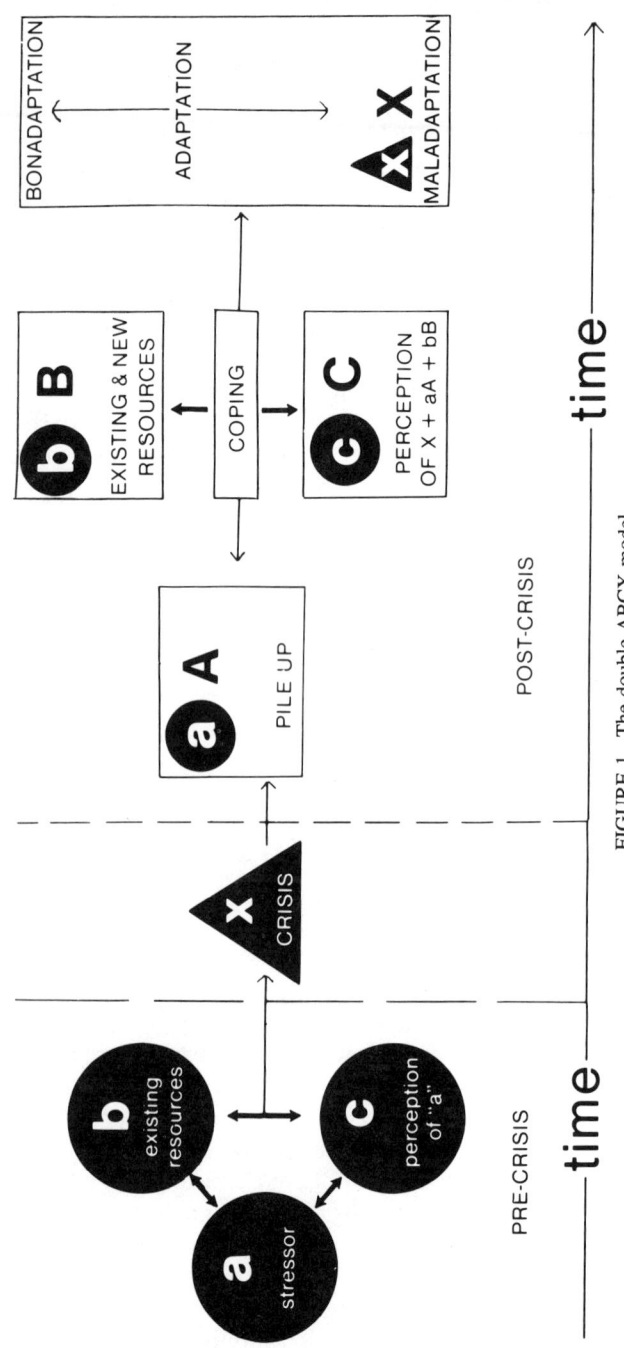

FIGURE 1. The double ABCX model

father role (McCubbin, Hunter, & Metres, 1974) which required solo decision making, disciplining of children, handling family finances, and managing children's health problems. Many wives experienced anxieties, frustrations, and feelings of insecurity and showed emotional symptoms of strain with the extended absence and uncertainty of their spouses' returns. Hardships, such as these, often are not readily resolved (as was true for these wives) and when they persist, they become additional sources of strain contributing to family distress.

Normative transitions. The demands of individual members and the family system are not static but change over time. For example, these families experienced the normal growth and development of child members (e.g., increasing need for independence), of adult members (e.g., mother's desire to pursue a career), of the extended family (e.g., death of grandparent, births) and family life cycle changes (e.g., school transitions, launching young adults). Such transitions occur concomitantly, but independently, of the initial stressor. These transitions or opportunities also place demands on the family unit since they require change.

Prior strains. It would appear that most family systems carry with them some residue of strain which may be the result of unresolved hardships from earlier stressors or transitions or may be inherent in ongoing roles such as parent, employer, etc. (Pearlin & Schooler, 1978). When a new stressor is experienced by the family, these prior strains are exacerbated and families become aware of them as demands in and of themselves. For example, wives whose husbands were missing became much more aware of the unresolved strains in their relationships with in-laws. Parent-child conflicts, which had existed when fathers were home, were often exacerbated for mothers functioning as single parents. These prior strains are not usually discrete events which can be identified as occurring at a specific point in time but rather, emerge more insidiously in the family. They do, however, contribute to the pile-up of demands families must contend with in a crisis situation.

Consequences of family efforts to cope. The fourth source of pile-up includes stressors and strains which emerge from specific coping behaviors the family may use in an effort to cope with the crisis situation. For example, wives acting as head of the household in their husbands' absence appeared to become more independent and self-confident. As mother changed her role and strengthened her authority and sought out new sources of emotional support, members of the kin network, especially in-laws concerned about possible divorce, challenged and questioned this style of coping. Their disapproval caused additional strain, contributing to the pile-up.

Intra-family and social ambiguity. Ambiguity is inherent in every stressor since change produces uncertainty about the future. Internally, the family may experience ambiguity about its structure. Certainly, having a spouse missing is most ambiguous in light of the unpredictability of his return. On the basis of systems theory and the symbolic interactionist perspective, Boss (1977) has suggested that boundary ambiguity within the family system is a major stressor since a system needs to be sure of its components, that is, who is inside of the system boundaries physically and psychologically, and who is outside. The concept of boundary ambiguity has also been applied to describe normative transitions (Boss, 1980) such as a young adult leaving home. Is this person in or out of the family unit?

Additionally, given the expectation that society will offer guidelines or blueprints for families coping with crises, it is probable that families will face the added strain of social ambiguity in those situations where needed social prescriptions for crisis resolution are unclear or absent. Families of the missing lacked legitimate procedures for resolution and were often confronted with conflicting or unclear messages about what to do. For example, powers of attorney expired, leaving wives with no legal power to sell jointly held property. Remarriage posed the threat of a bigamy conviction since there had been no declaration of death. The family's ability to manage stress may depend upon the efficacy and/or adequacy of the solutions the culture or community provide. However, these community solutions may lag far behind the times and offer little to families struggling to manage a difficult situation. As Hansen and Hill (1964) and Mechanic (1974) have pointed out, the fit between the family and the community may well be the major determinant of successful adaptation to stress.

Family Adaptive Resources (bB Factor)

Resources are part of the family's capabilities for meeting demands and needs and include characteristics (a) of individual members, (b) of the family unit, and (c) of the community. When viewed over time and in response to a crisis situation, the family's adaptive resources appear to be of two general types: existing resources and expanded family resources.

Existing resources. These resources are already part of the family's repertoire and serve to minimize the impact of the initial stressor and reduce the probability that the family will enter into crisis. Existing individual resources the wives in the longitudinal study appeared to use included the ability to nurture and meet the expressive needs of their children, manage the home, and to sublimate by engaging in hobbies, recreation, or work. They drew on the family resources of togetherness, role flexibility, shared values, and expressiveness. Community resources like friendships and religious involvement were also important.

Expanded family resources. The second type of resources (B of the bB factor) are those new resources (individual, family, and community) strengthened or developed in response to the additional demands emerging out of the crisis situations or as a result of pile-up. For example, wives availed themselves of educational opportunities to enhance their earning potential in anticipation of their spouse not returning. These opportunities for personal development also served to enhance their self-esteem and self-reliance. The family unit reallocated roles and responsibilities (e.g., oldest child member took a job to increase family income), involved extended kin in meeting family needs, relocated the family in a new community to gain a fresh start, and some remarried. Additionally, the family sought, and in some cases, created new community resources tailored to meet their needs. Wives joined the National League of Families, community-based counseling groups, and financial investment clubs. These groups offered various benefits such as encouragement, concrete guidance, empathic understanding, as well as a sense of membership.

One of the most important resources comprising the bB factor is social support. Social support has been defined as information that a family (a) is cared for and loved, (b) is esteemed and valued, and (c) belongs to a network of mutual obligation and understanding (Cobb, 1976). Families who have and are able to develop sources of social support (e.g., kin, friends, work associates, church, etc.) are both more resistant to major crises and are better able to recover from crisis and restore stability to the family system.

Family Definition and Meaning (cC Factor)

In the Double ABCX Model, the cC factor is the meaning the family gives to the total crisis situation which includes the stressor believed to have caused the crisis, as well as the added stressors and strains, old and new resources, and estimates of what needs to be done to bring the family back into balance.

While families with a husband/father missing struggled, they also appeared to reach a level of adaptive or functional stability—an outcome which could be attribued in part to wives' redefining the situation. For example, wives differentiated father's role (boundaries) in terms of his instrumental contributions versus his expressive contributions (Boss, 1977). Wives appeared to redefine the situation by endowing father's role with some value and meaning (i.e., as financial provider) and at the same time legitimate their personal efforts and the family's efforts to establish a new life for themselves (e.g., by developing new ways to meet expressive needs).

When families are able to successfully redefine the crisis situation and give it new meaning, it involves efforts to (a) clarify the issues, hardships, and tasks so as to render them more manageable and responsive to problem solving efforts; (b) decrease the intensity of the emotional burdens associated with the crisis situation; and (c) encourage the family unit to carry on with its fundamental tasks of promoting member social and emotional development. Generally speaking, family efforts to redefine a situation as a "challenge," as an "opportunity for growth," or to endow the crisis with meaning such as "believing it is the Lord's will" appear to play a useful role in facilitating family coping and, eventually, adaptation. Viewed in this way, the family's definition and meaning, or the cC factor, becomes a critical component of family coping.

Family Adaptive Coping: Interaction of Resources, Perceptions, and Behavior

Although family resources and perceptions have been studied independently and offer investigators a gauge of family capabilities used to meet demands, these same observations suggest that we could improve upon our understanding of family adaptation to crises by looking at these two variables simultaneously along with what families do to cope with the situation. Coping, then, becomes a bridging concept which has both cognitive and behavioral components wherein resources, perception, and behavioral responses interact as families try to achieve a balance in family functioning. Family coping efforts may be directed at (a) eliminating and/or avoiding stressors and strains; (b) managing the hardships of the situation; (c) maintaining the family system's integrity and morale;

(d) acquiring and developing resources to meet demands; and (e) implementing structural changes in the family system to accommodate the new demands (McCubbin, 1979; McCubbin & Patterson, 1982). What became apparent from observations of these families is that coping efforts following a crisis are directed at multiple stressors and strains (the pile-up) simultaneously. In other words, coping is not stressor specific, but involves efforts to manage various dimensions of family life at the same time, realizing that a "perfect" solution is never possible. Families learn to compromise, accepting the best possible outcome given their circumstances.

Family Adaptation Balancing (xX Factor)

Hill's x factor (1958), the amount of crisis in the family system, generally has been adopted as the major outcome variable describing disruptions in family routines in response to a stressor. Burr (1973) conceived of a crisis as a continuous variable, denoting variation in the amount of disruptiveness, incapacitatedness, or disorganization of the family. Given this definition, it might be concluded that the purpose of post-crisis adjustment or the goal of regenerative power (Hansen, 1965) is primarily to reduce or eliminate the disruptiveness in the family system and restore homeostasis. It might be argued, however, that family disruptions potentially help to maintain family relationships and even stimulate desirable changes in family life. Hansen and Johnson (1979) called attention to the restrictive focus of crisis and noted that "families are often observed 'accepting' disruptions of habit and tradition not so much as unwelcome problems; but more as opportunities to renegotiate their relationships" (p. 584). Systems theorists (Hill, 1971; von Bertalanffy, 1968) point out that it is characteristic of living systems to evolve toward greater complexity, and consequently, families may actively initiate changes to facilitate such growth. It is questionable then, whether "reduction of crisis" alone is an adequate index of a family's post-crisis adjustment.

Observations reviewed in this chapter suggest that family adaptation would be a useful concept for describing the outcome of family post-crisis adjustment. There are three elements to be considered in family adaptation: (a) the individual family member; (b) the family system; and (c) the community of which family members and the family unit are a part. Each of these elements is characterized by both demands and capabilities. Family adaptation is achieved through reciprocal relationships where the demands of one of these units are met by the capabilities at another so as to achieve a "balance" simultaneously at two primary levels of interaction.

Balance: Member to family fit. At the first level, a balance is sought between individual family members and the family system (e.g., family encouraging and supporting adolescent needs for independence and adolescent family member completing family maintenance tasks or participating in shared family activities). Based on the Double ABCX model, it could be hypothesized that family stress emerges when there is a demand-capability imbalance at this level of family functioning. Specifically, the demands an individual member may place on the family may exceed the family's capabilities for meeting these demands, thus resulting in an imbalance. For example, the stressor of a member entering adolescence may precipitate an imbalance by virtue of the family's demand for member adherence to rigid rules and their inability to alter expectations which would allow for the independence an adolescent needs for personal development. The family is therefore called upon to reconcile this matter and work to achieve a new "balance" between the individual member and the family unit.

Balance: Family to community fit. At the second level, a balance is sought between the family unit and the community of which this family is a part (e.g., family support of parental involvement in work and community activities and the employer's demand for extensive work time and commitment). It has frequently been observed that two social institutions, the family and the work community, compete for the involvement and commitment of family members which often results in stress—a demand-capability imbalance at this second level of family functioning. For example, the stressor of a wife-mother entering or returning to work may precipitate an imbalance if the family demands she make a priority commitment to family life and the children. Additionally, the family may be reluctant to modify its rules and behaviors (e.g., towards shared tasks, shared responsibilities) to permit the transitioning parent to invest in work-for-pay without the added burden of emotional guilt and the felt need to fulfill home and work responsibilities with equal competence. The family is called upon to reestablish and achieve a balance between family and work-community demands and capabilities.

Family coherence: A critical factor in adaptation. Even as families try to achieve bonadaptation by minimizing the discrepancy between family resources and demands, they are faced with the reality that there is no "perfect" fit where demands and resources are absolutely balanced. Successful adaptation in a less than perfect world calls for a general orientation by the family which reflects a sense of acceptance and understanding that this is the best they can do under the circumstances. Antonovsky (1979) describes this orientation as "coherence," that is, the pervasive, enduring, though dynamic feeling of confidence that internal and external environments are predictable and there is a high probability that things will work out as well as can reasonably be expected.

A family's sense of coherence is based primarily on its ability to balance two dimensions relative to its life circumstances: control and trust. For some life events and circumstances, a family can influence and shape the occurrence and/or the outcome. On the other hand, many life experiences of families cannot be directly controlled by them and they must trust that things will work out okay because other controlling factors—persons, institutions, a higher power—will act with their best interests in mind. Coherence is being able to differentiate when the family should take charge from when they should trust and believe in and support legitimate authority and/or power of other sources.

In the case of the families of the missing in action, many were able to trust the efforts of the United States to do what was best under the circumstances in terms of ending the war, finding and/or returning their spouses and establishing policies to help families. Many trusted God and their spiritual beliefs that somehow this was going to be okay for them. At the same time, these same families, wives in particular, were able to move ahead, get jobs, make decisions about child rearing and shape an acceptable, desirable (even though not perfect) future for themselves and their families. This realistic balance between trust and control leads to coherence and moves a family towards bonadaptation even when all demands are not absolutely met with available resources.

Therefore, family adaptation becomes the central concept in the Double ABCX model used to describe the outcome of family efforts to achieve a new level of balance in family functioning which was upset by a family crisis. In crisis situations the family unit struggles to achieve a balance at both the individual-family and the family-community levels of family functioning. Since the family is a social system and a change in one level affects the other, family efforts at adaptation always involve an attentiveness and responsiveness to both levels of family functioning simultaneously.

Outcome: Bonadaptation and maladaptation. The concept of family adaptation is used to describe a continuum of outcomes which reflect family efforts to achieve a balanced "fit" at the member-to-family and the family-to-community levels. The positive end of the continuum of family adaptation, called bonadaptation, is characterized by a balance at both levels of functioning which results in (a) the maintenance or strengthening of family integrity; (b) the continued promotion of both member development and family unit development; and (c) the maintenance of family independence and its sense of control over environmental influences. Family maladaptation, at the negative end of the continuum, is characterized by a continued imbalance at either level of family functioning or the achievement of a balance at both levels but at a price in terms of (a) deterioration in family integrity; (b) a curtailment or deterioration in the personal health and development of a member or the well-being of the family unit; or (c) a loss or decline in family independence and autonomy.

At the present time, family adaptation is but a descriptive criterion of family post-crisis outcomes rather than a clearly defined and operationalized set of measures. One obvious and complicating factor is that any form of adaptation may be viewed as having both long and short run consequences. What may be functional in meeting a family's or member's immediate needs, such as accepting a member who is abusing alcohol, may be maladaptive in light of the long-range, adverse consequences on family stability and the psychological well-being of its members.

FAMILY ADJUSTMENT
AND ADAPTATION RESPONSE—FAAR

Observations of Family Adjustment and Adaptation

Longitudinal observations of families faced with a prolonged war-induced separation (Benson, McCubbin, Dahl, & Hunter, 1974; Hunter, McCubbin, & Metres, 1974; McCubbin, Dahl, Lester, & Ross, 1976) revealed that these families changed over time in response to this predicament. Specifically, families appeared to go through three stages of adaptation which we have called resistance, restructuring, and consolidation.

Family resistance. Initially, when families found out their husband/father was missing, they focused their attention on the report of his absence. Some families sought evidence to disconfirm the report of their husbands being missing as a way to avoid the reality of the situation. Others defined the situation as temporary and made an effort to "wait it out" to see what would happen. In any case, the family resisted making any substantial change in the way the family unit was structured or functioned. Despite the ambiguity of this situation and sparsity of information, they were unwilling, in most cases, to believe their husbands would not be home soon and hence clung to maintaining their existing lifestyle and family structure as confirmation that nothing was different. They made only minimal changes in family routine to keep the family functioning and intact.

Over time, however, families came to realize that they needed to prepare for the possibility of father never returning and all the demands that this would place on them. Their existing coping strategies were not adequate to meet the family demands of a prolonged wait or to meet the demands of providing continuous attention to the developmental needs of family members. A family crisis emerged.

Family restructuring. The crisis situation called for families to make changes in the way they were organized and did things. Some reallocated family roles such as having an oldest child assume more parenting responsibilities. Some spouses decided to enter the work force or pursued further education as a way to prepare for the future. Some wives sought new male friendships to provide emotional support. Other wives began proceedings to terminate their marriage so they could begin a new life. This struggle for viable changes in the family structure was most characteristic of those families who defined the situation as a crisis and one that warranted changes in the family. Hill (1949) described this kind of response as "closing ranks" and viewed it as helpful in getting the family working together to shape their future. The changes in family structure were designed to manage the host of demands these families faced but there was no guarantee that all the hardships they were experiencing (e.g., need for income, loneliness, need for more information about their husbands, etc.) were well managed. In addition, changes in roles of family members were not always supported by all members even though they passively accepted or tolerated the changes. Consequently, the family unit was often disjointed and

disorganized, with minimal indices of coherent family functioning.
Family consolidation. The disorganization and incoherence in family functioning experienced by families in the wake of one or two major changes appeared to become a stimulus for making additional changes in an effort to restore stability to the family system. Family members did not always agree on what additional changes should be made. For example, as families altered old patterns (which worked with father present) and instituted new patterns such as mother taking on a career or mother dating with the possibility of remarriage, some members resisted making shifts in their own behavior which would accommodate mother in these new roles. However, many families were successful at shifting gears and making concomitant changes through compromise and negotiation. They developed a new orientation for their lives which included meanings such as, "we need to get on with our lives," "father would have preferred if we moved ahead," "it is God's will that our father is gone," and "we need to prepare for the future." As families worked to achieve a new level of stable internal functioning, they were also called upon to rework their fit with the community. Internal family changes often called for new friendships and changes in community networks to ensure a sense of acceptance and complementarity.

These observations were reconceptualized into a process model called the Family Adjustment and Adaptation Response—FAAR—which is graphically outlined in Figure 2. The FAAR processes are best viewed as occurring in two distinct phases: the Adjustment Phase in response to a stressor and the Adaptation Phase which occurs following a family crisis.

The Family Adjustment Phase

It is assumed that in the period of time preceding a family stressor event, family functioning is relatively stable. This stability does not preclude the possibility of some disturbing patterns of family interaction (e.g., marital conflict, sibling conflict, parent-child conflict). So, in reality, the family could be anywhere along the adaptation continuum from bonadaptation to maladaptation. Where families are along the continuum of adaptation influences their vulnerability to the impact of a subsequent stressor event or transition (Burr, 1973), but the important characteristic of the family before the impact of a stressor event or transition is their general

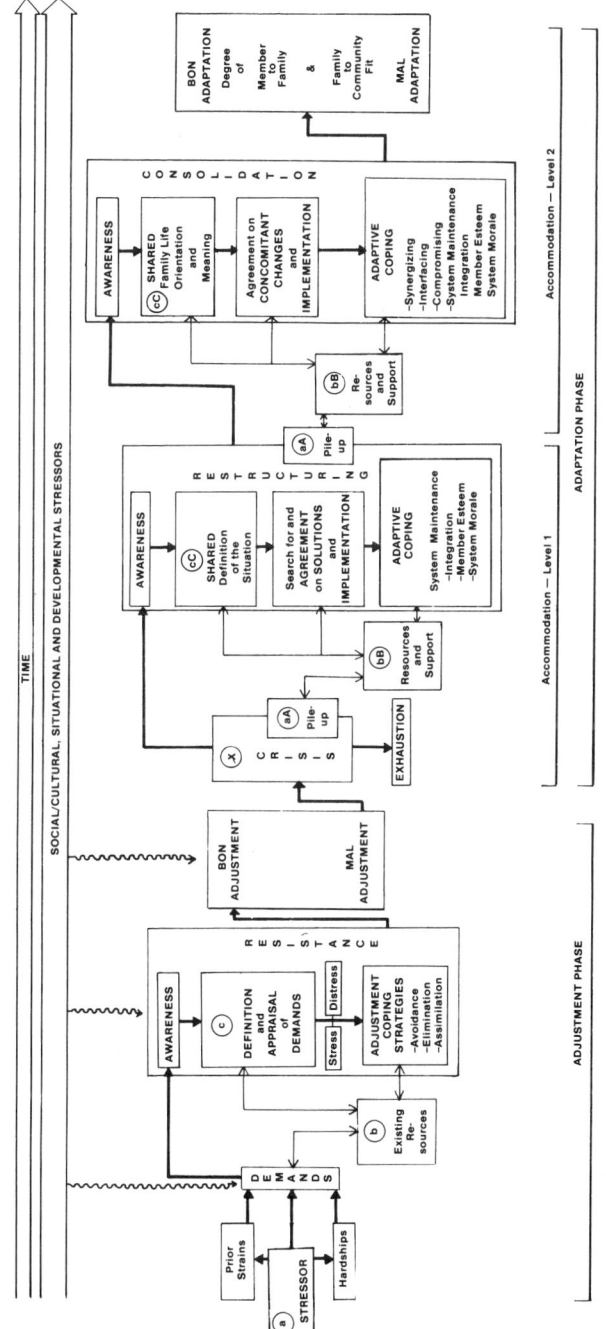

FIGURE 2. FAAR - Family adjustment and adaptation response

sense of satisfaction and stability about their structure and patterns of interaction.

When a family initiates or is confronted with a stressor event, i.e., an event of change with a discernable onset, a set of demands (see Figure 3) is placed on the family unit which includes: (a) the stressor event or transition; (b) the hardships directly associated with this stressor; and (c) prior strains already existing in the family system which may be exacerbated by the stressor and hence come into the awareness of one or more family members. In the usual course of action, the family attempts to make adjustments in their patterns of interaction, with minimal change or disruption of the family's established patterns of behavior and structure. These efforts can best be described as family *resistance* to change. The family resistance response begins with an *awareness* of the demands which is shaped by the intensity of the stressor (a factor), the extensiveness of related hardships, and the extensiveness of unresolved prior strains. The family arrives at a definition of the demands (c factor) and makes an appraisal of what needs to be done to manage the situation. They may experience *stress,* characterized by generally positive definitions, in contrast to experiencing *distress* where the family definitions are more negative and the situation is viewed as unpleasant or undesirable.

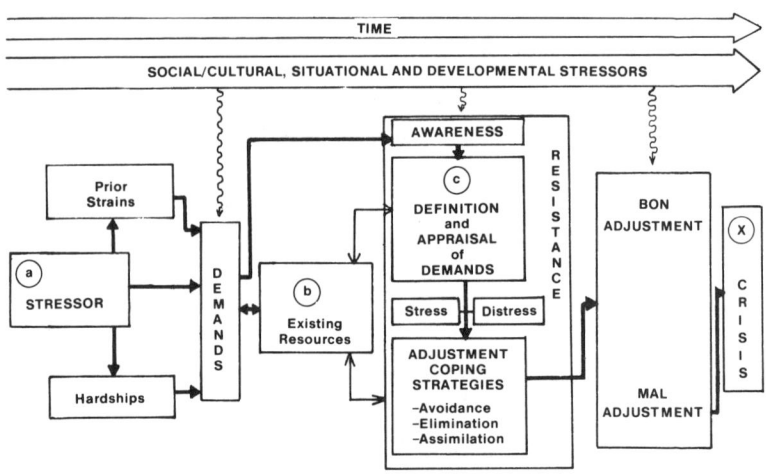

FIGURE 3. FAAR - Adjustment phase

During this phase prior to a crisis, the family makes an effort to protect itself from change by maintaining its established patterns. A family may employ at least three *adjustment coping strategies,* used alone or in combination, to bring about family adjustment: avoidance, elimination, and assimilation. *Avoidance* can be defined as family efforts to deny or ignore the stressor and other demands in the belief and hope that it will go away or resolve itself, and thus call for a negligible amount of internal family adjustment. *Elimination* is an active effort by the family to rid itself of all demands by changing or removing the stressor, or altering the definition of the stressor. Both avoidance and elimination responses serve to minimize or protect the family unit from having to make modifications in the family's structure. *Assimilation,* the third adjustment coping strategy, involves family efforts to accept the demands created by the stressor into its existing structure and patterns of interaction. The family absorbs the demands by making only minor changes within the family system (e.g., pay the debts, cut down on the amount of time at work, share in the housekeeping responsibilities, agree to utilize day care, etc.). Very little change is made, for the family unit has an adequate and appropriate supply of existing resources (b factor) which may be employed or reallocated. This supply of resources influences the definition and appraisal of demands, as well as which coping strategies are used. For example, inadequate resources might well contribute to a negative definition of demands, to a state of distress, and to coping directed at avoidance of the demands.

The outcome of these three family adjustment coping strategies in response to demands is *adjustment* which varies along a continuum from *bonadaptation* to *maladaptation.* It reflects the family's internal strengths and capabilities to respond with a single coping strategy or a combination of strategies most conducive to meeting the demands arising out of the family predicament. The changes made by the family are limited at this level to first order change (Montgomery, 1981; Watzlawick, Weakland, & Fisch, 1974) where the family structure remains intact and ways of interacting are modified only slightly. Adjustment (Melson, 1980), therefore, can be viewed as a short-term response by families, adequate to manage many family life changes, transitions, and demands. However, there are occasions when these adjustment oriented processes are insufficient to meet the demands to which families are exposed. This situation is likely to emerge in those circumstances in which (a) the nature of the stressor or transition involves a structural change in the family system (e.g., prolonged war-induced separation, transition to parenthood, death of a parent, etc.); (b) the nature, number, and duration of demands depletes the family's existing resources; (c) the number and persistence of prior unresolved strains also tax the family's resources; (d) the family's capabilities and resources are basically inadequate or underdeveloped to meet the demands; and (e) the family overtly or covertly seizes the opportunity to produce structural changes in the family unit as a way to promote family and member growth by allowing or facilitating a demand-capability imbalance or family crisis. Consequently, as the demand-capability imbalance persists and possibly increases, a family moves toward the maladjustment end of the continuum and eventually into a state of crisis.

Crisis, as already defined, involves disorganization and the demand for structural change(s) in the family unit to restore stability at its prior level or another (higher or lower) level of family functioning. This movement to initiate structural change in the family unit marks the beginning of the adaptation phase of the Family Adjustment and Adaptation Response. It is important to note that a family "in crisis" does not carry the stigmatizing value judgment that somehow the family has failed, is dysfunctional, or in need of professional counseling. Rather, many family crises are normative and include critical role transitions (see Mederer & Hill, Chapter 2) involving changes in family structure and established patterns of interaction to cope with developmental changes in family members and the family system. Other family crises are actively set in motion by family decisions to make structural changes (e.g., separation, dual careers, major shifts in family roles, etc.) or shifts in core family values or goals as a planful step to improve family conditions, reduce financial or emotional strains, and to enhance the overall functioning of the family unit.

The Family Adaptation Phase

Families in crisis, which face excessive demands and depleted resources (maladjustment), come to realize that in order to restore some functional stability and/or improve family satisfaction in their system, they need to make changes in their existing structure which may include modifications in established roles, rules, goals and/or patterns of interaction. Additionally, after they have made these in-

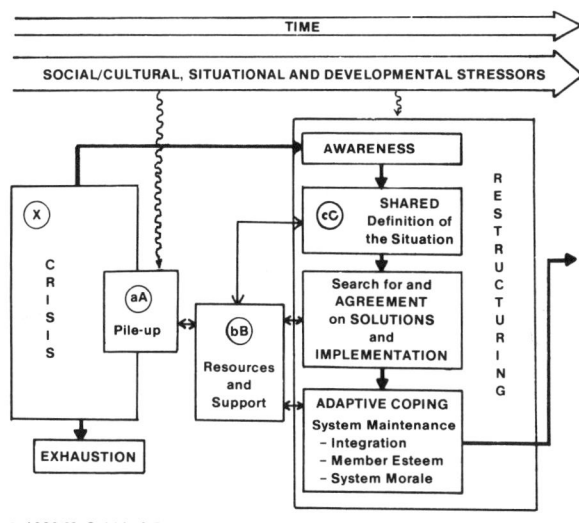

FIGURE 4. FAAR - Accommodation - Level 1: Restructuring

itial structural changes, the family is called upon to make subsequent changes in an effort to consolidate and bring the entire family into a coherent unit working together around and in support of the newly instituted changes. These processes of restructuring and consolidation suggest that there are two distinct levels of family accommodation which evolve over time as families work towards adaptation.

Family Accommodation - Level 1: Restructuring

Observations of families at the restructuring level of accommodation suggest that there are at least four components to this level: awareness, a shared definition of the situation, agreement on solutions and implementation, and adaptive coping strategies.

When a family experiences a crisis, what appears to emerge is an *awareness* by one or more family members that their existing structure and established mode of interaction are not adequate to meet the demands they now face (aA factor). This awareness may initially occur to only one member of the family unit who then attempts to influence others to share in this awareness that "something needs to change" in our family.

The second component of the restructuring process involves

family efforts to develop a *shared definition of the situation* (cC factor). Those members of the family who share an awareness of the need to change their system interact in a covert or overt way to develop a shared "label" or way of identifying what they perceive to be the family's problem. It is possible that the definition of the situation is never "shared" with another family member; in which case, it is one member's definition which becomes the basis for the restructuring which takes place. The way the crisis is defined is influenced by the pile-up of demands (aA factor) on the family, as well as the capabilities (bB factor) they have or lack to meet these demands.

Out of this shared definition, the family *searches for, agrees upon, and implements solution(s)* (structural changes) which they believe will solve the problem as they have defined it. A solution implemented during this restructuring phase of family adaptation involves a second order change (Watzlawick et al., 1974) where the family system itself changes. That is, accommodation takes place where the existing structure is altered to meet the specific demands to which the family is exposed. For example, the family may define their situation as "inadequate income to meet the family's financial demands" and may agree on the solution of one member of the family assuming a second job or, alternatively, they may agree on having a previously unemployed member enter the work force. While there may be more than one structural change in the family unit depending upon the demands and how the family defines this, the changes made in the family system during restructuring have primarily a singular focus (i.e., related to the defined problem) and the family is usually unaware of the full implication for the long-term stability of their system.

Families which successfully restructure their systems through the implementation of changes designed to solve their crises concomitantly employ the *adaptive coping strategy* of *system maintenance,* designed to keep the family functioning together as a unit, to maintain the esteem of members, and to maintain family morale.

Resources and support (bB factor) influence the family's transition through the restructuring phase of accommodation by buffering the impact of pile-up (e.g., using resources to resolve problems), by influencing the definition of the situation (e.g., positive appraisal, sense of mastery, communication skills), and maximizing solution(s) available (e.g., problem solving ability). The components of the restructuring process do not necessarily occur in an overt, carefully planned sequence by the family. They often evolve in a natural and spontaneous way with tacit and implicit understandings among family members.

From the clinical literature on family therapy techniques, it would appear that structural therapists (see Minuchin, 1974) often facilitate this first effort at family restructuring by finding the "nub," that is, the most potentially effective dimension or pattern of interaction where they can direct the family to make a second order change which will then set in motion other desirable changes in the family system.

The family's problem solving efforts and implementation of structural change(s) along with the adaptive coping strategy of maintaining family integration, member esteem, and system morale are all directed at (a) the management of specific demands; (b) changes in the family system to accommodate the demand(s); and (c) restoring organization and stability to the family system.

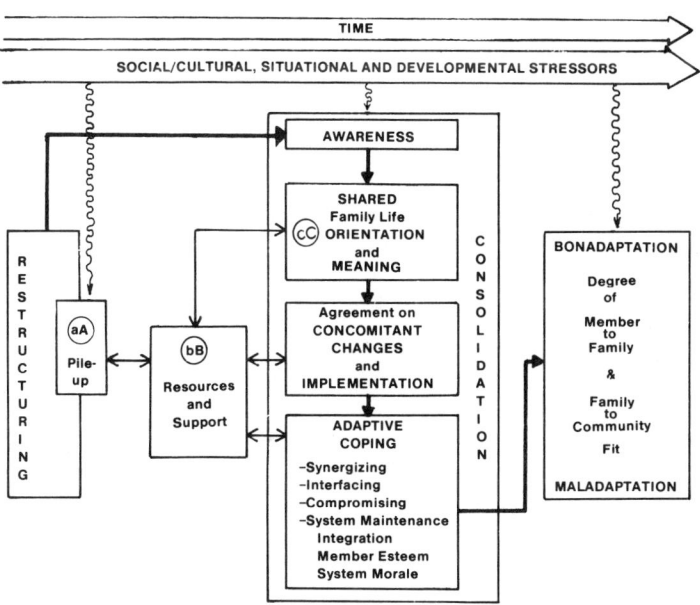

© 1982 McCubbin & Patterson

FIGURE 5. FAAR - Accommodation - Level 2: Consolidation

Family Accommodation - Level 2: Consolidation

Once the family has successfully initiated a second order change where their system has restructured itself in some way, the family moves into the second level of accommodation with efforts to consolidate and mold the family system into a coherent unit. It is a basic assumption of family systems theory (von Bertalanffy, 1968) that even as a system changes, it strives to maintain homeostasis. This dialectic between change and stability is inherent in social systems. If the structural change(s) made by the family during the restructuring phase of accommodation is to be integrated as a viable and stable component of the family system, the family unit is called upon to make additional changes in the family organization and structure to support and complement the newly instituted patterns of behavior.

As a first step in this consolidation phase of family accommodation, one or more members of the family has an *awareness* that the family has made a significant change which is incongruous with the family's prior structure and interaction patterns. An effort is made to develop a shared family awareness about the "goodness of fit" between the family's newly instituted structural change(s) and the family's established patterns of behavior and structure (see Hansen & Johnson, 1979). The total family system becomes involved in developing a *shared family life orientation and meaning* which would support and legitimate modification in some of their established patterns in an effort to be congruent with and maintain the newly instituted patterns and structural change(s). For example, families in the precarious situation of prolonged war-induced separations (with the unpredictable outcome as to father's return) sought to "close out" father's role in an effort to reorganize the family unit. While children often resisted this structural change, mothers were often able to develop an acceptable family orientation and meaning relative to the family's predicament by cultivating a shared belief that father (now absent) would have wanted this change, encouraged the family to move ahead, and defined these changes as a sign of a "good family."

Once having achieved an awareness and a new orientation and meaning (shared by the whole family either actively or at least through passive non-resistance), the family works to identify and initiate *concomitant changes* in the family system so that the family's new orientation will be coordinated, stable, and congruent. Thus the processes of assimilation and accommodation occur in tandem during this consolidation phase of family adaptation. Unlike the first level of accommodation where it is probable that only one or some members of the family or select dimensions of the family structure are involved in change, the successful negotiation of consolidation involves all members of the family unit.

The family then takes action through *implementation* of the changes agreed upon. This may involve some trial and error efforts by the family as they appraise the impact of each institutive change for the total family system. The family may decide that an agreed upon change isn't working or isn't congruent with other changes and patterns and thus abandon it in favor of an established pattern or different structural change.

Family efforts at consolidation are facilitated by the *adaptive coping strategies* of synergizing, interfacing, compromising, and system maintenance.

Synergizing refers to family efforts to coordinate and pull together as a unit to accomplish a shared life style and orientation which cannot be achieved by any member alone but only through mutuality and interdependence. Family members are attuned to each other as they work to synchronize and coordinate their respective perceptions, needs, and resources. Other stress scholars (Reiss & Oliveri, 1980) have emphasized that high coordination among family members appears to facilitate adaptation to stress.

Family efforts during consolidation are not limited to internal changes in the family unit. Because the family is a semi-closed system with commitments to and transactions with other social institutions (e.g., work, school, community groups, etc.), the restructured family also works at *interfacing* with the community to achieve a new "fit." The initial complementary relationship between the community and family life may be disturbed by the family's internal restructuring and therefore demand a new set of rules and transactions. Interfacing family needs and resources with community norms and resources appears to be a critical part of the family's overall effort to achieve a satisfactory level of family adaptation. In the case of families faced with prolonged separations and following restructuring (freezing out father's role), families often relocated to new communities, away from the pressures of military life which emphasized keeping father's role firmly in place.

Families are never able to achieve a perfect intra-family and family-to-community fit where all needs are absolutely met. Predictably, successful consolidation calls for *compromising* through a realistic appraisal of the family's circumstances and a willingness to accept and lend support to a less than perfect resolution. For example, families with a husband/father missing in war could not bring him home immediately, if ever. Some relocated to new communities and sought a new life style, even though they found the prior situation much more satisfactory and supportive. Compromise is also involved in consolidation as some family members push for more change and other members want to retain more of the established patterns.

As was true during the restructuring phase, successful consolidation requires coping efforts directed at *system maintenance,* i.e., integration, morale, and member esteem. This is especially important during consolidation because it is not unusual that when families experience crisis and struggle to make major changes, they also neglect the ongoing internal support function that sustains the family as a unit and enhances the quality of life. As the family works to restructure itself, it needs to know that there is something, i.e., the family itself, worth making all these changes for. It would appear that extended lack of attention to system maintenance may be a major contributor to family exhaustion.

The outcome of family efforts to accommodate at the two levels of restructuring and consolidation is adaptation. As previously defined, adaptation varies on a continuum from bonadaptation to maladaptation and reflects the family's ability to achieve a fit simultaneously at two levels of interaction: member-to-family and family-to-community.

Cycles of Adjustment and Adaptation

Families do not always progress in a direct, linear fashion through all the FAAR processes from crisis to adaptation. Quite possibly they can get stuck at one phase and may need to return to an earlier phase and work it through again. Figure 6 shows alternative cycles families may follow in an effort to achieve adaptation.

Family crisis revisited. Families may return to crisis from (a) restructuring; (b) consolidation; or (c) maladaptation. If, during restructuring, part or all of the family could either not decide on a major structural change which they believed would help solve their family problem or they could not implement the change(s), they may return to a crisis state. During consolidation, it may not be possible to get the family unit to make the concomitant changes

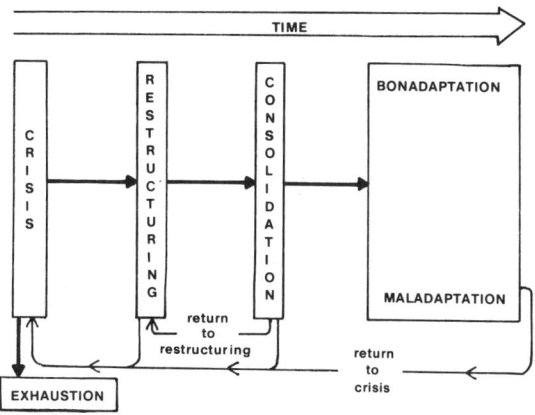

FIGURE 6. FAAR - Cycles of adaptation

necessary to achieve stability and congruence with the newly instituted family patterns (created during the restructuring phase). For example, if the family was restructured by mother's decision to return to work, consolidation may not occur if other family member(s) are unwilling to shift their roles to include sharing household maintenance and child supervision responsibilities. All the institutive changes made may be aborted, leading to disorganization, incapacitatedness and a return to crisis.

The family may reach adaptation having restructured and consolidated their system but with a resulting large discrepancy between the needs and resources (more demands than resources) at the member-to-family and/or family-to-community levels. The family would be close to the maladaptation end of the continuum. Predictably, a maladapted family system would be particularly vulnerable to a crisis if they experienced even a minor change or stressor event. For example, if one member became dissatisfied with the institutive changes (e.g., new roles, expectations, etc.) and refused to fulfill agreed upon role responsibilities, this change may well propel the family back to crisis. In fact, it is not an uncommon occurrence that the family will move back into crisis from any of these phases due to the experience of an additional stressor event which casts a new light on the changes just made or that they are in the process of making. If, for example, a family was in one of the processes of accommodating (i.e., restructuring or consolidation) to a post-crisis pile-up of demands, and a member died or had a serious accident, a new family crisis would ensue.

Exhaustion: An exit from crisis. Whenever families are in crisis, it is always possible that one outcome may be a state of exhaustion when the family is unable or chooses not to resolve the crisis situation. Particularly, if family resources are depleted because they had few to begin with, were unable to acquire or activate additional ones, and essentially used all their resources to meet the pile-up of demands, exhaustion is the likely outcome. Families are particularly apt to move toward exhaustion if they have repeated these adaptation phases several times and have been unsuccessful at restructuring and consolidation. Family dissolution is often the concomitant occurrence of exhaustion.

Return to restructuring. A return to restructuring from (a) consolidation or (b) maladaptation are two additional cycles families may experience in their efforts to achieve adaptation. If the family is unable to consolidate their system around an institutive change made during restructuring, they may decide to try a different approach. For example, if father took on a second job in an effort to resolve the crisis of mounting financial debts, the family may find it impossible to consolidate around this change because it is incongruent with the value the family places on "actively doing things together." They may return to restructuring and decide instead that mother should take on a part-time job and then the family works to consolidate around that change (e.g., use day care, have father help with household chores, etc.).

SUMMARY AND CONCLUSIONS

Predictably, as family researchers move ahead with the development of operational definitions of family level measures of the Double ABCX variables and the FAAR processes (see Olson, Portner, & Bell, 1979, 1982; McCubbin & Patterson, 1981), we can expect an expansion of research efforts to test the efficacy and limitations of this framework. Additionally, it is reasonable to argue that the next decade of research has much to offer the theorist, researcher, and clinician. The Double ABCX model and FAAR processes were introduced in an effort to foster our understanding of how families manage or even thrive on life's hardships. With this perspective in mind, we can envision, or at least hope for, a wealth of research which will add in an appreciable way to our understanding of why families struggle with change, the creative ways in which they approach and manage life demands, and why families are so resilient in the face of predictable transitions and adversities.

REFERENCES

Aldous, J., Condon, T., Hill, R., Straus, M., & Tallman, I. (Eds.), *Family problem solving: A symposium on theoretical, methodological, and substantive concerns.* Hinsdale, IL: The Dryden Press, 1971.
Angell, R. D. *The family encounters the Depression.* New York: Charles Scribner, 1936.
Antonovsky, A. *Health, stress and coping.* San Francisco: Jossey-Bass, 1979.
Benson, D., McCubbin, H. I., Dahl, B. B., & Hunter, E. J. *Waiting: The dilemma of the MIA wife.* In H. I. McCubbin, B. B. Dahl, P. Metres, E. J. Hunter, & J. Plag (Eds.), *Family separation and reunion.* Washington, DC: U.S. Government Printing Office, 1974.
Berardo, F. (Ed.), Special issue: A decade review. *Journal of Marriage and the Family,* 1980, *42*(4).
Boss, P. G. A clarification of the concept of psychological father presence in families experiencing ambiguity of boundary. *Journal of Marriage and the Family,* 1977, *39*, 141-151.
Boss, P. G. Normative family stress: Family boundary changes across the life span. *Family Relations,* 1980, *29*, 445-450.
Broderick, C. Beyond the five conceptual frameworks: A decade of development in family theory. In C. Broderick (Ed.), *A decade of family research in action.* Minneapolis: National Council on Family Relations, 1970.
Burr, W. F. *Theory construction and the sociology of the family.* New York: Wiley, 1973.
Caplan, G., & Killilea, M. *The family as a support system.* New York: Grune & Stratton, 1976.
Cobb, S. Social support as a moderator of life stress. *Psychosomatic Medicine,* 1976, *38*, 300-314.
Cavan, R., & Ranck, K. R. *The family and the Depression.* Chicago: University of Chicago, 1938.
Figley, C., & McCubbin, H. I. *Stress and the family,* Volume 2. New York: Brunner/Mazel, in press.
Hansen, D. Personal and positional influence in formal groups: Compositions and theory for research on family vulnerability to stress. *Social Forces,* 1965, *44*, 202-210.
Hansen, D., & Hill, R. Families under stress. In H. Christensen (Ed.), *Handbook of marriage and the family.* Chicago: Rand McNally, 1964.
Hansen, D., & Johnson, V. Rethinking family stress theory: Definitional aspects. In W. Burr, R. Hill, F. I. Nye, & I. Reiss (Eds.), *Contemporary theories about the family,* Volume I. New York: The Free Press, 1979.
Hill, R. *Families under stress.* New York: Harper & Row, 1949.
Hill, R. Generic features of families under stress. *Social Casework,* 1958, *49*, 139-150.
Hill, R. Modern systems theory and the family: A confrontation. *Social Science Information,* 1971, *72*, 7-26.
House, J. *Work stress and social support.* Reading, MA: Addison-Wesley, 1981.
Hunter, E. J., McCubbin, H. I., & Metres, P. Religion and the POW/MIA wife. In H. I. McCubbin, B. B. Dahl, P. Metres, E. Hunter, & J. Plag (Eds.), *Family separation and reunion.* Washington, DC: U.S. Government Printing Office, 1974.
Klein, D. Family problem solving and family stress. In H. I. McCubbin, M. B. Sussman, & J. M. Patterson (Eds.), *Social Stress and the Family: Advances and developments in family stress theory and research.* New York: Haworth Press, 1983.
Klein, D., & Hill, R. Determinants of family problem solving effectiveness. In W. Burr, R.

Hill, F. I. Nye, & I. Reiss (Eds.), *Contemporary theories about the family.* Volume 1. New York: The Free Press, 1979.

Koos, E. L. *Families in trouble.* New York: King's Crown Press, 1946.

Lazarus, R. *Psychological stress and the coping process.* New York: McGraw-Hill, 1966.

McCubbin, H. I. Integrating coping behavior in family stress theory. *Journal of Marriage and the Family,* 1979, *41*(3), 237-244.

McCubbin, H. I., & Boss, P. G. (Eds.), *Family stress and coping: A special issue of Family Relations.* October 1980, *29*(4).

McCubbin, H. I., Dahl, B. B., Lester, G., & Ross, B. The returned prisoner of war and his children: Evidence for the origin of second generational effects of captivity. A preliminary report. In R. Spaulding (Ed.), *Proceedings of the third Department of Defense medical conference on prisoners of war.* Washington, DC: Department of the Navy, 1976.

McCubbin, H. I., & Figley, C. (Eds.), *Stress and the family.* Volume 1. New York: Brunner/Mazel, in press.

McCubbin, H. I., Hunter, E. J., & Metres, P. Adaptation of the family to the prisoner of war and missing in action experience. In H. I. McCubbin, B. B. Dahl, P. Metres, E. J. Hunter, & J. Plag, (Eds.), *Family separation and reunion.* Washington, DC: U. S. Government Printing Office, 1974.

McCubbin, H. I., Joy, C., Cauble, A., Comeau, J., Patterson, J., & Needle, R. Family stress, coping and social support: A decade review. *Journal of Marriage and the Family,* 1980, *42,* 855-871.

McCubbin, H. I., Olson, D. H., & Patterson, J. M. Beyond family crisis: Family adaptation. In J. Trost (Ed.), *Families in disaster.* Sweden: International Library, in press.

McCubbin, H. I., & Patterson, J. M. Family adaptation to crises. In H. McCubbin, A. Cauble, & J. Patterson (Eds.), *Family stress, coping and social support.* Springfield, IL: Charles C. Thomas, 1982.

McCubbin, H. I., & Patterson, J. M. Family stress and adaptation to crisis: A Double ABCX model of family behavior. In D. H. Olson & B. Miller (Eds.), *Family studies review yearbook.* Beverly Hills, CA: Sage Publications, in press.

Mechanic, D. Social structure and personal adaptation: Some neglected dimensions. In G. V. Coehlo, D. A. Hamburg, & J. E. Adams (Eds.), Coping and adaptation. New York: Basic Books, 1974.

Mederer, H., & Hill, R. Critical transitions over the family life span: Theory and research. In H. I. McCubbin, M. B. Sussman, & J. M. Patterson (Eds.), *Social Stress and the Family: Advances and developments in family stress theory and research.* Haworth Press, 1983.

Melson, G. *Family and environment: An ecosystem perspective.* Minneapolis, MN: Burgess, 1980.

Merton, R. *Social theory and social structure.* New York: The Free Press, 1968.

Mikhail, A. Stress: A psychobiological conception. *Journal of Human Stress,* 1981, *7,* 9-15.

Minuchin, S. *Families and family therapy.* Cambridge, MA: Harvard University Press, 1974.

Montgomery, J. *Family crisis as process.* Washington, DC: University Press of America, 1981.

Moos, R. *Family environment scale and preliminary manual.* Palo Alto, CA: Consulting Psychologists Press, 1974.

Olson, D. H., Portner, J., & Bell, R. *Family adaptability and cohesion scales (FACES I).* St. Paul, MN: Family Social Science, 1979.

Olson, D. H., Portner, J., & Bell, R. *Family adaptability and cohesion scales* (FACES II). St. Paul, MN: Family Social Science, 1982.

Pearlin, L., & Schooler, C. The structure of coping. *Journal of Health and Social Behavior,* 1978, *19,* 2-21.

Reiss, D., & Oliveri, M. Family paradigm and family coping: A proposal for linking the family's intrinsic adaptive capacities to its responses to stress. *Family Relations,* 1980, *29*(4), 3-16.

Reiss, D., & Olivieri, M. Family stress as community frame. In H. I. McCubbin, M. B. Sussman, & J. M. Patterson (Eds.), *Social Stress and the Family: Advances and developments in family stress theory and research.* New York, Haworth Press, 1983.
Reiss, I. *The family system in America.* New York: Holt, Rinehart & Winston, 1971.
Satir, V. *Conjoint family therapy.* Palo Alto, CA: Science and Behavior Books, 1964.
Satir, V. *Peoplemaking.* Palo Alto, CA: Science and Behavior Books, 1972.
Selye, H. *Stress without distress.* New York: Lippincott & Crowell, 1974.
Waller, W., & Hill, R. *The family: A dynamic interpretation.* New York: The Dryden Press, 1951.
Watzlawick, P., Weakland, J., & Fisch, R. *Change.* New York: W. W. Norton, 1974.
Whitaker, C., & Keith, D. *Functional family therapy.* In A. Gorman (Ed.), Handbook of family therapy. New York: Brunner/Mazel, 1981.
von Bertalanffy, L. *General systems theory* (Revised edition). New York: George Braziller, 1968.

Chapter 2

Critical Transitions Over the Family Life Span: Theory and Research

Helen Mederer
Reuben Hill

INTRODUCTION

To even the most casual observer of family life it is apparent that families change over their lifetimes. Despite variations in family form, most families go through a cycle of expansion, stability and contraction in size. The nature of the relationships between the family and external institutions such as work, voluntary organizations, and kinship and friendship networks also varies over time. Inside the family, predictable patterns of behavior among members in role structures of decision making, affection, communication, and division of tasks are renegotiated continually to meet changing family and individual member needs. The proposition that families change, then, is widely accepted. There is less agreement among scholars about the nature of family change. Families have been described as changing from one stage of development to the next through a series of critical transitions; however, the precipitators of transition and the nature of the transition process are poorly understood.

The main problematic issue is to understand what combination of circumstances precipitates a shift in families from one stage of structural equilibrium to the next. Why should families, which prize order and predictability as much as any other group, give up their

---

Helen Mederer is Assistant Professor and Reuben Hill is Regents Professor, Department of Sociology, University of Minnesota, Minneapolis.

© 1983 by The Haworth Press, Inc. All rights reserved.

scripted roles, rules and procedures to regroup around a different allocation of roles and duties, thereby entering a new stage of development? The second issue is to understand how the change occurs by identifying phases of the transition process.

This chapter addresses these issues of developmental change by reviewing recent work in family development theory and by drawing on the work in family stress and critical transition theories. The purpose of this chapter is to present a reworked model of family development which emphasizes the precipitators of transition in families, the phasing of critical transitions, the process of reorganization and the resultant changes in family role structures.

A REVIEW OF FAMILY DEVELOPMENT THEORY

A Description of Traditional Family Development Theory

Family development is the primary theory which deals with family change. This perspective has traditionally described family life over time as divided into a series of stages. Stages are defined as periods of relative structural stability which are qualitatively and quantitatively distinct from adjacent stages.

The most frequently employed system currently for categorizing family life into stages was developed by Evelyn Duvall and Reuben Hill (1948). Using the criteria of (a) major change in family size, (b) the developmental stage of oldest child, and (c) the work status of the breadwinner, they identified eight stages of development:

1. Establishment stage (childless, newly marrieds)
2. First parenthood (infant to 3 years of age)
3. Family with preschool child (oldest 3-6 years)
4. Family with school child (oldest 6-12 years)
5. Family with adolescents (oldest 13-20 years)
6. Family as launching center (leave taking of children)
7. Family in middle years (empty nest)
8. Family in retirement (breadwinner 65 and over)

The scheme delineated above rests on an assumption of high member interdependence; namely, that families are forced to change the rules for interrelating of members each time one or more members are added or leave the family and each time the oldest child[1] changes in his or her own individual developmental stage requiring redefinition of his or her roles vis a vis other members. Duvall and Hill specified individual developmental tasks for members and, later, Duvall (1957) did this for the family as a whole for each of the eight stages of the family life cycle. A favorite dictum from child development was also assumed for families, namely, that success in one stage of family development made for success in later stages and vice versa, that failure in one stage handicapped families in later stages.

Stages, as demarcated by Duvall-Hill, allow the analyst to view the processes of development in phases and to concentrate on the role reciprocities and role conflicts at different periods in the family's development. The stage model is a description of the structural stability found within each stage. In recent papers, Klein and colleagues (Klein, Bourne, Jache & Sederberg, 1978; Bourne, Jache, Sederberg & Klein, 1979) commented that the stage model of family development makes stages discrete entities so that, both quantitatively and qualitatively, we should expect differences between adjacent stages in such phenomena as marital adjustment and task allocation (see Figure 1). The stage-discrete model assumes that variables such as marital adjustment, task allocation and child discipline techniques will vary by stage of the family career.

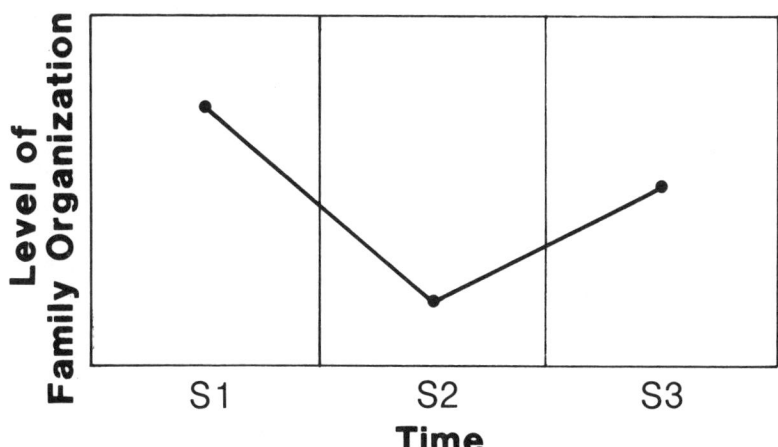

FIGURE 1: Model of development as "stage-discrete": What happens *in* the stage

Structurally, family development views the family system as the unit of analysis made up of social positions of husband-father, wife-mother, daughter-sister, and son-brother.[2] Each position has an associated set of roles, such as breadwinner, disciplinarian, and nurturer, which are, in turn, made up of norms about attitudes and behaviors for those roles. As a primary group, the family system maintains predictable patterns of role relationships among members which are defined as the role structures of division of labor, communication, affection, and decision making. Transactionally, the family maintains relationships with external institutions, such as work, voluntary organizations and schools, and with friendship and kinship networks. Within each stage of the family career these structures are in a state of relative equilibrium, but the equilibrium is disrupted and new structures negotiated during transitions between stages.

A Critique of Traditional Family Development Theory

As a descriptive theory, family development has several important applications. It increases understanding of families at different points in their family careers. It also generates descriptions of typical family careers. But the focus on structural stability within stages also places severe restrictions on the scope and generalizability of the theory.

A major deficiency of the stage discrete family development model is that it does not provide insight into the processes of developmental change by which families differentiate and transform their interaction structures. Most family development research has focused on descriptions of family life *within stages* with some attention to typical sequences of family careers. To our knowledge, none of this research has described developmental processes. The focus on stability has resulted in several limitations. For instance, there is a tendency to ignore variations in initial levels of family organization prior to transitions because of the assumption that families are able to achieve and maintain equilibrium within each stage. The theory has implied, although without empirical investigation, that stages are relatively long and enduring, while transitions that punctuate them are short periods of disorganization and reorganization of minor interest (see Figure 2). Researchers differ in their views of which is more characteristic of families over developmental time,

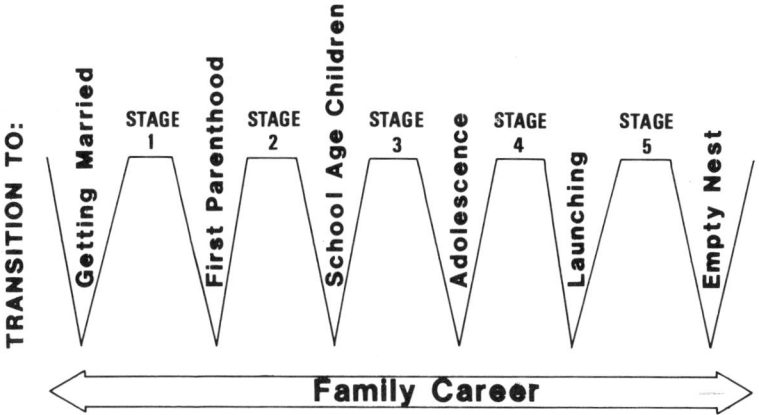

FIGURE 2: Equilibrium states and transitions in traditional family development theory

equilibrium or structural change. In recording family histories by retrospective interviews, many respondents have reported that the stages seemed to merge into one another imperceptibly without sharp breaks between stages (a position taken theoretically by Menaghan, 1982; Neugarten & Hagestad, 1976; Rosow, 1976). The concept of "ease of role transition" from stage to stage was created (Burr, 1972) to account for this variability among families; some experience rough transitions and others smooth changes in structure from stage to stage. Hansen and Johnson (1979) provide a sound theoretical rationale for this phenomenon through their concepts of "established" and "institutive" interaction patterns. Established patterns of interaction are familiar regularities of everyday family life as well as the established emergency routines which family members may bring into play when confronting individual or collective problems. Hansen and Johnson (1979) note,

> In most families under "normal" or endemic stresses of everyday life, these established routines display a general persistence. Close observation also reveals a slow and continual disruption of these patterns, so we speak of *variable disruption of established patterns*. (p. 585)

Institutive patterns of interaction are regularities that are of recent origin and not fully routine, familiar or accepted.

Institutive patterns can also be seen in most families under the "normal" stresses of everyday life, but the range and number are highly variable, both from family to family, and within any family from time to time.... We will speak of variable negotiations of institutive patterns. (p. 585)

The major point is that Hansen and Johnson view "established" and "institutive" interaction patterns as varying independently, so that both can coexist. Smooth transitions, then, would result when established patterns are gradually phased out and institutive patterns are gradually phased in.[3]

Another shortcoming of the stage discrete model is that it has left residual the "adaptive" transitions which make possible the subsequent achievement of family stability. For instance, the entrance of the wife-mother into the labor force may require extensive reorganization, but it also may make possible the achievement of financial security, thereby increasing family stability. Additionally, family development makes the untested assumption that structural change is uniform and consistent, and that each role structure is different within each stage. Empirical evidence is accumulating which suggests that changes in role structures may not be uniform, and that role structures may vary independently of each other. Thus, transitions between stages do not necessarily change all roles, rules and patterns of interaction. Family development theory might profit by analyzing not only what changes, but also what remains stable in family role structures over time.

Finally, family development is limited in the respect that it deals primarily with developmental events and changes, which are predictable, ubiquitous changes such as births of children, launching of children and retirement. It does not deal with changes brought about by idiosyncratic family characteristics or cohort and historical influences. This results in a normative and restrictive view of change in family systems. The effects of other types of nondevelopmental stressors on family functioning and development have not been adequately conceptualized and researched.

Recent work in family development theory (Bourne et al., 1979; Hill & Joy, 1980; Klein et al., 1978; Mederer, Hill, & Joy, 1981) is beginning to address these limitations. The remainder of this chapter describes the contributions of family stress theory and critical transitions theory to a reworked model of family development.

FAMILY STRESS, CRITICAL TRANSITIONS AND FAMILY DEVELOPMENT: A SYNTHESIS

Family Stress Theory and Family Development

Family stress theory and family development theory are similar in their foci. Both theories take, as the unit of analysis, the family as a small group association with respect to its reactions to events, disorganization, renegotiation, and reorganization. Indeed, Rodgers (1973) felt that family stress theory was essentially a special case of family development theory. Despite their similarities, these theories have tended to emphasize reactions and adjustment to different types of life events. Family development has tended to focus on internal, normative, ubiquitous events while family stress has examined primarily the impacts of acute, unanticipated and severe external events (Elder, 1974; Hill, 1949; 1958; McCubbin, Hunter, & Metres, 1974; Mccubbin, Dahl, Lester, & Ross, 1975; McCubbin & Dahl, 1976), or more recently the effects of chronic, persistent stressors that bring long-term hardships on families (McCubbin, Patterson, McCubbin, Wilson, & Warwick, in press).

If change and adaptation are viewed as consequences of both normative developmental situations as well as non-normative stressor events, the disparate emphases of stress and developmental theories might be seen as different aspects of the same problem, namely, family adaptation to stress over time. This complementarity has not yet been fully detailed. A brief description of family stress theory and research helps to identify potential areas of compatibility.

Attention to families' reactions and adjustments to stress has been a long tradition in family research. Hill (1949) provided the major conceptualization of the process of reaction to stressor events in his model of family crisis.

> A (the stressor event)—interacting with B (the family's crisis meeting resources)—interacting with C (the definition the family makes of the event)—produce X (the crisis).

The distinction between these variables has often been confounded in research, e.g., stressors are identified in terms of their effects, and these effects are then taken to be evidences of stressors or the distinction between "stress" and "crisis" often has not been made clear.

The "A" and "X" factors. The above mentioned problems are largely due to the inability to view stress as a process, a deficiency which both Mechanic (1974) and Hansen and Johnson (1979) identified. Recent attention has addressed these problems by defining stressor events as problem situations which present themselves to the family for resolution (Howard & Scott, 1965). Scott and Howard (1970) propose that problem conditions might be categorized by the locus of their initiation: (a) the internal physical environment (of the family); (b) the external physical environment; (c) the psychological environment (of family members); and (d) the social culture. Other typologies of stressor events have been offered (cf. Hill & Rodgers, 1964; Lipman-Blumen, 1975; McCubbin et al., 1980; McCubbin & Patterson, 1981). Hill (1973) introduced the notion of "pile-up" of stressors to account for the fact that most families can accommodate to one or two stressor events, but are forced into reorganization if the stress engendered by the stressors exceeds a certain threshold. This notion helps to explain why stressor events may have different impacts on different families, and the importance of the immediate context in shaping adjustment.

The X factor of crisis is also messy. Hill (1949) defines "crisis" as any sharp or decisive change for which old patterns are inadequate. However, not all disruptions in family capacities and routines should be termed crisis. A case can be made that high levels of disorganization in some cases might be essential to the maintenance of family relationships, and may push families to creative solutions in problem solving (Hansen & Johnson, 1979). The crisis variable might be better viewed as one end of a stress continuum. Hansen's and Johnson's (1979) definition of stress as a condition of "heightened ambiguity" in family roles is similar to Hill's (1949) definition, a situation of sharpened insecurity which blocks the usual patterns of action and calls for new patterns. More recently, Croog (1970) has defined stress as a condition of tension within the individual which occurs as a response to one or more stressors. These definitions leave open the possibility that stress may bring forth adaptive change. McCubbin and Patterson (1981) sharpen this distinction by differentiating between stress and distress. They see the former as a state which arises from a "demand-capability imbalance" in the family's functioning, which is characterized by a non-specific demand for adaptive behavior. Distress, then, is defined as an unpleasant or dysfunctional state which arises from a condition of stress. Their scheme has the advantage thereby of removing the negative connotations from stress.

What does all of this have to offer to family development? For one, it provides us with a taxonomy of concepts which are general enough to include both changes associated with developmental events and changes associated with severe, unanticipated crises.

Any problem condition which the family experiences may, under certain conditions, produce a feeling of unresolved tension, or heightened ambiguity in family roles. The ambiguity, then, calls for a response of adaptive behavior as the family moves into a period of negotiation and reorganization.

Two questions remain: (a) what are the conditions under which problems produce the outcome of heightened ambiguity or tension? and (b) how do members change their interaction patterns in response to ambiguity? The first question is a structural question, while the second question is a process question. We will return to this latter question in the discussion of recommended research.

The B and C factors. One of the major advantages of the ABCX model is that it provides both a description and an explanation of why families move into transition. The focus is to understand the conditions under which families move to adapt to problem situations. The model identifies general intervening variables which affect the probability that families will move into transition. These include the B factor of family resources and the C factor of perception of the seriousness of the situation.

The B factor of family resources has received much attention. Four types of resources utilized in research were identified by McCubbin et al. (1980). These are (a) family members' personal resources; (b) the family's internal resources; (c) social support; and (d) coping. The functions of resources are to reduce tension, to manage conflict and to fulfill family needs brought about by the stressor situation.

The C factor, the family's definition of the situation, also intervenes (in the original ABCX model) between the stressor and the resulting degree of stress (or crisis). Hill (1949) defined this factor as the degree to which the situation is seen as a threat to family status, goals, or objectives. Hansen and Johnson (1979) note that the concept's utility lies in the conceptualization of family members' efforts to coordinate their interaction with other members. The perceptual factor (C), then, affects the degree to which family interaction is characterized by role playing (established interaction patterns) versus role making (new institutive patterns of interaction) (Hansen & Johnson, 1979). This idea provides a basis for looking at phases of transition in family development and level of adjustment as families move into a new stage.

Adjustment to stress. Hansen and Johnson (1979) view the adjustment process as the renegotiation of new interaction patterns among family members under conditions of heightened ambiguity. Throughout the family career, families experience a series of problem situations which cannot be resolved using established interaction patterns. For instance, most families have the experience of first parenthood. The types of hardships inherent in this event may be impossible to cope with using established patterns of decision making. Because one parent may become primary caretaker of the baby, he or she may have more say than the noncaretaking parent in decisions concerning the baby. Communication and affection patterns between husband and wife are interrupted by the baby's own schedule. The situation may become more ambiguous if other family structural or family organizational changes occur simultaneously (Hill's notion of pile-up).[4] The response of the family to the ambiguity is to start experimenting with other interaction patterns to see what can be modified and still achieve role fit among members. Moreover, since developmental events can be anticipated, the family can start to experiment with new patterns slowly, while retaining the comfort of old patterns on which to fall back when ambiguity becomes too high. In this scenario, the distress is minimal, and the transition proceeds smoothly. Conversely, rough transitions might result if established patterns were not retained while new patterns were being explored, a result of an unexpected and severe problem situation, or if the repertoire of experimental interaction strategies is limited, and the family is stuck in old patterns which do not work.

Traditionally, family development has attempted to incorporate essentially structural models of adjustment to stress. Hill (1949) provided the first model of adjustment in his roller coaster model (see Figure 3). He proposed a period of disorganization while the family was destructuring and restructuring, followed by a new level of re-equilibrium. The new level might be lower or higher than the previous level of adjustment.

Recently, McCubbin and Patterson (see Chapter 2) have defined more precisely the elements in the process. Noting that the original ABCX model focused primarily on precrisis variables, these re-

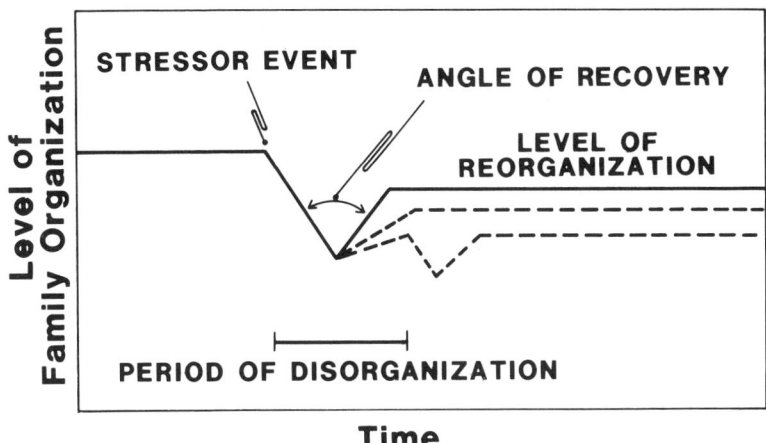

FIGURE 3: Hill's "roller-coaster" profile of family reactions to a crisis-provoking event

searchers created the "Double ABCX Model," which focuses on family efforts over time to recover from a crisis situation. The double ABCX adds post-crisis variables to the original ABCX model in an effort to describe additional concurrent stressors the family may be experiencing which would affect recovery from the original crisis, the new as well as previously existing resources used by families in the recovery process, their perceptions and evaluation of their post-crisis situation, and the outcome, or degree of adaptation.

Another stream of research is worth noting. Farber (1964) created a "crisis process" for the changes which the stressor event trips off. His stages of adjustment offer nuances lacking in the ABCX models:

1. First, an attempt is made to handle the event within existing role structures—by denying that the stressor is harmful, viewing the condition as temporary and expecting that restoration will occur.
2. Unless the situation is righted a second stage of realism is reached and the problem is faced with its implications for former family commitments.
3. The problem becomes public and extra-familial ties are altered as required.

4. Role reorientation occurs with a revision of expectations accepted by family members.
5. Finally, a "freezing out" of the offensive behavior occurs or if necessary the removal of the stress-bearing member from the home occurs (the alcoholic, the mentally retarded, or mentally disturbed, or the delinquent) so that the family unit can get on about its business.[5]

Adams (1975) undertook a useful synthesis of the ABCX and Farber models about responses to stress by conceptualizing types of stressors along temporary-permanent and voluntary-involuntary continua, against the likely-phased responses of families to these types of stressors (see Table 1). Different stressors result in different typical responses: freezing out the behavior and reinstating the individual or temporarily reorganizing and reinstating, or freezing out the individual and permanently reorganizing. Families may "freeze out" their deviant members from the problem solving process until they are able to enter into renegotiation with the remainder of the family.

Critical Transitions Theory and Family Development

The theoretical and empirical contributions of Rhona Rapoport (1963, 1964) in her work on normal family crises and family structure have clarified the process of transition and adjustment. Rapoport noted the close parallels between the responses to the hardship-bearing stressor events of the family crisis studies and the

TABLE 1: MOST LIKELY FAMILY RESPONSES TO CHANGE AND CHALLENGES (STRESSORS)

TYPE OF STRESSOR (with example)	RESPONSES
Voluntary-Temporary (illegitimacy)	Freeze out behavior reinstate person (if persistent, other stressors may follow)
Involuntary-Temporary (unemployment)	Ignore or deny; or else admit temporarily reorganize reinstate
Voluntary-Permanent (divorce)	Reorganize
Involuntary-Permanent (retardation)	Admit freeze out person reorganize (death: admit reorganize)

Source: Bert N. Adams, The Family: A Sociological Interpretation. (Chicago: Rand-McNally, 1975), page 341.

normal developmental challenges requiring family reorganization which punctuate the family's life span. Termed "normal crises of transition" because they are encountered by all families bearing children, she identified them in sequence as (1) the crisis of getting married; (2) the crisis of parenthood; (3) the crisis of deparentalization; (4) the crisis of leavetaking or launching; and (5) the crisis of retirement.[6] She invoked crisis theory to account for the behavior of families as they moved through "points of no return" from one crisis to the next. If the crisis is handled advantageously, it is assumed that the result is some kind of maturation or development. If the crisis is not handled well, old tensions may be renewed and new conflicts may arise. It should be noted that the developmental crises carry no stigma, no label of deviancy, which characterize a number of the crises depicted in the family crisis literature. Hill (1973) offered a tentative way of operationalizing Rapoport's concept of critical transition to generate stages of family development. He noted that stages of development, by definition, were marked by multiple sharp changes in the family's role complex. Most families can sustain one or two changes in their role scripts but are forced into major reorganization if there is a pile-up of role complex changes. Hill singled out three types of structural events which might be expected to be stressful and hypothesized that, if they occurred within the same period of time, they would precipitate a critical transition demarcating a new stage of development:

1. Changes in numbers of family members (accessions and losses of spouse and/or children, return of divorced and widowed adult children).
2. Age composition changes:
   Changes in age norm content due to individual developmental status change, school status change, and so on of:
   oldest child
   middle child
   youngest child
3. Major status changes of:
   Cohabitating, engaged, married, divorced, widowed statuses
   Childless, parenthood, stepparenthood, grandparenthood, emptynesthood statuses
   Changes in conjunctive roles affecting priorities in role cluster and role sets:
   Entering and leaving school (Fa, Mo, Ch)

Entering labor force, changing careers, and leaving labor force (Fa, Mo, Ch)
Entering and leaving military service (Fa, Mo, Ch)
Entering and leaving hospital as patient (Fa, Mo, Ch)
Residential status and location changes:
Renter, homeowner, renter
Network affiliation changes

Hill suggested that it is a matter of judgement how many of these several role complex changes might be used for formulating discrete categories of the family life cycle depending on the research problem and the availability of data. A family stress score to reflect the pile-up of critical life events occurring over a limited period might be constructed as has already been done for life course stresses by Holmes and Rahe (1967) to predict mental breakdown and recently tested by McCubbin and Patterson (1981). Examples of critical transitions generated by four or more critical events occurring simultaneously, are shown in Table 2. What is not shown in this table is any evidence of periods of equilibrium in between the critical transitions which the formulation in Figure 2 earlier depicted. The number of critical transitions generated, however, are roughly the same as the number of stages of development generated by the Duvall-Hill criteria.

Based on Rapoport's (1963, 1964) work, Klein and colleagues (1978, 1979) have highlighted a model of development called "stage transitional," which makes the transition from one stage to the next the key phenomenon of interest (see Figure 4). Best illustrated by the research on the "crisis of first parenthood," the approach sees stages as relatively uneventful periods and stage transitions as capturing the variables of interest.

Klein et al. (1978) note the differences between the stage discrete model of development (Figure 1) and the stage transitional model; namely that the discrete stage model ignores the question of how families get from one stage of development to the next, while the transitional stage model ignores possible difference before and after the transition is made. They offer a merger of the two (see Figure 5) which makes family development a stage-transitional branching process. Using the conceptualization of stage transitions as a point of departure, they add the idea that changes result in varying levels of re-equilibrium, an idea anticipated by Magrabi's and Marshall's (1965) game tree model. Figure 5 offers a hypothetical illustration

Table 2.

SEQUENCES OF CRITICAL TRANSITIONS GENERATED BY STRESSFUL IMPACT OF SIMULTANEOUS STRESSORS AND/OR CHANGES IN FAMILY ROLE COMPLEX

Possible Stressors &/or Disjunctive Role Complex Changes	Type of Critical Transition	Possible Stressors &/or Disjunctive Role Complex Changes	Type of Critical Transition
Disengaging from sibling and filial roles (H & W)		Oldest child shifts orientation to peers, disengagement from family	IV.
Leaving parental residence (H & W)	I.	Youngest child enters school	Critical transition to dual earner family organization & disengagement of children, expanded role sets with several conjunctive roles
Leaving school (H & W)	The critical transition of getting married (disengagement from parental families & friends & becoming a settled married couple.)	Mother reenters school and/or labor force	
Taking job (H & W)		Life cycle squeeze of deficit financing	
Taking on marital status (H & W)			
Changing friend network (H & W)			
Taking on an in-law status (H & W)		Oldest child leaves school, enters labor force	
Accession of infant member, plurality pattern change to triad.		Oldest child marries	
Taking on parental status with father & mother roles activitated	II.	Oldest child leaves home	V.
Leaving labor force (W)	Critical transition of first parenthood	Plurality patterns change as children launched	Critical transition of launching children, placement of children into jobs and marriage
Kinship network reactivitated (Grandparents, aunts, & uncles)		Youngest child disengages from parents & shifts to peers	
Residential change to accommodate infant needs		Parents become in-laws	
Oldest child enters school		Change in residence to smaller quarters	VI.
Youngest child born	III.	Return to dyadic pattern	Critical transition to companionate marriage and to grandparenthood
Residential changes to accommodate growing children's needs	Critical transition to transactional relations with schools & neighbors.	Retirement from parenthood	
Change from renter to home owner status		Taking on roles of grandparenthood	
Network change from open to close knit		Reduction in many conjunctive roles	
		H & W retire from labor force	
		H & W lose leadership positions, status losses	VII.
		H & W close boundaries by disengagement	Critical transition to retirement & disengaged status of aged
		Residential status change to renter or to nursing home resident	

of four possible paths (A through D) which couples might follow in the level of their family organization following the birth of the first child:

— Path A: The birth adversely affects the level of spousal adjustment temporarily but a full recovery to the prebirth level eventually occurs.
— Path B: The birth erodes spousal consensus to such a degree the relationship ends through divorce or separation.
— Path C: The birth adversely affects the level of marital adjustment but the couple stabilizes at a lower level than before.
— Path D: The birth adversely affects the couple temporarily but in reorganization the couple eventually achieves a higher level than before.

This third model amalgamates a variety of notions which

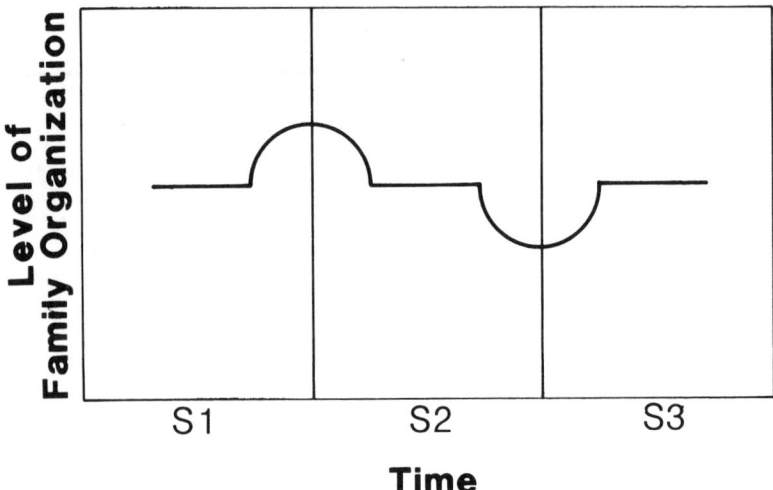

FIGURE 4: Model of development as "stage-transitional": What happens *between* stages

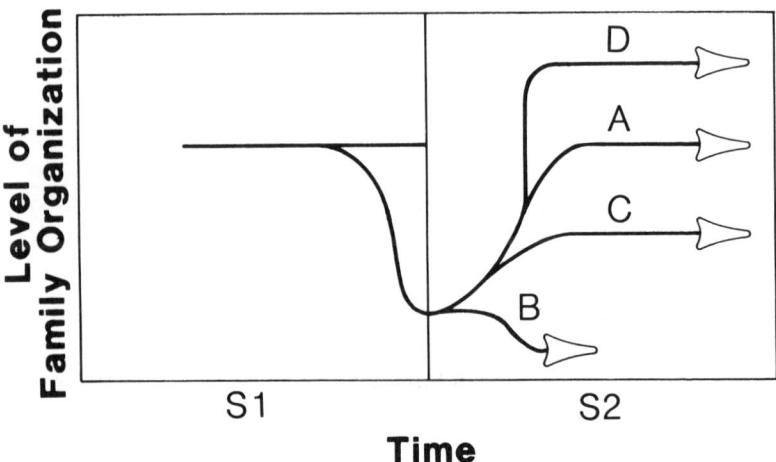

FIGURE 5: Model of development as "stage-transitional branching process": What level of organization the family returns to after transition

developmental scholars have advanced to describe the process of development: dynamic equilibrium; critical transitions; morphogenesis; and family crisis and adaptation. It offers a heuristic synthesis of much of the foregoing review of family development, family stress and critical transition theories. Comparison of the three models, namely, Figure 1, Stage Discrete Model; Figure 4, Stage Transitional Model; and Figure 5, Stage Transitional Branching Model illustrates clearly why empirical efforts to "measure" development have produced ambiguous results. Typical statistical procedures will not detect the processes of development described by the second and third models. The only model with which current linear and curvilinear association procedures are compatible is the first of these, the Stage Discrete Model. It is important to note, however, that the statistical problems stem directly from the methodologies favored by family development researchers.

Researchers who investigate these issues, especially family sociologists, heavily utilize the interview and questionnaire as research tools to the exclusion of other methods. We tend to rationalize our choice of self-report methods by relying on the symbolic interaction dictum: what persons (i.e., respondents) believe to be true are true in their social consequences. However, it is becoming increasingly evident that families are often not their own best informants. Families may know what they believe to be true, but they are not always fully aware of how they behave (Brody & Endsley, 1981; Yarrow, 1968). They are also too close to the process of change to be fully cognizant of the change.

If we are going to understand the processes of negotiating institutive versus established patterns of interaction as families cope with ambiguity, observational methods are required to supplement self-report methods. Observational data, taken at short time intervals, over a period of time can be systematically coded and subjected to time series analysis techniques. Through observational methods, we may be able to learn more about the process of negotiation in families.

PROGRESS, PROBLEMS AND RECOMMENDATIONS FOR FUTURE RESEARCH

It is perhaps obvious that the family development perspective has been limited by its reliance on the Stage Discrete model of development (Figure 1), since it is not an adequate description of the processes of developmental change and may overgeneralize differences between family career stages. The stage transitional branching process (Figure 5) seems to depict more accurately the course of developmental changes because of its focus on transitions and recognition of differences in resulting levels of reorganization. If we adopt this as our model, the research questions become: (a) what precipitates families into transitions; (b) what are the phases of transitions; (c) how does the family reorganize itself; and (d) what are the possible outcomes of reorganization? This chapter has set the stage for addressing these questions by discussing the complementarity among family stress theory, critical transitions theory and family development theory.

These research questions are both structural and processual in character. To understand why families enter transitions we need to know the structural conditions under which problem situations posed to the family produce the outcome of heightened ambiguity or tension. Variables which have been identified include both characteristics of the problem situations as well as characteristics of the family. Researchers have made some progress with this question; however, our methods still do not allow us to identify operationally the onset of transitions or the exit from transitions as evidenced by behavioral or attitudinal change. Theoretically, Hansen's and Johnson's (1979) contributions allow us to identify the onset of the transition process as a time of "heightened ambiguity" in family rules and roles. They propose that during periods of heightened ambiguity, families experiment with "institutive patterns of interaction," but do not necessarily give up their "established patterns of interaction" immediately. Interaction is restructured through a process of experimenting with new patterns within the safety of familiar interaction patterns. The transition process is then broken down into phases of experimental versus old interaction patterns.[7] Hypothetically, it may be possible to operationalize phases of transitions as different ratios of established to institutive interaction patterns, if we utilize observational techniques to supplement survey methodology.

The third research question, how does the family reorganize itself, examines the process by which institutive patterns become incorporated as established patterns. Some efforts have been made to identify the negotiation between family members which characterizes this reorganization process (see Mederer, Hill, & Joy, 1981). It may be hypothesized that families negotiate new structures by utilizing both old family rules of negotiations as well as their rules-about-rules (metarules) (Broderick & Smith, 1979). When the family becomes disorganized, they eventually define their situation as undesirable and then mobilize their resources to take action, that is, to make a decision as to what can be done. The alternatives are:

1. Dissolve the family.
2. Pull the family back into line by creating more rules to suppress overt signs of dissatisfaction. Emphasize the preeminence of family organization over individual members' growth. This technique has been labeled "negative feedback," leading to morphostasis. The use of psychological coping strategies which buffer the family through altering the perception of the situation is prominent. Established patterns are emphasized.
3. Start another process of negotiaton to identify members' needs and wants and balance them with effective family functions. In effect, this alternative moves the family into transition. In the negotiation process, the formerly established rules of organization and role structures of decision making and communication are altered, and these alterations affect changes in other role structures of affection, division of tasks, and the family's relations with the near environment. New patterns are actively encouraged. Psychological coping strategies may be used to ease the perception of difficulty of the transition, but the predominant strategy is sociological coping, i.e., structural change.

In this line of research, our theoretical understanding again outdistances our methodological sophistication.

The fourth research question about possible outcomes of reorganization was addressed in Figure 5. Outcomes of transition may temporarily erode family consensus (Path A), permanently erode family consensus to the point of dissolution (Path B), reduce family consensus to a lower level (Path C), or increase family consensus to a higher level than before the transition (Path D). These hypotheses may not be exhaustive, and remain to be tested in research.

At this point, we stop and evaluate where we are in understanding the processes in family change over the family career. The main integrating issue of family development, family stress and critical transition theories is: how do families go about changing their structures to reflect changing membership, changing member and family needs, and changing expectations from their external social networks? The theoretical bases for understanding this issue are becoming more elaborate as more disciplines become interested in developmental issues, but our propositions remain at an exploratory or, at best, descriptive level of analysis. Interdisciplinary, multimethod research is an important next step. This chapter has provided the preliminary theoretical integration necessary to undertake such research.

REFERENCE NOTES

1. Lansing and Kish (1957) chose the youngest child as the indicator of family change since it has an emancipating effect for the parents, such as return of the mother to school for additional training or to reenter the labor force.
2. Not all of these positions are necessarily occupied at any one time.
3. Menaghan (in press) may provide empirical evidence that smooth transitions are generally typical of family transitions. She found in her sample of families who were experiencing normative transitions that expected changes in household composition and development of the oldest child did not produce high levels of disorganization. Using Hansen's and Johnson's concepts, institutive patterns over time may have replaced established patterns smoothly for Menaghan's sample. In contrast, Nock (1981) found in a longitudinal study that family transitions negatively affected subjective evaluations of life. He found that the effects of transitions were modest, and all but one were negative, suggesting that transitions are experienced as challenging and perhaps unpleasant events.
4. Menaghan (personal correspondence) has suggested that this may not always be the case since some simultaneous events may serve to mitigate the effects of other events. Her example was: a pile-up of birth of child, residential move to larger quarters, and wife-mother leaving the labor force. In this scenario, the last two events are both stressors in their own right and *coping responses* to create discretionary time and space in dealing with the first stressor event.
5. Hansen's and Johnson's (1979) theory is compatible with steps (1) through (3) above; however, their model is an elaboration of step (4).
6. It should be noted that there is some coincidence in time of the Rapoport transitions and some of the Duvall-Hill stages described earlier although they have been derived from different principles.
7. David Reiss (1981) recently has proposed an interesting parallel view to that of Hansen and Johnson. His framework proposes that family disorganization may occur in three separate stages: (a) the emergence of rules as the family's repertoire of background understandings, shared assumptions, and traditions disappear; (b) the emergence of an "explicit family" as a social construction, as rules begin to coalesce into more rigid systems of control; and (c) the rebellion of individual members against the "explicit family." At this point, according to Reiss, the family withdraws into itself, ceases its "task orientation" and becomes "process oriented." That is, the family withdraws its investment in managing identifiable tasks and instead struggles with itself. To reorganize, the family must recognize that it is in crisis and begin to develop some shared concept of that crisis. They are able then to start the process of reorganization.

REFERENCES

Adams, B. N. *The family: A sociological interpretation.* Chicago: Rand-McNally, 1975.
Aldous, J., & Hill, R. Breaking the poverty cycle. *Social Work,* 1969, *14,* 3-12.

Bourne, H., Jache, A., Sederberg, N., & Klein, D. *Family chronogram analysis: Toward the development of new methodological tools for assessing the life cycles of families.* Paper presented at the Theory-Methods Workshop of the National Council on Family Relations Annual Meeting, Boston, 1979.

Broderick, C., & Smith, J. The general systems approach to the family, in W. Burr, R. Hill, F. Nye, & I. Reiss (Eds.), *Contemporary theories about the family, Volume 2: General theories/theoretical based orientations.* New York: The Free Press, 1979.

Brody, G., & Endsley, R. Researching children and families: Differences in approaches of developmental and family researchers. *Family Relations,* 1981, *30*(2), 275-280.

Burr, W. Role transitions: A reformulation of theory. *Journal of Marriage and the Family,* 1972, August, 407-416.

Croog, S. The family as a source of stress. In S. Levine & N. Scotch (Eds.), *Social Stress.* Chicago: Aldine, 1970.

Duvall, E. M. *Family development* (First Edition). Philadelphia: Lippincott, 1957.

Elder, G. *Children of the Great Depression.* Chicago: University of Chicago Press, 1974.

Farber, B. *Family organization and interaction.* San Francisco: Chandler, 1964.

Hansen, D., & Johnson, V. Rethinking family stress theory: Definitional aspects. In W. Burr, R. Hill, F. Nye, and I. Reiss (Eds.), *Contemporary theories about the family. Volume I: Research based theories.* New York: The Free Press, 1979.

Hill, R. *Families under stress.* New York: Harper & Row, 1949.

Hill, R. Generic features of families under stress. *Social Casework,* 1958, *49*, 139-150.

Hill, R. *Family life cycle: Critical role transitions.* Presented at Thirteenth International Family Research Seminar, Paris, 1973.

Hill, R., & Joy, C. *Conceptualizing and operationalizing category systems for phasing of family development.* Unpublished paper, 1980.

Hill, R., & Rodgers, R. The developmental approach. In H. Christensen (Ed.), *Handbook of marriage and the family.* Chicago: Rand-McNally, 1964.

Holmes, T., & Rahe, R. The social readjustment rating scale. *Journal of Psychosomatic Research,* 1967, *11*, 213-218.

Howard, A., & Scott, R. A proposed framework for the analysis of stress in the human organism. *Behavioral Science,* 1965, *10*, 141-160.

Imig, D. Accumulated stress of life changes and interpersonal effectiveness in the family. *Family Relations,* 1981, *30*(3), 367-371.

Klein, D., Bourne, H., Jache, A., & Sederberg, N. *Family chronogram analysis: Toward the development of new methodological tools for assessing the life cycles of families.* Unpublished manuscript, University of Notre Dame, 1978.

Lansing, J., & Kish, L. Family life cycle as an independent variable. *American Sociological Review,* 1957, *22*, 512-519.

Lipman-Blumen, J. A crisis framework applied to macrosociological family changes: Marriage, divorce, and occupational trends associated with World War II. *Journal of Marriage and the Family,* 1975, *27*, 889-902.

Magrabi, F., & Marshall, W. H. Family developmental tasks: A research model. *Journal of Marriage and the Family,* 1965, *27*, 454-461.

Mattessich, P., & Hill, R. Family development and life cycle research and theory revisited. In M. Sussman & S. Steinmetz (Eds.), *Handbook of marriage and the family.* New York: Plenum Press, in press.

McCubbin, H., Hunter, E., & Metres, P. Adaptation of the family to the prisoner of war and missing in action experience. In H. McCubbin, B. Dahl, P. Metres, E. J. Hunter, & J. Plag (Eds.), *Family separation and reunion.* Washington, DC: U. S. Government Printing Office, 1974.

McCubbin, H., Dahl, B., Lester, G., & Ross, B. The returned prisoner of war: Factors of family reintegration. *Journal of Marriage and the Family,* 1975, *37*, 471-478.

McCubbin, H., & Dahl, B. Prolonged family separation in the military: A longitudinal study. In H. McCubbin, B. Dahl, & E. J. Hunter (Eds.), *Families in the military system.* Beverly Hills, CA: Sage Publications, 1976.

McCubbin, H., Joy, C., Cauble, E., Comeau, J., Patterson, J., & Needle, R. Family stress and coping: A decade review. *Journal of Marriage and the Family*, 1980, *42*(4), 855-870.

McCubbin, H., & Patterson, J. *Systematic assessment of family stress, resources and coping: Tools for research, education and clinical intervention.* St. Paul, MN: Family Stress and Coping Project, Department of Family Social Sciences, University of Minnesota, 1981.

McCubbin, H., Patterson, J., & Wilson, L. *Family inventory of life events and changes.* St. Paul, MN: University of Minnesota, 1979.

McCubbin, H., Patterson, J., McCubbin, M., Wilson, L., & Warwick, W. Parental coping and family environment: Critical factors in the home management and health status of children with cystic fibrosis. In D. Bagarozzi, T. Jurich, & I. Jackson (Eds.), *New perspectives in marriage and family therapy: Issues in theory, research and practice.* Palo Alto, CA: Human Science Press, in press.

Mechanic, D. Social structure and personal adaptation: Some neglected dimensions. In G. Coelho, D. Hamburg & J. Adams (Eds.), *Coping and adaptation.* New York: Basic Books, 1974.

Mederer, H., Hill, R., & Joy, C. *Bridging theory via multi-methods: Questionnaire and interview design for capturing critical transition processes in family development.* Paper presented at the Theory-Methods Workshop of the National Council on Family Relations Annual Meeting, Milwaukee, Wisconsin, October 1981.

Menaghan, E. Assessing the impact of family transitions on marital experience: Problems and prospects. In H. McCubbin, A. E. Cauble, & J. Patterson (Eds.), *Family stress, coping and social support.* Springfield, IL: Charles C. Thomas, 1982.

Neugarten, B., & Hagestad, G. Aging and the life course. In R. Binstock & E. Shanas (Eds.), *Handbook of aging and the social sciences.* New York: Van Nostrand Reinhold, 1976.

Nock, S. Family life cycle transitions: Longitudinal effects on family members. *Journal of Marriage and the Family*, 1981, *43*(3), 703-714.

Rapoport, R. Normal crises, family structure and mental health. *Family Process*, 1963, *2*(1), 68-80.

Rapoport, R. The transition from engagement to marriage. *Acta Sociologica*, 1964, *8*, 36-55.

Reiss, D. *The family's construction of reality.* Cambridge, MA: Harvard University Press, 1981.

Rodgers, R. *Family interaction and transaction: The developmental approach.* Englewood Cliffs, NJ: Prentice-Hall, 1973.

Rosow, I. Status and role change through the life span. In R. Binstock & E. Shanas (Eds.), *Handbook of aging and the social sciences.* New York: Van Nostrand Reinhold, 1976.

Scott, R., & Howard, A. Models of stress. In S. Levine and N. Scotch (Eds.), *Social Stress.* Chicago: Aldine, 1970.

Yarrow, M., Campbell, J., & Burton, R. *Child rearing.* San Francisco: Jossey-Bass, 1968.

Chapter 3

Family Stress as Community Frame

David Reiss
Mary Ellen Oliveri

The study of family stress has become a coherent field. There is a widening consensus on its origins, its significant historical junctures and current prospects. Indeed, two recent reviews have very successfully delineated the accomplishments of the field so far as well as delineated its major problems (Hansen & Johnson, 1979; McCubbin, Joy, Cauble, Comeau, Patterson, & Needle, 1980). Further review of the past seems unnecessary now. Rather, a clarification of existing problems is more useful—particularly if it serves to improve future research and practice. In this connection, it is ironic that the concept of family stress remains a central problem for the field. There is both ambiguity and disagreement about how family stress is to be defined. This chapter sketches an approach to this definition. Simply put, we suggest that family stress can be defined not with respect to the family itself, but with respect to the social community in which the family lives. We will clarify this definition, suggest strategies for measuring family stress in this way and indicate some of the advantages of this approach to defining family stress.

David Reiss is Professor and Mary Ellen Oliveri is Assistant Research Professor, Center for Family Research, Department of Psychiatry and Behavioral Sciences, George Washington University Medical Center, Washington, D.C.

Preparation of this paper was supported by a grant (DHEW MH 26711) from the National Institute of Mental Health.

CURRENT DEFINITIONS OF FAMILY STRESS

In previous work in the field, there seems to be a consensus on distinguishing between family stress and family crisis. Hill's (1949, 1958) influential formulation talked of four critical components of family stress. He proposed a well-known sequence: a stressor event interacts with the family's crisis-meeting resources, as well as its definition of the seriousness of the event, to produce a crisis. The critical distinction here is between the stressor event—a demarcated occurrence afflicting the family—and the crisis which refers to the family's disorganization and subjective distress. Thus family stress is generally held to refer to circumstances, events or experiences with which the family must somehow cope. There is also a recognition among most workers in this field that there is no easy way to decide whether an event or circumstance might be stressful for any given family. Hill recognized this by emphasizing the importance of the family's subjective appraisal of the event; if the family itself saw the event as trivial, others, including researchers, could profit little from regarding it as stressful. The problem of defining stress becomes particularly clear in studies which seek to compare families in their response to stress. A basic question here is why some families cope well with stress whereas others are thrown into intense crises. Equally important are questions as to why some families, whatever the depth of short-term crisis in response to stress, recover effectively whereas others do not. These contrasts between family's *responses* to stress become meaningful only if the stress itself, as well as its magnitude, can be measured or assessed independently of the impact it makes on the family. There have been three approaches to defining family stress which have attempted to solve this problem.

First, stress can be defined and measured by attention to the objective qualities of the event itself and its correlates in the family's environment. Few workers have used this approach exclusively although it is the one we will develop in this paper. Hill, however, spoke to this perspective in arguing that the hardships associated with any event determine, in part, the stress it provides. Thus, in his study of war-induced separations of fathers from their families (1949) he found that some families—as a consequence of the separation—had to endure major economic deprivation, relocations and significant changes in relations with kin; for other families there was relatively less hardship and a few had an improvement in their situation as defined objectively.

A second approach reflects most workers' views that even when objective hardships are great, some families will perceive them as terrifying whereas others will see them as transitory or masterable. Thus, this second perspective argues that the family's own perception of the event is the *sine qua non* condition of family stress. As we have pointed out, Hill recognized the central role of family definitional process in his influential model. More recently, Hansen and Johnson's stimulating resynthesis of Hill's model (1979) weaves this notion of subjective definition around the central idea of ambiguity. In effect, Hansen and Johnson argue that stress confronts a family when they *cannot* define a situation: when their capacities to solve the dilemma or the potential resources for help are simply indeterminate. Thus, stress comes at times of most rapid and thorough change in the environment but, imply Hansen and Johnson, change as defined by the expectations and understandings of the family—not the outside observer.

A third approach is the option pursued by Elder (1974). He views stress as a genuine interaction between the family and its environment—a view conditioned by his decade-long research on the impact of the Great Depression. For Elder, economic hardship—conceived of in terms very similar to Hill's notion of hardship—clearly constituted a necessary but not sufficient cause of family stress. These hardships must interact with factors Elder refers to as "claims" and "controls." "Claims" constitute the family's sense of what it needs from its environment and "controls" refer to its awareness of its own capacities to meet those needs. Where claims exceed controls— as the family defines it—serious stress is unavoidable.

The second and third approaches clearly depend on family definitional processes to conceptualize family stress. We see two difficulties with these perspectives because of this dependence. First, they underestimate the effect of the family's definitional processes. They overlook the likelihood that the family's definitional processes not only determine the magnitude of experienced stress but also shape its coping with and recovery from the impact of that stress. Second, these two perspectives—because of their dependence on the family definitional process—weaken our efforts to identify properties of the environment that constitute "generic stress" for its component families. By "generic stress" we mean events that are likely to be stressful for the typical family in a specific social community. Let us consider each of these objections in turn.

Underestimation of the Pervasiveness of Family Definitional Processes

In a previous paper (Reiss & Oliveri, 1980), we have argued that a family's definition of the event and the social context in which it arises is crucial to all phases of its response to challenges, threats and disruptions. For example, the family's most immediate coping efforts will be determined by its perception of the event and its context. If the family sees the event as masterable and understandable, its first efforts will be to explore the event, learn more about it and come to some preliminary diagnosis or conclusion. On the other hand, if the family sees the event as capricious, obeying no laws and unfathomable, its initial approach to coping will be quite the opposite. The family will tend to retreat and protect itself. As Dill, Feld, Martin, Beukema, and Belle (1980) point out, this perception of threat may be based in a realistic appraisal of the environment; an appraisal of this kind is exemplified by the low-income mothers in their study who confronted endless obstacles in their efforts at coping in their deprived and unresponsive environment. In our own studies, we showed that these perceptions of danger and disorder in the environment may, in many instances, be traced to a characteristic of the family itself—a pervasive disposition to see themselves as unequal to any severe challenge. After their immediate efforts to cope with the challenge, a family's long-term recovery from the impact of the challenge may also be shaped by its initial and continuing subjective definition of the event itself. For example, a family's appraisal that its solution to the challenge was due to its own collective efforts will lead the family to a sense of shared accomplishment and solidarity which may exceed what it felt before the challenge. Likewise, a family which perceives itself as a continuing and helpless victim of a challenge will, at the conclusion of its fruitless coping, intensify its experience of itself as defeated, fractionated and depleted; it may be particularly vulnerable to any subsequent challenge. Recognizing the crucial role that the family definitional process plays in both the family's efforts to cope with the stress as well as its mode of recovery helps us to see that *the family's subjective appraisal of the event is itself a coping process.* Families who can see a major event as circumscribed and manageable are already engaged in an effective coping process. It follows that in studies where we wish to contrast and compare the coping styles and recovery processes in different families, we must have a concept of family stress which is independent of family definitional processes. Without such a concept we confound the nature and magnitude of the challenge with the family's response to it.

Identifying Stressful Properties of the Environment

Conceptions of family stress which rely heavily on the family definitional process are also inadequate for another important line of investigation: They do not permit us to explore systematically the family's social environment for generic sources of stress to families. A particularly instructive example is unemployment. What is the impact on a family when, for example, a local plant is shut down and the father becomes unemployed? There are two fundamentally different questions we can ask concerning the relationship between the plant closing and family stress. The first is, what accounts for the differences between families in their response to this event? Some families seem unperturbed but in others there is unremitting crisis. Concepts of stress woven around a family definitional process will be helpful in answering this question. However, we are very likely to discover that the features which lead families to be relatively invulnerable to this particular challenge of unemployment are very similar to those which lead to invulnerability to a broad range of other challenges.[1] Using a family definitional approach in conceptualizing family stress, we will learn very little about why this particular plant closing was disruptive to families and why the closing of another plant in a different community, at roughly the same time, was not. We will need a different perspective on family stress to understand why, for example, the closing of an urban plant can have devastating effects on its employees and their families but a rural plant closing may not (Gore, 1978), or why unemployment in the 1970s and 1980s may have less of an impact on families than unemployment during the Great Depression (Thomas, McCabe, & Berry, 1980).

A COMMUNITY-BASED PROPOSAL FOR DEFINING FAMILY STRESS

Our proposal suggests we replace the family's subjective definition of the event with another subjective definition: that of the social community in which the family lives. Our hypothesis is that all communities develop some consensus on events that happen within them and their potential impact on families. Moreover, communities have specific conceptions of the family: its technical sufficiency for causing the event in the first place (its accountability), its moral obligation for dealing with it (its duty), and its capacity for carrying out its responsibility (its competence). In simpler societies, "culture" and "community" may be regarded as roughly synonymous. The prevailing standards and practices of the family's community (village, tribe, etc.) are a single-voiced expression of the prevailing beliefs and values of the culture. In more complex societies, the community is more heterogenous and, though by no means mute on the issue of events and families, may speak with several voices. Moreover, for highly mobile families or even for sessile families with cosmopolitan perspectives it may be difficult to define the "community" whose values and conceptions are most influential. Nonetheless, for simplicity's sake, we will define a family's community as those social settings of its everyday life. In urban settings, these will include neighborhood, major friendship and kin networks and occupational and school settings. In a complex urban setting each of these might constitute separate social worlds—perhaps with conflicting perspectives, images and values. It is important that many of them are not simply voluntary but that the family is actively recruited or coerced into some by law (school) or by need (occupational setting).

Our proposal was anticipated by the comprehensive Hill model which speaks of the salience of the "cultural definition" (of the event) formulated by the community (1958). Hill sees this process as relevant to the experienced magnitude of the event but regards it as less important than family definitional processes. Lipman-Blumen (1975) has provided a more elaborate notion; she argues that an entire national community can define and experience a number of aspects or components of stressful events. Applying her own approach to World War II as a severe challenge, she suggests that all of America experienced the onset of the war as sudden, external, pervasive, unexpected with long-range implications and perhaps not solvable (winnable). Lipman-Blumen's data suggest that this community-conceived stress had profound effects on the structure of American families. In our own proposal we suggest there are four aspects of the community's subjective definition of family-related stress. First, is the community's *image of the event.* Communities can define the seriousness or magnitude of the event according to a clearly-established set of assumptions and perspectives. Communities also can provide, using Jackson's term, the *punctuation of an event:* its consensually-perceived "beginning" and "ending" and the events that are clearly connected to it. A third component of the community's definition concerns its *definition of the family's relationship to the event:* the family's accountability, its duty and its competence. Finally, a community's definitons vary in their *coherence* from simple, single-voiced conceptions to complex and competing conceptions to the chaotic and deteriorating conception of a community in a state of transition or decay.

The Community's Image of an Event

Goffman (1974) has argued that social communities share a set of core beliefs and assumptions which permit their members to explain and understand rapidly "what it is that is going on here." Goffman refers to these as primary frameworks. An act or event takes on intense and vivid meaning because the primary framework provides an immediate sense of its cause, its intent and probably consequences. For example, in a medical setting (or community) the pelvic examination of a woman patient by a male physician is perceived as not only appropriate but as professionally conscientious. The same act interpreted under a different framework—in a neighborhood community—might be perceived as a rape. Although frameworks are inherent in the organization of communities themselves, their components are not usually explicitly known to or describable by the members of that community. Single communities can, of course, embrace several frameworks and have principles for applying one or the other in particular circumstances. Thus, the same community can apply a naturalistic or medical framework under certain circumstances and a more social one under others. Each provides very different explanations of the very same behavior.

These frameworks provide a shared matrix for interpreting the seriousness of events. A particularly illustrative example is provided by the work of Scotch (1963) on hypertension (high blood pressure) in a rural and urban sample of Zulus in South Africa. Hypertension was viewed by Scotch as the result, in part, of cumulative and sustained stress. Among the most striking findings was that in rural Zulu communities the appearance of menopause was strongly correlated with hypertension in women but the number of children was not; just the reverse findings were found in women in the urban Zulu communities. To explain these differences, Scotch delineated constrasting frameworks in the two communities. In the more traditional rural community, the continuity and stability of the community was understood to rest substantially on the women bearing children; indeed, we may safely surmise that the birth and rearing of children constitutes a central concern of a society that sees itself as continuing indefinitely in time. The urban community consisted, however, of migrants struggling to stay alive, on a moment to moment basis, by finding whatever employment was available; again we can surmise a foreshortened time perspective in which the community's central preoccupation was day-to-day survival. In this setting, childbearing is stressful because it impairs the woman's capacity to work for pay while menopause brings surcease. A frame of continuity versus survival in the rural versus urban community provides an entirely different meaning for the same two events: childbirth and menopause. This little example illuminates an ongoing debate within the family stress field as to whether the birth of a healthy child into a family constitutes a significant "normative" family stress (Hobbs, 1965; 1968; Laceby, 1969; LeMasters, 1957; Miller & Sollie, 1980). Menopause has been studied less frequently (Notman, 1979), but presumably could be ensnared in a similar debate.[2] These debates can be turned on their side; the community's frame delineates the magnitude of the challenge imposed on the family. Whether or not any particular family *experiences* stress is part of their unique coping repertoire. In effect, the event interacting with the community's frame defines the magnitude of the stress inherent in an event as it presents itself to the family's boundary of experience; the family takes over from there. We may well imagine a white, hypervigilent middle-class couple discussing the wife's recent gynecologic exam and "suspecting" that the doctor had hidden, dangerous sexual motives. With a firm knowledge of the community's endorsement of a medical frame for this event the researcher is justified in looking further "into" the family for the determinants of their idiosyncratic response. Consider, however, a black, poor family in a community gulled and manipulated by white merchants and professionals. Their community cannot endorse a neutral, medical frame for any encounter between a white professional and a member of the community. In this case, the researcher is on softer ground when he looks "into" the family to determine the idiosyncratic basis of their perception. Indeed, it becomes a primary concern in socially or geographically mobile families to adopt, albeit with some struggle, a primary frame of their new community. Thus, Jewish migrant families coming to New York's lower East Side at the turn of the century struggled to grasp that the local political system was available to them to exploit; they need not regard themselves as helpless victims of its destructive, capricious and violent excess as they had so perceived it (with full justification) in Eastern Europe (Howe, 1976).

The Community's Punctuation of an Event

The family therapy pioneer Don Jackson introduced the concept of "punctuation" into family studies (Greenberg, 1977); it is equally applicable to our related concerns about the community. He called attention to how social construction defines the beginning and ending of sequences in ways that provide intense personal meaning to events. His initial use of the concept was to explore conflicts between marital partners. A frequent example used by Jackson was the alcoholic marriage where the husband reports that he drinks because his wife nags him and the wife says she finds her husband drinking and then has to push him to sober up. The husband's sequence begins with wife's nagging; the wife's begins with the husband's drinking. Golda Meir recognized that communities in conflict also have contrasting punctuations. In considering the long-standing Arab-Israeli conflict, she commented that in deciding who was right, it all depended on where you started history. In the Israeli view, their military strikes into Arab territory are preemptive defensive manuevers to prevent the repetition of murderous and unwarranted attacks by Arab terrorists; in the Arab Palestinian view, their forays into Israel are efforts to secure recognition of their rights to their homeland, prevented by Israeli militarism. But conflict is not essential to punctuation. Central characteristics of the culture's frame are revealed by their linking of events. For example, Zborowski's (1952) classic in-hospital studies of response to pain led him to identify contrasting punctuations in Italian-American, Jewish-American and "Old Protestant" American sub-cultures. He was struck that Italian patients were sensitive to pain and complained bitterly until the symptom was relieved by the doctor. Jewish patients also complained freely about pain but were relieved only when they were satisfied that the root cause had been diagnosed and treated properly. The old-line Americans were more stoic, actively participating in the treatment of their condition. Zborowski explored the cultural differences behind these contrasts. The Italian typically sees pain as the consequence of some foolishness or poor judgment. This punctuation is clear from the mother's search for the misbehavior or poor judgment that must have preceeded the child's complaint of pain. Did he foolishly injure himself in sports or get caught in a draft or eat too much? Pain is the second element in a sequence which must always begin with a misdeed of the sufferer. Jewish parents are also concerned with the causes of pain but take a more naturalistic or folk-biologic perspective. They look for the sign of the biologic malfunction underlying the pain. Thus, they are apt to link even the slightest clue to this illness with the pain itself. Does he feel hot? Is he out of breath? Has he been tired recently? Was he exposed to the pneumonia of that child in school? The punctuated sequence for the typical Jewish parent then, is first a sign of impending illness and then the pain. The "old line" American punctuation, in sharp contrast, has pain at the beginning. Zborowski delineated a prevailing perspective, that pain is an indication of a problem to be solved. Thus, pain is linked to the available option for understanding and controlling it. Following pain is the apprehension of who and what is available to understand and eliminate it. The punctuated sequence then is pain first, grasp of alternative solutions second. It follows that a stoic problem-solving response is most appropriate.

The Community's Concept of the Family

In his influential book, *The Psychology of Interpersonal Relations,* Fritz Heider (1958) presented the notion of "naive psychology." People, in their interaction with one another, must be able to understand each other's behavior in order to make appropriate responses. Was the behavior intentional, what were its aims, what can be done to change it? Each person develops his own, personal psychological principles to phrase and then answer such questions. These naive psychologies are patterned, similar across individuals and capable of systematic, cumulative study; indeed much of Heiderian thought is an effort to explore the nature and function of these intuitive systems. Similarly, Reiss, Costell, Berkman and Jones (1980) have explored what might be called a "naive family sociology." Families develop elaborate appraisals of psychological and social attributes of other families. They can readily define alliances and similarities in members of other families they know; they can often decipher the dynamics underlying relationships in other families. Further, they seem to have a set of dimensions and structured relationships among these dimensions that functions as an abstract system for making particular judgments of other families. Nor is it surprising that this is so. In order for families to appraise their own functioning, to establish their own norms and role allocations they must have some sense of how and why other families perform these same functions.[3]

Barber (1961) was perhaps the first to articulate clearly the notion that social communities have organized conceptions about their component families. Indeed, Barber proposed the term "family status" as another way of assessing social stratification, a way based on these evaluations of families by their communities. According to Barber's analysis, communities develop a consensus on what constitutes a "good" family. Usually this consensus focuses on the family's history in performing desirable services for both its own members and for the community as a whole. High status is afforded families who meet these community standards. We extend Barber's notions to argue that this community consensus on the family includes three components: a conception of the family's accountability, duty, and competence. Although these notions are closely intertwined, it is useful for analytic purposes to delineate the special properties of each.

Accountability. By accountability we mean the community's conception of family dynamics or family process. We suggest that all communities have some shared notions of causal sequences in families—what sorts of interactions, arrangements and role relationships lead to what sorts of consequences for individual family members and for the outside world. Perhaps the most universal concerns in this regard are child development and health and illness. Communities may be distinguished by their conception of the family's influence and power over these processes. If a child is either a great success or a miserable failure can one find the root causes in the family or are the peers, genes or gods more to be held to account? An historical account of these contrasts is given in Aries' *Centuries of Childhood* (1962). In the Middle Ages, Aries argues, there was no conception of childhood as an extended and vulnerable phase of human development. Quite the contrary, the child was very rapidly perceived as a little adult whose development unfolded within the social forces of public life. To ask whether the family could influence this development in significant ways was to suggest not only the impossible but the inconceivable: The child was simply not seen as responsive to such influences.

A particularly interesting contemporary example may be found in current psychiatric practice. There has been an interesting evolution of psychiatric thinking over the years on the causes of schizophrenia. During the later '40s and early '50s, the concept of the "schizophrenogenic mother" (Fromm-Reichmann, 1948) became transformed into a widespread conception that disordered family process somehow caused schizophrenia in the offspring (Broderick & Pulliam-Krager, 1974). More recently, as brain biology has become a dominant influence on psychiatric practice, there is a central conviction that vulnerability to schizophrenia is genetically transmitted and becomes clinically manifest when certain brain amines become elevated or the receptors to them become too sensitive. In fact, the family, genetic and biochemical data are all intensely disputed—for good scientific reasons. However, where psychiatric researchers can luxuriate in debates on issues of sampling, validity of instruments and appropriate statistical analyses, practitioners must take action. They are daily faced with the profound behavioral disturbances of schizophrenia and the emotional turmoil in the patient's family that often accompanies these disturbances (as either cause or effect or both). Action often requires that practitioners form a clear conception of the malady they treat, however ambiguous the data may be. Years ago, a number of psychiatric hospitals—and these may be regarded as organic, bounded communities—focused their treatment efforts on the family, seeking to correct the relationship problems that presumably gave rise to the schizophrenia in the first place. The clear conception of psychiatrists, social workers and nurses in these communities was that the family was accountable for the schizophrenic illness.[4] In sharp contrast, today there are many psychiatric hospital communities where the exactly opposite concept is presented: the family is in no way accountable for this disorder because schizophrenia is viewed as a genetically transmitted brain disease.

Duty. Duty is a somewhat different concept and reflects the community's conception of what the family should do about the event, if anything, whatever its level of accountability for the event in the first place. This area of community conception is most squarely addressed by Barber's notion of a community-based family status. A particularly striking example of a community conception of this sort is provided by John Demos' (1970) analysis of family life in Plymouth Colony. He titled his book *A Little Commonwealth* to emphasize that the family had primary responsibility for carrying on virtually all the functions of community life. Not only was it a central unit of economic production, but the family was assigned, by the community, a broad range of educational, religious, and welfare functions as well. Parents were charged by law to provide education to their children, daily home worship was a clear community expectation, wayward youths and even adults were assigned, for correction, to well-respected families, and orphans were given to families for long-term care.

Competence. This aspect of the community's view of the family is closely related to accountability and duty. Many communities have an implicit conception of what a typical family can handle—in the way of severe challenge—and when it is likely to be overwhelmed and need help.

Elsewhere, we have tried to reconstruct a picture of family life in the mid-nineteenth century Great Plains (Reiss, 1981) from sources such as Hamlin Garland (1914), Willa Cather (1949), and Laura Ingalls Wilder (1937). After the passage of the Homestead Act of 1862, thousands of families streamed West to establish their own farms and ranches on territory provided without fee by the United States government. This rush of families into the wilderness bespoke an image, often illusory, of their hardiness and competence to do without the support of town and city life typical of their East Coast or European origin. This wave of migration was different than many others because *individual families* established their own self-sufficient way of life often at a great distance from any other family. Indeed, Pa Ingalls would move his family further into the wilds whenever another family moved close enough for him to see the smoke from their chimney. Other migrations often involved groups of families moving together as outfits or re-establishing close inter-family ties in their new setting. Garland, Cather and Wilder convey an image of the family as isolated and self-sufficient—an image these families not only developed for themselves, but an image that was a driving force in the loosely knit community of migrating pioneers.[5]

More typically, communities regard the family in a more balanced position: it is competent to deal with some of the severe challenges of everyday life but requires help with others. Thus, the communal healing rites of the Navajo (Kluckholn & Leighton, 1958) require that extended family members travel for many miles across the reservation's semi-arid plains to participate with the nuclear family in the ceremonies. Healing is the responsibility of far-flung extended kin; the more restricted family alone is not competent to produce the cure. Likewise, Jewish tradition regards the nuclear family as unable to bear the grief of death alone. More specifically, Jewish tradition emphasizes that once grieving has occurred, the survivors are to be encouraged to return to life and participate in it fully. Jewish tradition conceives of the family as incapable of doing this alone and prescribes the ceremony of sitting *shiva* where the grieving family is supported through the day by visits and prayer in the home until a week after the death (for a variety of interpretations of Jewish practices following death, see Katz, 1977, and Reimer, 1974).

Coherence and Breadth of the Community Frame

It is easier for the researcher to define the community frame—particularly as it relates to family stress—when the community is simple and stable. It is for comparable reasons that anthropologists flocked to the world's simpler cultures (while they still existed). As we have already indicated, in more complex societies, particularly urban settings, communities are more difficult to delineate. A family, in actuality, is a member of several communities. Perhaps more important for our current analysis is that communities differ in the coherence and breadth of their frames. In this complex domain, we will consider only two of many possible points of analysis in order to provide a preliminary sketch of processes here. The first will be to note the impact on families of periods of rapid change in the surrounding social community, times when the frame may be in a state of chaos. The second will be unprecedented events for which the community frame is inadequate.

Richard Sennett (1970) provides an absorbing analysis of middle-class families in the rapidly developing city of Chicago during the 1870s and 1880s. Sennett focuses on a particular neighborhood on the West Side, Union Park, where the family became a particularly intense island of stability and rootedness. He paints a picture of the city itself as immense, with enormous economic uncertainty, with job opportunities and paths for advancement opening up without warning and as suddenly collapsing. Further, the relationship among families in the neighborhood itself was distant and impersonal. In short, during this period of remarkable but uneven economic growth and community development, there was no structured human community to provide a context for family life. In this setting, the family withdrew into itself; all demographic indicators suggested its boundaries were extremely impermeable and that only the father and adult sons ventured much into the city and then only for employment. It seems unlikely that either Chicago as a whole or any of its components or the Union Park neighborhood itself could successfully provide a community frame either for defining the magnitude of family stress inherent in any event or a concept of the family's accountability, duty or responsibility. In fact, all major events arising in this urban context may well have been stressful and the family, in this extreme situation, had only its own history—unaided by a community frame— to define its relationship to them.

An intriguingly similar reaction can occur when a community—whatever its stability and coherence—cannot encompass an event or challenge because that event has no precedent. This seems to be the case for a group of families we are now studying in our laboratory where one member has end-stage renal disease and must receive lengthy dialysis treatments thrice weekly to stay alive. The ill member is also physically weak, usually unemployed, must make a radical change in his diet and often suffers frightening complications (bleeding, disorientation, heart attacks). The maintenance of human life by a machine—a life so imperiled by debilitating disease and death—is a challenge to the family with which no community is prepared to deal. The family's social community—its social network, its church, its kin, its neighbors—while it has some clear concepts of acute illness, terminal illness and death, seems utterly lacking in referents for this uniquely grotesque medical situation. As the families in Chicago, the families of patients on long-term dialysis appear to withdraw; they develop almost impermeable boundaries. However, the boundaries are not usually erected between the family and its social community but rather between the family and the disease. A typical response is for the family members never to accompany the patient to the dialysis center, to reduce time spent with the patient, to learn nothing about the illness and to fail utterly to keep up with changes and developments in the illness. They regard the patient either as if he were healthy or as if he were no longer a member of the family. This reaction is unwittingly abetted by the medical community at the dialysis centers which sees its job exclusively as to provide only the dialysis, a technical service having nothing to do, in their view, with the patient's family.

ASSESSING THE COMMUNITY FRAME

If we begin from the perspective of any particular family there are two fundamental assessments that are required for delineating the community frames relevant to it. First, we must identify the community or communities in which our family holds membership. In simpler societies we may need to delineate only one such community. In more complex societies there may be two or more; one of these may clearly be regnant, as in the case of well-demarcated ethnic communities and economically privileged communities in this country. The second assessment, of course, is to define the community's frame by delineating the magnitude of importance or of expected disruption it assigns particular events, its punctuation of those events and its conception of family accountability, duty, and competence. To be sure, we will depend on sensitive, empathic and intuitive observation to identify the relevant communities, delineate their boundaries and decipher their frames. For example, Scotch's measurements of high blood pressure in the Zulus was medically precise but it took his empathic, anthropologist's eye to grasp the meaning of child rearing in the two different Zulu communities.

We are, however, not entirely dependent on wholistic and intuitive appraisals in assessing the community frame. Seeds are available for developing a more systematic and quantitative methodology; these come from an unlikely source, the original work on stressful life events by Holmes and Rahe (1967).[6] They were initially interested in the effects of stressful life events on the appearance of somatic illness. They recognized that some events are more disruptive to individuals than others and selected a panel of judges to rate the events for their potential for disrupting ordinary life patterns and thus requiring readjustment. In the work of Holmes and Rahe, and those who have followed in the tradition they established, these judges have been samples of convenience: co-workers and other individuals more or less readily at hand.[7] The aim of Holmes and Rahe was to have a standardized scale reflecting the environment's input into the development of somatic illness. The judges were used to measure the objective stress, external to any particular individual, inherent in events. To them, the issue was one of *psychometrics*. We contend, instead, the issue is one of *community frames*. In effect, Holmes and Rahe were asking their judges to read their community. They might very well have prefaced their request by asking, "In *your community*, what readjustment would these events require?" In this connection it is interesting that Masuda and Holmes (1967) submitted Holmes and Rahe's original 42 life events to a Japanese sample of judges and found that they differed significantly from their American counterparts on 17 of these items. Moreover, these differences seemed clearly related to differences between American middle class and Japanese middle class frames. For example, the Japanese rated minor violations of the law and detention in jail much higher than the Americans; this in keeping with the Japanese perspective that misbehavior not only reflects on the individual but his family and thus entails a more intense loss of prestige and status in the community at large. Equally interesting, the Japanese judges rated several items related to marital discord as of lesser magnitude than did the Americans. This seems in keeping with the Japanese conception of marriage organized around clearcut role segregation and concepts of obligation of husband and wife to one another. It is quite plausible that Japanese respondents see these highly formalized marital rules as able to withstand occasional though severe interpersonal strain between a marital couple. Perhaps equally important, Japanese are less dependent on their marital relationships for self-confirmatory love and for the satisfaction of their dependency needs. Even in middle-class Japan of today, large peer groups, particularly those based in one's place of employment, offer more sustained emotional support than any comparable structures in American society. (For an authoritative account of post-war Japanese middle-class families at the time of the Masuda & Homes study, see Vogel, 1963).

In our own laboratory we used a sample of 48 families, each with two parents and an adolescent, to serve as both the source of a list of events likely to disrupt family routines and as a panel of judges for rating these events. Our technique encourages families to tell us what they regard as stressful events in contrast to most other investigators who have compiled events lists according to individuals' reports of what events should be stressful. It is instructive, then, that from a relatively small sample of families, 63 of the 170 events they reported cannot be found on standard life events lists such as the extremely comprehensive 102-item list of Dohrenwend (1978) and on the even more comprehensive, preliminary 171-item list of McCubbin (1979), the Family Inventory of Life Events (FILE). What all these lists miss are certain aspects of the family's environment which have a significant impact on its routine. Thus, among the unique items on our list were many which concerned transportation (e.g., "family member starts using a new form of transportation," or "child learns to drive"), quality and functioning of the neighborhood school ("quality of child's school deteriorates," "time schedule of child's school changes"), changes in the friendship network (e.g., "friends move," "parent's friends begin to retire"), and changes in the neighborhood ("highway is built in the family's neighborhood," "robbery occurs in family's neighborhood," "property near family's home is sold for development").

We were interested to see if this sample of families, again each family working as a group, could help us read the community frame by judging these events. Since these families were all drawn from just two high school districts in middle-class Washington, D.C. suburbs, their readings are pertinent to just these communities and those which are demonstrably similar. We might have obtained ratings of a very different sort had we moved two or three miles into the inner city of Washington or several miles to the southwest into the Virginia hunt country. We asked our families to make two judgments on a scale of 1 to 9. The first was a judgment of the seriousness of the event. Here, for each event, we asked families "how much impact would this event have on the average family" and to give a rating of 1 if the event's impact was "minimal or none" to 9 if the event's impact was "severe." The second was a rating of the family's accountability for the event. Again, we asked them to use a nine-point scale to answer the question "what kind of factors led to this event's occurrence?" A rating of 1 reflected "only factors internal to the family" and 9 reflected "only factors external to the family." We asked the two parents and a teenage child in each family to work together to make each of the 340 ratings (170 events each rated for seriousness and family accountability). We reasoned that this procedure would bring us closer to reading the community's frame. As we have already indicated, we believe the community frame develops and is sustained by each family's need to appraise itself and its functioning in the light of its appraisals of other families. If this assumption is correct, and we did not directly test it, then the appraisal process we chose for our study is a more accurate model of community process related to family stress than the more typical procedure in which single individuals do the ratings.

Our initial results have been quite intriguing. First the reliability of the judgments of magnitude and accountability has been quite high. We used a stringent criterion for reliability, the intraclass correlation coefficient, which assesses the level of agreement between families on the absolute values of the ratings. For magnitude the correlation was .51 ($p < .0001$) and for accountability it was .61 ($p < .00001$). While the other interpretations are quite plausible, these high coefficients are consistent with the view that community perceptions, images and conceptions exert considerable influence on the individual family's appraisals of magnitude and accountability. In other words, the agreement among families may reflect the fact that all families, under constraint of the community frame, see events in the same way.[8]

While our findings concerning individual items for magnitude are interesting, the specific findings for accountability yield a particularly intriguing glimpse of the community frame of our suburban high school districts. As expected, some items received very high scores (no family accountability): "quality of child's school deteriorates" (score = 8.4, S. D. = .91) and "highway is built in family's neighborhood" (score = 8.6, S. D. = 1.38). Somewhat more surprising was almost equally high scores for events that happen to kin. For example, the item "relative retires" received an 8.4 (S. D. = 1.25) whereas the comparable item referring to the nuclear family itself, "parent retires," received a 5.1 (S. D. = 1.77). Likewise, the item "relative's health improves" received a score of 8.0 (S. D. = 1.32) whereas the comparable item, "(nuclear) family member's health improves" received a 5.6 (S. D. = 1.95). Thus, although our families saw the average family as modestly accountable for changes in employment and health status of its own immediate members, it saw its accountability for comparable changes in its kin as negligible as that for school closings and highway construction.[9] In our Northern Virginia suburb, then, the family is viewed as technically insufficient to effect major changes in either its physical environment or kin, but at least moderately accountable for the employment and health status of its own adults. In this respect, if our judges are accurately reading it, the community conceives of the nuclear family as quite bounded and having virtually no influence over major life transitions in its kin. Presumably, the same is true in reverse: the community sees major transitions in lives of nuclear family members as equally uninfluenced by kin. The nuclear family, however, is clearly accountable for the academic pacing and success of its children. Some of the lowest scores were given to these items: "child starts preschool" (3.3, S. D. = 1.17) "child drops out of high school" (3.8, S. D. = 1.67) and "child starts college" (3.5, S. D. = 1.71). The family is evidently held somewhat less accountable for its children as they mature, however, because the event "child drops out of college" received a higher score (4.7, S. D. = 1.60).

These findings are a preliminary glimpse at a qualitative method for exploring the community frame. The method will have to be employed in contrasting communities. Further, more qualitative assessments of the community frame will be required as critical data to be integrated into an overall picture of the community frame.

SUMMARY

We have sketched a preliminary model picturing family stress as originating in community-based frameworks; these frameworks provide for an understanding of the structure and meaning of events as well as their relationships to the families which compose the communities. These shared understandings of events and families may arise, or are at least maintained, from the needs of families to appraise their own function in reference to their evaluation of how other families around them function. Four features of the community's conception of events may interact to produce a high likelihood of disruption to families: when the community frame defines the event as of great magnitude, when the family is held accountable, when the community regards the family as duty-bound to deal with the event, and when the community frame is blurred through heterogeneity, insufficient breadth or social chaos. The community frame also provides guidelines for family coping and for community patterns of assistance in the face of threat or challenge to families. The community's punctuation of the event provides to its families a conceptual nucleus for understanding that event. The community's concept of the limits of a family's competence can set in motion community-based systems or practices of support for challenged families.

NOTES

1. It is remarkable, however, how little this issue has been addressed empirically.
2. It seems clear that one learns little from studies addressed to this question. If one wants to learn simply whether or not childbirth constitutes a generic stress, one might examine the response of families in a particular community to see if most of them show evidence of stress in response to this event. An investigator will have to pay exquisite attention to sampling, however: he must scrupulously define the community in which he has an interest ("middle class Americans" just will not do) and make sure he has a representative sample. However, even data collected in this way will not be very illuminating unless—using a community perspective—we understand why childbirth is more stressful in community A but less so in community B.
3. The community frame concerning family stress is, we contend, built up by the community's families themselves. A variety of community institutions allow families to interact with and observe one another and to collaboratively fashion and sustain the shared perspectives inherent in the community frame. From a theoretical perspective this is crucial. It means that a family who is engaged in its community knows the community frame the way it knows or apprehends any community-wide value. It is an integral part of the patterned interaction of the community which itself reifies community standards and perspectives. Thus, the community frame is not a sequestered set of constructs which reaches some families but not others. It is an immediate given of the family's experience of its community and is realized or objectified by the family's own community participation.
4. Intellectually sophisticated and sensitive clinicians in this genre could hold to these concepts without blaming the family and making them feel guilty. In less sure hands the family was implicitly though painfully blamed for the evolution of the schizophrenic psychosis in one of their offspring.
5. To be sure, individual families experienced fears, anxieties and more than an occasional wish to go back to safer, more protected and more familiar settings. These feelings within families, and presumably acknowledged between families, do not detract from a remarkable sense of family self-sufficiency fostered by the community of migrants.
6. The original work in this field by Holmes and Rahe is often cited in the family stress literature. Indeed, recently McCubbin and his group have adapted the Holmes and Rahe approach for the construction of an event list, weighted for seriousness as judged by individual family members, more pertinent to the family. However, most family researchers seem unaware of the significant though disputatious development of the "life event" field since Holmes and Rahe (1967). A central issue has been whether the ratings of magnitude of events by a panel of judges, no matter how those judges were selected, accurately assess the amount of stress inherent in the event. Critics of this approach, such as the British sociologist George Brown (1974), have argued that one must take into account the specific meaning of the event to the individual. This debate seems to follow quite precisely the same groove as the one in the field of family stress to which we alluded earlier in this paper.
7. We know of only two exceptions: the work of Miller, Bentz, Aponte, & Brogan, (1974), in rural North Carolina and of Dohrenwend, Krasnoff, Askenasy, & Dohrenwend (1978) in New York City. Both teams of investigators chose random samples of individuals to serve as judges.
8. It is entirely plausible, however, that the events we asked families to rate are universals; that any group of families from any community would rate them the way our families did. This counter-hypothesis, of course, needs testing by more systematic comparisons between communities of families' ratings. However, the findings we have cited from Masuda and Holmes, and more recent data from Dohrenwend et al. (1978) suggest that individual

ratings are significantly influenced by the culture or community from which the raters are drawn and that these differences are interpretable by the concept of a community frame.
9. Given the data we have presented, a very simple interpretation is possible: the nuclear family is held accountable only for events that one of their members actually initiates. However, events connected to individual nuclear family members receive a full range of ratings suggesting that other considerations are operating here.

REFERENCES

Aries, P. *Centuries of childhood.* New York: Random House, 1962.
Barber, B. Family status, local community status and social stratification: Three types of social ranking. *Pacific Sociological Review,* 1961, *4,* 3-10.
Broderick, C. B., & Krager-Pulliam, H. Family process and child outcomes. In W. R. Burr, R. Hill, F. I. Nye, & I. L. Reiss (Eds.), *Contemporary theories about the family.* New York: The Free Press, 1979.
Brown, G. W. Meaning, measurement, and stress of life events. In B. S. Dohrenwend & B. P. Dohrenwend (Eds.), *Stressful life events: Their nature and effects.* New York: Wiley, 1974.
Cather, W. *My Antonia.* New York: Houghton Mifflin, 1949.
Demos, J. *A little commonwealth.* New York: Oxford University Press, 1970.
Dill, D., Feld, E., Martin, J., Beukema, S., & Belle, D. The impact of the environment on the coping efforts of low-income mothers. *Family Relations,* 1980, *29,* 503-509.
Dohrenwend, B. S., Krasnoff, L., Askenasy, A. R., & Dohrenwend, B. P. Exemplification of a method for scaling life events: The PERI life events scale. *Journal of Health and Social Behavior,* 1978, *19,* 205-229.
Elder, G. H. *Children of the Great Depression.* Chicago: University of Chicago Press, 1974.
Fromm-Reichman, F. Notes on the development of treatment of schizophrenics by psychoanalytic psychotherapy. *Psychiatry,* 1948, *11,* 263-273.
Garland, H. A. *Son of the middle border.* New York: MacMillan, 1941.
Goffman, E. *Frame analysis.* Cambridge, MA: Harvard University Press, 1974.
Gore, S. The effect of social support in moderating the health consequences of unemployment. *Journal of Health and Social Behavior,* 1978, *19,* 157-165.
Hansen, D. H., & Johnson, V. A. Rethinking family stress theory: Definitional aspects. In W. R. Burr, R. Hill, F. I. Nye, & I. L. Reiss (Eds.), *Contemporary theories about the family.* New York: The Free Press, 1979.
Heider, F. *The psychology of interpersonal relations.* New York: Wiley, 1958.
Hill, R. *Families under stress.* Westport, CT: Greenwood Press, 1949.
Hill, R. Generic features of families under stress. *Social Casework,* 1958, *39,* 139-150.
Hobbs, D. F., Jr. Parenthood as crisis: A third study. *Journal of Marriage and the Family,* 1965, *27,* 367-372.
Hobbs, D. F., Jr. Transition to parenthood: A replication and an extension. *Journal of Marriage and the Family,* 1968, *30,* 413-417.
Hobbs, D. R., Jr., & Cole, S. P. Transition to parenthood: A decade replication. *Journal of Marriage and the Family,* 1976, *38,* 723-731.
Holmes, T. H., & Rahe, R. H. The social readjustment rating scale. *Journal of Psychosomatic Research,* 1967, *11,* 213-218.
Howe, I. *World of our fathers.* New York: Simon & Schuster, 1976.
Jacoby, A. P. Transition to parenthood: A reassessment. *Journal of Marriage and the Family,* 1969, *31,* 720-727.
Katz, S. T. *Jewish ideas and concepts.* New York: Schocken Books, 1977.
Kluckhohn, C., & Leighton, D. *The Navaho.* Cambridge, MA: Harvard University Press, 1958.
LeMasters, E. E. Parenthood as crisis. *Marriage and Family Living,* 1957, *19,* 352-355.

Lipman-Blumen, J. A crisis framework applied to macrosociologic family changes: Marriage, divorce and occupational trends associated with World War II. *Journal of Marriage and the Family,* 1975, *37,* 889-902.

Masuda, M., & Holmes, T. H. The social readjustment rating scale: A cross-cultural study of Japanese and Americans. *Journal of Psychosomatic Research,* 1967, *11,* 227-237.

McCubbin, H. I., Joy, C. B., Cauble, A. E., Comeau, J. K., Patterson, J. M., & Needle, R. H. Family stress and coping: A decade review. *Journal of Marriage and the Family,* 1980, *42,* 855-871.

Miller, F. T., Bentz, W. K., Aponte, J. F., & Brogan, D. R. Perception of life crisis events. In B. S. Dohrenwend & B. P. Dohrenwend (Eds.), *Stressful life events: Their nature and effects.* New York: Wiley, 1974.

Miller, B. C., & Sollie, D. L. Normal stresses during the transition to parenthood. *Family Relations,* 1980, *29,* 459-465.

Notman, M. Midlife concerns of women: Implications of the menopause. *American Journal of Psychiatry,* 1979, *136,* 1270-1274.

Reiss, D., & Oliveri, M. E. Family paradigm and family coping. *Family Relations,* 1980, *29,* 431-444.

Reiss, D., Costell, R., Berkman, H., & Jones, C. How one family perceives another: The relationship between social constructions and problem-solving competence. *Family Process,* 1980, *23,* 239-256.

Reiss, D. *The family's construction of reality.* Cambridge, MA: Harvard University Press, 1981.

Reimer, J. *Jewish reflections on death.* New York: Schocken Books, 1974.

Scotch, N. A. Sociocultural factors in the epidemiology of Zulu hypertension. *Journal of Public Health,* 1963, *53,* 1205-1213.

Sennett, R. *Families against the city.* Cambridge, MA: Harvard University Press, 1970.

Thomas, L. E., McCabe, E., & Berry, J. E. Unemployment and family stress: A reassessment. *Family Relations,* 1980, *29,* 517-524.

Vogel, E. F. *Japan's new middle class.* Berkeley: University of California Press, 1963.

Wilder, L. I. *On the banks of Plum Creek.* New York: Harper & Row, 1937.

Zborowski, M. Cultural components in response to pain. *Journal of Social Issues,* 1952, *8,* 16-30.

Chapter 4

Family Problem Solving and Family Stress

David M. Klein

The thesis of this chapter is that the study of family stress, crisis, and coping (which I will designate as SCC for economy) and the study of family problem solving (PS) have diverged historically in their emphases. The theories and empirical researches in these areas have come to take on mutually independent status, with the result that the two streams of work have failed to benefit from one another in ways which would be advantageous to both and to the field as a whole. A major objective of this paper, therefore, is to show how SCC and PS might be reunited around shared conceptual, theoretical, and methodological concerns.

VOCABULARIES AND RESEARCH NETWORKS

If two sets of researchers use different concepts to designate phenomena, we can be fairly sure that they have either become isolated intellectual groups or are studying different phenomena. A recent review of SCC literature in the 1970s highlights the concepts of stressor event, resources, stress, crisis, social support, and coping (McCubbin, Joy, Cauble, Comeau, Patterson, & Needle, 1980). The same review also draws attention to the concepts of hardship, vulnerability, regenerative power, adjustment and the definition of the situation. It seems significant that none of these concepts, with the possible exception of the last one, appears in the lexicon of PS researchers. The latter researchers are more inclined to emphasize such concepts as problem, problem solving, group structure, struc-

---

David M. Klein is Assistant Professor, Department of Sociology and Anthropology, University of Notre Dame, Notre Dame, Indiana.

© 1983 by The Haworth Press, Inc. All rights reserved.

tural complexity, social placement, interaction, and effectiveness (Klein & Hill, 1979). On the face of it, then, there seems to be little overlap between these two areas of study. It is quite likely, however, that the terminological differences mentioned above mask some shared concerns.

Placing the two streams in historical context may help us see how they came to evolve distinctive conceptual tools. SCC as a focus of family research goes back at least to the 1930s and to a concern with the ways in which families responded to the Great Depression. By the mid-1960s, Hansen & Hill (1964) were able to provide a comprehensive review of the SCC literature, drawing attention to many themes and issues requiring further study. The ideas of "family problem," "problem solving," or other notions now standard features of the PS stream of work were not visible in the Hansen-Hill review because those ideas had not yet been articulated by family scholars.

Among the earliest studies to use the PS perspective were those of Tallman (1961) and Straus (1968). Tallman's study was designed to develop a measure of parental skill in dealing with childrearing problems, based on the content analysis of open-ended questions administered to parents during interviews. Problem solving skill was defined in terms of the parent's adaptability and was divided into the conceptually independent but empirically related components of flexibility, empathy, and motivation. Tallman viewed the "problem of raising a child as a day-to-day and moment-to-moment affair" and considered the action chosen by a parent to be "determined by his perception of the specific situation" (p. 652).

Straus (1968) set the stage for much subsequent research on PS by developing a simulation game, SIMFAM, allowing the researcher to directly observe family interaction. This innovative procedure enabled the researcher for the first time to calculate scores for the problem solving ability of the family as a group instead of having to focus on the problem solving ability of one member, as was the case in Tallman's earlier study. Experimental manipulations of the game permit the researcher to increase the difficulty of the problem, presumably leading to increased stress to the point where a crisis might be said to exist. The cross-cultural and cross-class application of SIMFAM in this study make it clear that social-structural factors would be important in explaining the problem solving efforts of families.

At about the same time that Straus published his first work on

SIMFAM, Reiss began a program of research on problem solving in families which also relied on a laboratory simulation (Reiss, 1971; 1981). It is significant that Reiss, a psychiatrist, and Straus, a sociologist, developed their PS research programs quite independently of one another. Tallman joined Straus and Hill at the University of Minnesota in the 1960s and, along with Aldous and their students, a brief tradition of PS research was set into motion (Klein & Hill, 1979). Reiss developed his own program with colleagues at George Washington University. The result has been the elaboration of two distinctive vocabularies and theoretical approaches for describing and explaining the PS process in families as well as two parallel but distinctive strategies for conducting research.

OBJECTS OF STUDY

The primary object of study for SCC researchers has been the "crisis." Although defined in a variety of ways, a crisis is generally viewed as a relatively severe disruption of the family's previously established state of affairs. The impression created by the use of the crisis label is that disruptions may reach nearly catastrophic proportions. The precedent for this view clearly goes back to the early studies of family crisis. These studies emphasized sudden and sharp economic losses during the Great Depression as well as family role changes caused by the separation and return of husband-father during World War II. Whereas life itself may be seen to produce stresses and strains within some "normal" range, SCC has focused on situations which go beyond this range. The classification of stressor events provided by Hansen and Hill (1964) adds credence to this conclusion. The disruptions caused by dismemberment, accession, or demoralization cannot be easily interpreted as modest or mild. These are not "mere" problems.

In sharp contrast, PS researchers have focused on the more routine and expectable disruptions and dislocations of family life. This emphasis is, no doubt, a reflection of the heritage of PS work in the social psychology of small groups. The problems of organizing to meet the demands of developmental change, the ongoing struggle to make sense of the puzzles of life, these and other more routine exigencies have occupied the attention of PS researchers.[1]

Embedded in this difference of emphasis are value orientations toward change and disruption. SCC scholars have generally viewed stress and crisis as negative or detrimental. Recognizing this orientation as unnecessarily limiting, efforts have recently been made to highlight concepts such as "eustress" (Selye, 1980), and the creative potential inherent in crisis situations (Hansen & Johnson, 1979; McCubbin et al., 1980). Again in sharp contrast, PS researchers have typically avoided the negative connotation of family problems. Instead, families are said to function effectively to the extent that they seek out, create, or persist in defining situations in problematic terms (Aldous, 1971; Tallman, 1970).

SCC researchers have not limited their attention to the negative consequences of experience with crises, of course. Indeed, one of the earliest insights from research on families in disaster was that some families seemed to emerge from the experience strengthened beyond the level of pre-disaster functioning (Hill & Hansen, 1962). The point about differing value orientations associated with crises and problems is that most people do not ordinarily wish crises on their families if they could be avoided, whereas problems are much more likely to be seen as inevitable and as challenges through which the family can demonstrate its skills and resources.

The imagery of distinctive objects of study is further enhanced when one compares "coping" with "solving." A family copes with a crisis by managing its affairs in whatever manner it can and to the best of its ability. A family solves its problems by eliminating the difficulty or completely overcoming it. There is the sense here in which crises, because of their severity, can only be assuaged, accepted and handled on their own terms. Problems, on the other hand, are subject to control and eradication.

This difference in imagery is reinforced by the way SCC researchers have recently attempted to incorporate problem solving into their discussions. The tendency has been to view problem solving skills as a resource or problem solving activity as a strategy which might be employed in times of crisis (Day & Raschke, 1980; McCubbin et al., 1980). Reiss and Oliveri (1980) describe problem solving styles as pre-established perspectives, operative in "quiescent periods," which might be invoked during periods of more severe stress (p. 431).

The above considerations suggest that the SCC and PS streams of research and theory can be profitably viewed as operating at different locations on a series of continuous dimensions. Severity, disruptiveness, ambiguity, and controllability may all be seen as variables. By viewing SCC and PS as differing mainly in degree, we are led to ask new questions and to explore the relationship between the two bodies of work. For example, when do families transform problems into crises and vice versa? At what point do existing problem solving strategies no longer serve a family well because it is in a period of crisis for which established patterns of response no longer work? Only comparative investigations which simultaneously study family crises and family problems, as well as the responses families make to both, will shed light on such questions. These comparative studies have not yet been conducted, a symptom of the split between the two research domains, but there is no obvious reason for this separation of focus to continue.

DEPENDENT VARIABLES

The most widely recognized theory of SCC, summarized by Burr (1973), contains three separate dependent variables: crisis, vulnerability, and regenerative power (or recovery). Focusing on the first of these, effort is directed toward explaining why a situation becomes a crisis. The ABCX model proposed by Hill (Hansen & Hill, 1964) is the explanation usually examined. Focusing on vulnerability, the effort would logically seem to be directed at explaining the amount of disruption which occurs once a crisis exists. Finally, focusing on regenerative power, the effort would logically seem to be directed at an explanation of the rate and degree of recovery from disruption. The dependent variables of vulnerability and regenerative power are embedded in the "roller coaster" pattern which Hill adapted from Koos (Hansen & Hill, 1964; Hill & Hansen, 1962). A crisis is said to bring about a period of disorganization, which is followed by a period of recovery, and finally by a new level of reorganization that may or may not return the family to its state of pre-crisis equilibrium. It is the charting of the sinuous path of family organization over time which invokes the metaphor of the roller coaster. A family's vulnerability to stress would be indicated by the angle and magnitude of its disorganizing phase, and a family's regenerative power would be indicated by the angle and magnitude of its recovery phase.

This reliance on three dependent variables seems advantageous. It reminds us that SCC occurs in a process over time and that the three dependent variables represent successive points in the process. It seems, however, that having three separate dependent variables has sometimes created more confusion than it is worth. Some research has been devoted to explaining the likelihood that crises will occur (Pearlin & Schooler, 1978), but the other two dependent variables have resisted empirical study. Hansen and Johnson (1979), for example, now see these two variables as hopelessly ambiguous and difficult to measure. A related difficulty is that Burr (1973) and most other theorists who follow his lead tend to explain vulnerability and regeneration with the same set of antecedent variables. With some exceptions, whatever increases vulnerability is seen as decreasing regenerative power. The logical fallacy of this parallelism should be apparent but has not usually caught the eye of SCC analysts. According to Burr's version of the theory, if a family is invulnerable, it should experience little disruption requiring recovery. On the other hand, if a family is highly vulnerable, it will not have the tools to make a recovery. By drawing greater attention to the temporal and substantive differences between vulnerability and regeneration, advances may yet be made in seeing them as requiring fundamentally different explanations.

A parallelism between vulnerability and regeneration seems more evident in Burr's rendering of SCC theory than in earlier treatments (Hansen & Hill, 1964; Hill, 1949; 1958). There may be some advantage, therefore, in returning to these earlier formulations to search for insights about the causes of and connections between the disorganizing and reorganizing phases of response to family crises. One recent attempt to rethink the linkage between phases has been provided by McCubbin and Patterson (1982). Their "double ABCX model" posits that the process leading to a crisis continues to operate well after the crisis has arisen and is joined with emergent features of the post-crisis period. Future tests of this model will require repeated measures in a longitudinal design. Hence, no evidence has yet been brought to bear on the argument that there is a repetition after the crisis of processes at work in producing a crisis.

Recent dissatisfaction with the three basic dependent variables in SCC theory has led scholars to search for other dependent variables. One dependent variable that has recently surfaced in SCC is "coping efficacy." For Pearlin and Schooler (1978) efficacy is the ability of resources and coping behaviors to reduce the causal impact of a stressor event upon the definition of the event as a crisis. "(E)fficacy is simply the extent to which a coping response attenuates the relationship between the life-strains people experience and the emotional stress they feel" (p. 8). The difficulty with this conceptualization of coping efficacy is that "attenuation" is not the same as reduction over time. Presumably, a person feels something (stress), then acts (attempts to cope), and then experiences a reduction in the stress. Such a sequence is required in order to conclude that the coping has been efficacious. Pearlin and Schooler measure all these variables at one point in time, however. Hence, the causal process implied but carefully avoided in their definition of efficacy is incompatible with the research design they employ. Quite independently, Day and Raschke (1980) have developed a similar approach to efficacy in their theory of post-divorce adjustment.

In a series of studies, McCubbin and his colleagues (McCubbin, 1979) have examined coping patterns and strategies, and they clearly see efficacy of coping as a dependent variable worthy of explanation. They conclude their study of the strategies wives employ to deal with their husbands' absences due to military service by calling for research on the efficacy of coping repertoires (McCubbin, Dahl, Lester, Benson, & Robertson, 1976). This step is undoubtedly important, especially if the teleological notions of functional and dysfunctional coping strategies are to be maintained. As of yet, however, few propositions have been developed to account for variations in coping efficacy, and no research has directly tested hypotheses in which the coping efficacy of families serves as the dependent variable. We can infer that whatever coping behaviors are reported to have been used have worked, but we cannot tell how well they have worked nor the conditions under which they work or are used but do not work (McCubbin et al., 1980, p. 866).

In contrast to SCC, which appears to have been in a continuous and tumultuous search for appropriate dependent variables, PS has traditionally had a single dependent variable which has been accepted without challenge. This dependent variable is "problem solving effectiveness," usually defined as the ability of the family to solve its problems to the mutual satisfaction of its members (Klein & Hill, 1979). This is a deceptively simple idea, and there may be some advantage for SCC scholars to borrow it and rename it something like "coping effectiveness." We can hope, however, that in opting for this organizing concept the processual nature of coping is not abandoned. There has been a tendency in PS research to see the dependent variable as something which can only be assessed after the problem solving activity is over, perhaps because PS episodes tend to be seen as short in duration. The original imagery of SCC theory may be closer to reality. That is, we may still need a series of dependent variables, each corresponding to a separate phase in the process. Furthermore, both streams of work have, in theory at least, emphasized that episodes of coping or problem solving have consequences beyond their immediate evaluation. These episodes may produce or exacerbate other crises or problems (McCubbin et al., 1980; Weick, 1971). Research designed to unpack these processual issues ought to have a high priority in both areas.

UNITS OF ANALYSIS

As the traditions of theory about SCC and PS have developed, one unifying theme has remained apparent. Both streams of work are concerned with the family and not the individual, not even the individual who happens to be a family member. Despite their shared commitment in principle to the family as the unit of analysis, SCC and PS researchers have diverged in their recent empirical studies. PS research has remained faithful to the group level; SCC research has not. Valuable as it might be in suggesting hypotheses about coping by families, the work of Pearlin and Schooler (1978) only addresses the coping of individuals with stresses created in their family roles. Day and Raschke (1980), concerned with post-divorce adjustment, leave moot whether they are describing the divorced individual or the single-parent family. In their impressive series of studies of coping, McCubbin, Boss, and their colleagues only report information collected from wives about what they themselves have done (Maynard, Maynard, McCubbin, & Shao, 1980; McCubbin, 1979). Hence, their results describe how individual family members cope in or on behalf of families, not how families cope as groups or collective entities. PS researchers, because they invariably collect data on family interaction patterns, have kept their sampling units consistent with the group level in their theory.

Even if all scholars were to agree that the family is the appropriate unit of analysis, an issue would still arise concerning the properties of individual members as explanatory factors in family coping and problem solving. Boss and her colleagues (1979), for example, suggest that selected psychological variables warrant inclusion in Burr's (1973) formulation. The question is, how are these psychological properties to be combined to yield some predictable effect on the group? One possibility is to suggest that if wives act in one way (or possess certain traits), while husbands act in another way (and perhaps children in still another way), then some family property such as coping effectiveness will be enhanced. This approach seems cumbersome, however.

Because the same issue has emerged in PS theory, it may be valuable to see how it has been handled there. Klein and Hill (1979) argue that the characteristics of family members, along with their behaviors during problem solving, are crucial to an understanding of the PS process. They also argue, however, that these characteristics and behaviors cannot legitimately be included in the theory as separate independent variables, not if one is explaining the effectiveness of the *family* as a problem solving group. Therefore, Klein and Hill invoke the notion of "distributive effects." It is the degree to which the characteristics of members and their actions are similar or concentrated as opposed to being differentiated or dispersed which constitutes their importance for the process.

Another version of the unit of analysis issue concerns the "group fallacy" (Klein & Hill, 1979). Hansen and Hill (1964) noted several years ago with some trepidation that "crisis researchers even speak of family definitions as if the family presented a unified mind to all situations" (p. 862). If the hazard of blatant reductionism to the level of individual behavior is tempting, so, apparently, is the hazard of assuming that groups have the properties of individuals.

One recent attempt to overcome the group fallacy has been provided by Reiss and Oliveri (1980; Reiss, 1981) and it seems promising. They argue that families develop "paradigms," or unified cognitive appraisals of themselves and their relation to the environment. This premise is based on patterns of family activity during problem solving which have been observed in the laboratory. The notion of the family paradigm is compelling in some respects, but it is flawed in other respects. One dimension of a family's paradigm is said to be "configuration," or the degree to which the family senses orderliness in the environment and feels that it can master the social world (p. 435). While it may be the case that families vary from high to low on configuration, are we to assume that there is more variation among families than within families on this dimension? It seems reasonable to suppose that a sense of mastery is learned gradually by the child as he or she matures. If so, it also seems reasonable that families with young children will have a great deal of variation among members in their sense of mastery. How are we to label the paradigm of a family that has some members with high scores on configuration and other members with low scores? Reiss and Oliveri imply that this is an uncommon occurrence, but it seems premature to accept that position uncritically.

Similar issues surround the other defining features of the family paradigm. For example, the dimension called "coordination" refers to a family's sense of itself as a group. Families high on coordination seem well synchronized, with members attuned to one another and sharing many similar views (Reiss & Oliveri, 1980, p. 436). What is to be said of families who are rated low on coordination? Are they groups in the usual sense of the term? Is there any shared orientation or paradigm in such families beyond a philosophy of each member going his own way and doing his own thing?

Of the SCC and PS streams of work being assessed here, neither seems immune from individualistic reductionism or group reification. Still, scholars interested in either phenomenon need to be careful about these matters, perhaps more so than they have been. Further research is called for which demonstrates that the properties ascribed to families, such as their degrees of integration or their orientation toward the environment, are emergent properties of the group and not just convenient theoretical constructs without suitable empirical referents.

PROCESS MODELS

Both the SCC and PS streams of work emphasize the processual nature of social forces and human activity. Each stream does so, however, with a somewhat different slant. A comparison of the two streams in this respect reveals several of their strengths and weaknesses.

The Causes of Crises and Problems

Attention to factors which precipitate crises has been a central feature of SCC theory. Hill's ABCX model argues that crises (X) result from the interaction of stressor events (A), a family's resources (B), and the family's definition of the situation (C) (Hansen & Hill, 1964). Notice that the antecedent conditions are not said to independently and additively influence crises. Instead each condition is necessary but insufficient alone to produce a crisis. Hence, for example, evidence that the A, B, and C elements are intercorrelated is not evidence for the ABCX model, despite claims to the contrary (McCubbin et al., 1976). Such correlations only serve to show that the causes of a crisis either coexist or do not, and this provides no explanatory leverage. The model receives support only *if* a crisis results when an experienced stressor is accompanied by inadequate resources and the shared cognition or perception by family members that the situation is indeed a crisis.

There is a serious question as to whether the ABCX model is a causal model at all. For it to be one, there must be some way to measure a crisis apart from the three conditions said to cause it. Because it has been extraordinarily difficult to develop such an independent measure of crisis, perhaps it is more fruitful to view the ABCX model as an analytical definition.[2] Hence, there is no way to either support or refute the model with empirical evidence. Instead, it is simply a conceptual and measurement tool. The three necessary conditions are, therefore, functionally equivalent to a crisis and not causally antecedent to it.[3]

There is nothing in PS theory comparable to the ABCX model. Whether that model is a causal one or simply a formal definition, it would seem advantageous to have some ground rules about the conditions necessary for the existence of a problem. This point will be elaborated when we consider conceptual frameworks underlying SCC and PS theory.

Family Structure

A central feature of both SCC and PS theories is their concern for family structure. The general argument in both is that the family's structure at the beginning of or just prior to a crisis or problem influences the family's response and the outcome of their response. Hansen and Hill (1964) draw attention to three central concepts of structure: the family's values, its communication pattern, and its role organization. The same analysts and others have also emphasized such structural concepts as integration, adaptability, and positional vs. personal relationships. Most of the antecedent variables in Burr's (1973) formal model can be viewed as a catalogue of these structural variables.

PS analysts have also catalogued family structural variables, placing greatest emphasis on structures of social status, communication, affection, power, and composition (Aldous, 1971; Klein & Hill, 1979; Straus, 1978; Tallman, 1970). The recently developed notion of the family paradigm (Reiss & Oliveri, 1980) can also be viewed as a structure of shared perception and cognition. The suggestion that such paradigms emerge out of or are sustained by a family's problem solving efforts but may be severely challenged in times of high stress or crisis (Reiss & Oliveri, 1980, pp. 434-435) poses an interesting issue worthy of further study.

How do family paradigms originate and how are they transformed? For example, since marriage brings together persons raised in different families, we must assume either that the mate selection process works to sort into couples those with homogeneous paradigms or else that paradigm conflict and negotiation are central features of marital relations. The conflict over what childrearing practices shall be employed may be seen as a struggle not only between parents but between generations over what paradigms shall govern behavior. Conflict over paradigms is doubtlessly a problem and occasionally a crisis in a substantial number of families. Equally interesting is the question of how family paradigms, once established, are transformed. A sample of families could be exposed to or asked to report on a series of experiences ranging from problematic to crisis in proportions in order to determine at what point their paradigms fracture and to examine how they become reconstructed. The same strategy could be used to study changes in other structural dimensions of family life, especially those involving social roles.

At this point in the development of SCC and PS theory, there is little to distinguish the two streams in their perspectives on family structure apart from the labels given to some of the structural variables. A systematic comparison of these variables across streams would be a fruitful way to integrate the two bodies of work. More pertinent may be the deficit in both regarding the place of family structure in the causal process. Both theories anticipate that structural changes can result from crisis-coping and problem solving, respectively. The research conducted to date out of both theories has, however, tended to view family structure only as a conglomerate of antecedent variables. The process of living goes on after crises and problems are handled, whether successfully or not, and researchers can devote greater attention to the continuities and discontinuities of this "afterlife."

Stages of Family Activity

It was mentioned earlier that SCC theorists, by postulating three separate dependent variables, acknowledge that the family's activity progresses through a series of stages. PS theorists have also given considerable attention to the stages or phases of activity during problem solving (Aldous, 1971; Klein & Hill, 1979). In both streams of work, however, there has been some reluctance to explore the phasic nature of the process.

If one examines Burr's (1973) model of SCC, for example, one is not encouraged to see phases of activity. A series of discrete independent variables is depicted as affecting a series of discrete dependent variables. There is little sense of flow and movement as one goes from one part of the model to another. Indeed, it can be argued that Burr's model does not capture family interaction at all. Instead, certain abstract entities or states such as "family integration" seem to influence other abstract entities or states such as "regenerative power."

It is probably in response to previous models such as Burr's, which relegate family interaction into the background, that certain new trends have emerged in the SCC literature to revitalize the concept of interaction. The recent emphasis on coping can be viewed in this light (McCubbin, 1979; McCubbin et al., 1980). It was argued earlier in this paper, however, that coping in and of itself does not guarantee a focus on family interaction. In particular, interaction remains illusory when coping is seen only as the behavior of individuals. Only if we were to detect a collective increase in, for example, religious rituals during mealtime would we be entitled to say that the *family* was doing something that might be classified as coping (See McCubbin and Patterson, Chapter 1).

Another attempt to revitalize family interaction appears in the complex analysis of SCC by Hansen and Johnson (1979). One of their missions seems to be the reconceptualization of variables formerly considered structural into interactional terms. So, for example, "appeals to relativity and emergence" as well as "established vs. institutive patterns" clearly refer to what family members are doing together during a crisis and not what sort of group they are at the outset of a crisis.

PS theory and research has probably been more consistent than its sister domain in attending to family interaction. Klein and Hill (1979) attempt to capture the essential aspects of family problem solving activity in their theory.[4] The likely reason for this relative emphasis on family interaction is that PS researchers have traditionally observed directly and measured family interaction as an integral part of their studies.

While it is tempting to encourage SCC researchers to borrow the insights of PS researchers about family interaction, some issues remain unresolved here. For example, there is not complete agreement among PS researchers that PS activity can be separated into meaningful phases. Reiss and Oliveri (1980), for example, are adamant in disclaiming any sequential pattern for their own model of phases. Furthermore, PS researchers have not often analyzed their interaction data in terms of phases of activity. The recent study of PS in marriage by Craddock (1980) is a solitary exception. Adapting the procedures of Bales and Raush (Bales, 1950; Raush, Barry, Hertel, & Swain, 1974), Craddock partitions the problem solving process into "introductory," "conflict," and "resolution" phases. Further research is needed to demonstrate that these or some other set of phases capture the content and sequence of problem-solving or crisis-coping episodes.

The Community Context

One major asset of SCC has been its concern for the community context. Hansen and Hill (1964) saw this as an underdeveloped aspect of SCC theory at the time of their writing, but their attention to the matter helped keep the issue alive. McCubbin et al. (1980) have pointed with appropriate enthusiasm to a variety of recent attempts to investigate social networks as sources of support in family stress management. To date, however, the emphasis has been on describing these sources of support and not on identifying the conditions under which they are used or used effectively.[5] PS theory and research can be criticized for virtually ignoring this aspect of the community context altogether. The reason for this deficit is probably traceable to research on *ad hoc* small groups, which has heavily influenced the PS tradition. The community context is also ignored in the small groups literature.

Some caution needs to be exercised, however, before rallying around social networks as a key feature of SCC or PS. Hansen and Hill (1964) remind us that ties to the community do not operate only as sources of support. The community can also be the cause of family stress and crisis. We should be prepared to ask, for example, what sort of situation exists and what sort of crisis coping or problem solving occurs when the family's relationship with the community or with social networks *is* the problem or *is* the crisis. The community is not just a source of family strength and support; it can also bedevil families, creating considerable distress, anxiety, or despair, and not because of the resources it fails to provide, but because of the oppressive demands it imposes.

In SCC theory, the primary relevance of the community is that it ties individual family members into relationships with individuals and groups outside of the family. In PS theory, the community context surfaces as well, but at an entirely different level of analysis. Compared with SCC research, PS research has been significantly energized by social class differences and cross-societal differences in family behavior (Straus, 1968; Tallman & Miller, 1974; Tallman, Marotz-Baden, & Pindas, 1981). Klein and Hill (1979) have attempted to capture this concern in their theory under the rubric of "social placement." The general idea is that problem solving activity and its effectiveness are different depending on a family's status in a society's stratification system and depending on the type of society in which the family finds itself. The evidence marshalled in support of this idea remains scanty, but it is sufficient to warrant further investigation. No comparable focus exists in SCC theory or research.

We may conclude that SCC and PS have each attended to the social world outside the family, but have done so in different ways. SCC has focused on the immediate environment of social contacts and relationships whereas PS has focused on aspects of social structure at large. Neither emphasis is fundamentally superior to the other, so that both streams of work have something to gain by incorporating the strength of the other stream.

Socialization for Crisis Coping and Problem Solving

One final aspect of the process models in SCC and PS remains to be explored. This refers to the learning or socialization process. One facet of PS research is concerned with how families socialize their children to become effective problem solvers (Aldous, 1975; Bee, 1971; Tallman, 1972; Tallman et al., 1981). The emphasis is on the development of analytical skills, exploratory behavior, and creative judgement. Certain kinds of parental behaviors are thought to encourage the problem solving abilities of children, often with unanticipated consequences such as social activism in young adulthood (Tallman, 1972).

Of course, both theoretical traditions implicitly acknowledge that experience with crises and problems acts as a learning device to prepare families for later bouts with crises and problems. What is lacking from the SCC side, however, is the same detailed treatment found on the PS side of the family as a training ground for the management of life's major and minor difficulties. This deficit is understandable if we view crises as catastrophic, undesirable, and unpredictable. Furthermore, there is some evidence that crisis-proneness in families is passed on from one generation to another, suggesting that whatever learning has occurred must not be very effective in certain families where structural constraints, such as poverty, are endemic (Geismar & Ayres, 1959). The suspicion remains, however, that socialization for crisis-management does occur in families. A fruitful avenue for future research would be to trace the long-term impacts of previous experience with crises. This suggests, for example, that life histories of crisis experience might be collected and perhaps supplemented with investigations of crisis experiences occurring in the present. Attention would be given not only to the families with repeated failures and repeated conquests, but also to instances of crossover in which "miracle success stories" and "shocking collapses" occur without any obvious precedent.[6]

CONCEPTUAL FRAMEWORKS

A tension has existed for some time between two competing frameworks for the analysis of SCC. Hansen and Hill (1964) point out that symbolic-interactionism and structure-functionalism provide dissimilar images of the SCC process. A strength of the interactional perspective is that it focuses on the dynamic quality of relationships among family members. A strength of the functional perspective is that its focus is on the community context and the transactions which occur between the family and its environment. Similarly, interactionism tends to see individuals and groups as active and constructive, not the pawns of impersonal social forces but the very creators of those forces. Functionalism, in contrast, tends to emphasize the reactive quality of human conduct and in particular views family behavior as heavily determined by social forces at the societal level. Finally, interactionism tends to be subjectivistic in that it views social reality from the perspective of the participants themselves, whereas functionalism tends to be objectivistic in that the explanations for social phenomena have validity regardless of whether or not the participants are aware of them.

In some respects, this tension has waned or at least been forgotten in SCC theory and has never arisen in PS theory. Both theories seem to incorporate elements that would be consistent with features of both frameworks. There are indications, however, that skirmishes at the metatheoretical level remain or might crop up in the future.

SCC theorists have usually considered a clearly subjective notion, the definition of the situation, to be a variable which can be analytically distinguished from other variables in the causal process (Burr, 1973; Lipman-Blumen, 1975). More recently, however, complaints have been registered that this compromises the interactional perspective too much (Reiss & Oliveri, 1980, p. 442; Hansen & Johnson, 1979). Hansen and Johnson are explicit about this when they argue that:

> unless we attend more closely to the meaning aspects of familial relations, seeking an interpretive perspective on the individual member's efforts to coordinate with other members, we will miss essential qualities of the stress processes. (p. 585)

PS theorists have been more inclined to place objective and subjective accounts on an equal footing. The very definition of problem-solving effectiveness contains both facets, as to situational characteristics and other components of the theory (Klein & Hill, 1979, p. 499, 529, 541-542).

Moving to empirical inquiry, SCC researchers have seldom asked family members how they view the situation they are in, and yet we do tend to get their own assessments of what they do and with what effect from their responses to interviews and questionnaires. By contrast, PS research has been decidedly objectivistic. PS researchers tend to impose situations on research subjects, define the situation for them, and analytically infer the meaningfulness of the observed patterns without finding out what they mean to the family members or even how stressful they are. Only one published study on PS to date has supplemented objective measures of problem solving effectiveness (time to solution, number of correct solutions, number of creative suggestions) with subjective assessments of satisfaction with the process or result (Craddock, 1980).

The tension between symbolic-interactionism and structure-functionalism can be viewed as a healthy one. At the present time, SCC and PS theory appear to be leaning toward the interactional side while their research leans more toward functionalism, at least on the objectivity-subjectivity dimension and with regard to the inclusion of structural variables.

Another conceptual framework for the study of the family, developmentalism, is beginning to be employed in SCC and PS work. Not so long ago, Burr was compelled to treat SCC and life-cycle transitions with separate theories (1973, Chs. 6 and 10). More recently, McCubbin et al. (1980) include the study of "normative stress" over the life cycle in their review of recent SCC work, even though the literature suggests that these situations resemble problems more often than crises (such as, for example, research on the transition to parenthood). Similarly, PS theory has remained sensitive to developmental issues. Weick (1971) notes that the "developmental confound" helps to distinguish families from other problem solving groups. Klein and Hill (1979) include both stages of the family life cycle and "developmental flexibility" as variables in their model. In research, however, the developmental context of PS remains to be examined. With rare exceptions, such as the work on socialization and Craddock's (1980) study of newlyweds, PS has been studied primarily in families with a young adolescent child. Further research is required to determine how problem-solving behavior and effectiveness are conditioned by stages in the family life cycle and by type of stage transition.

Still another very serious challenge can be mounted against the PS stream. Goulet's (1977) critical analysis of modernity theory points to values shared by PS theorists which limit the scope of their orientation.

Goulet argues that four basic values are embedded in the technological apparatus of contemporary Western societies:

— *rationality:* Every experience is viewed "as a problem which can be broken down into parts, reassembled, manipulated in practical ways, and measured in its effects." (p. 17)
— *productive efficiency:* "Production looks to the amount of final output; productivity, to some proportion between what is put in and what comes out . . . Behind this form of reasoning lies a mechanistic engineering mentality." (p. 18)
— *problem solving stance:* ". . . an expert steps back some distance from reality, breaks it up and analyzes its component parts, devises means for solving difficulties in the most effective way, and then dictates a strategy or policy." (p. 19)
— *Prometheanism:* "Natural forces as well as human institutions are viewed by adepts of technology as objects to be used and manipulated." (p. 20)

The entire rhetoric of PS theory and research seems to fit precisely this sort of value system. It is remarkable that SCC theorists have not "succumbed" to it, given that SCC is also largely about American families as seen through the eyes of American family scholars. Exceptions among PS theorists are Aldous (1971), Simmons, Klein, and Thornton (1973), Tallman et al. (1981), and Weick (1971), who note that families are not perfectly rational, efficiency-oriented, or manipulative. Many of the families studied seem to be forebearing, bound to sentiments of attachment, and simply too busy with other things to adopt a "rational efficiency" approach to family problems. In their comparative study of Mexican and American families, Tallman and his associates (1981) found Mexicans much more rational and efficient problem solvers than middle-class Americans who seemed to be adopting a deliberately more relaxed, playful, and spiritual or emotional approach to their family difficulties.

RESEARCH DESIGNS

Of all the contrasts between SCC and PS, none is as distinctive as their differing styles of research. SCC relies heavily on the survey technique, PS on direct observation supplemented with interviews with a few recent exceptions (McCubbin & Patterson, 1981; Patterson & McCubbin, in press). SCC uses an *ex post facto* method, capturing families after and occasionally during a crisis, whereas PS follows families throughout the course of the problem-solving process. SCC relies heavily on field studies with naturalistic features. PS relies heavily on laboratory games and simulations which can be conducted in the home with experimental variations. Other differences have been alluded to earlier in this paper. While PS has had a few cross cultural studies, SCC has not yet moved in this direction. SCC studies typically rely on a single family member as the informant, while PS studies typically involve two or three members of the same family. Neither stream includes systematic investigations of whole families, though clinical case studies suggest the feasibility of this strategy.

These sharp contrasts are not particularly surprising. It is inefficient and difficult to gain access to a reasonable sample of families just before a crisis is predicted to occur. There would be serious ethical questions about experimentally inducing a crisis in the family. The external validity of studies of simulated family crises could easily be questioned. Due to reactivity, it may be difficult to induce panic or the other distressful responses which are found in natural family settings. Reiss (1981) has turned this difficulty into an asset in his PS research by assuming that his families are responding to a research environment rather than to one without scientific observers. At this point, of course, claims about the external validity of SCC simulations are presumptive because direct tests have not been performed.

Where both streams of research have fallen short is in their strategies for sampling situations. In both SCC and PS theory, the nature of the situation looms large as a causal or contingency factor affecting the entire process. SCC studies, taken together, have covered a vast territory of varying crisis situations. Each particular study, however, tends to look at a single type of crisis. Even programs of research often confine themselves to a narrow range of situational variation. The consequences of this strategy are important for theory development. For example, one of the coping patterns which has emerged in all of the husband-separation studies by the McCubbin team is "establishing independence" through self-development or self-sufficiency (McCubbin, 1979). While this may indeed be a universal coping pattern when an adult member is absented for a period of time, it is probably not applicable to many other types of crisis situations such as the severe illness of a child, or a flood which destroys much of the family's property.

The piecemeal investigation of narrowly defined situations is not peculiar to SCC research. PS studies have also tended to be confined in the same way. Since the history of PS research is shorter than that of SCC research, the lack of situational variation across PS studies is especially noticeable. In one of the few PS studies to look at multiple problems systematically, situational variation in behavior and outcome turned out to be one of the major findings (Craddock, 1980). Families apparently have varied repertoires for coping with crises and attempting to solve problems, and there is little evidence that they deal with different situations in a uniform way.

The classification of crises and problems has proceeded to the point where testable predictions about situational variation deserve to be formulated and empirically studied (Hansen & Hill, 1964; Klein & Hill, 1979; Lipman-Blumen, 1975; Tallman et al., 1974). If one of the key dimensions of the situation is severity or disruptiveness, so that we may speak of crisis-like situations and problem-like situations, then studies which combine the two types of situations have the potential of greatly contributing to the integration of SCC and PS theory. Such an integration would be pushed a step further if multimethod strategies could be devised to take advantage of the current strengths of SCC and PS research designs.

DATA ANALYSIS STRATEGIES

We conclude our examination of the SCC and PS work by looking at the techniques both use to analyze their data. There is little to differentiate here between the two bodies of work. Both tend to use quantitative and multivariate techniques appropriate to the data collected, although qualitatively rich case studies were popular in the early decades of SCC research (Angell, 1936; Hill, 1949).

One particular data analysis strategy suitable for the study of PS has been underutilized. Given the available data on family interaction, researchers have ordinarily limited themselves to summary scores based on frequency counts. Straus (1968), for example, calculated the total volume of intrafamily communication. Tallman and Miller (1974) compared PS scores for elaborate and restrictive speakers. Craddock (1980) and Reiss (1981) counted the total number of acts which occurred in a variety of categories and compared these frequencies across different types of family units. None of the published reports of PS in families have examined the temporal sequence of interactions in action-response units as they have evolved during a PS episode, although Aldous (1981) is currently exploring this approach. As systems for coding interaction develop and methods for assessing stochastic processes become more widely available, we should expect greater utilization of sequence analysis techniques (Bales & Cohen, 1979; Filsinger & Lewis, 1981; Gottman, 1979). These tools will facilitate answering questions such as what happens next when one family member defines for the others what a situation means or suggests a particular course of action. Of course, there is no reason in principle why these data analysis techniques could not be used to study family interaction during the process of coping with crisis, the only limitation to date being that the relevant data have not been collected.

Factor analysis may be thought of as a technique for sorting cases along a continuum. When multiple factors are identified and distinguished by means of orthogonal rotation, cases may be thought of as being simultaneously sorted along several independent continua, one per factor, so that the score for a case on one factor is more or less unpredictable from the scores for that case on each of the other factors. Because a factor represents a variable or dimension, it is important to attend as much to low scores as to high scores. The point is that "each person (or case) has a score on the factor" (Nunnally, 1967, p. 291).

The several factors which McCubbin and his colleagues have identified and called coping patterns and strategies are interesting for the questions they raise about behavioral repertoires. The repeated discovery that self-sufficiency, for example, is a coping pattern (McCubbin, 1979) is most interesting in the context of the other coping patterns identified in their data sets. We might ask, for example, (a) what proportion of wives cope with stress by becoming self-sufficient, (b) what other coping patterns do they exhibit in conjunction with that particular one, and (c) how are the coping attempts arranged in a sequence over time?

The first question is simply a matter of calculating frequency distributions, yet we know less than we should about the frequency with which family members cope in various ways. There may be differences between members within a family and important implications of *not* engaging in certain activities while attempting to cope. McCubbin and associates (1976) have already discovered, for example, that the wife's self-sufficiency is negatively related to indicators of her husband's social status. Further issues worth exploring are what family members do in the face of highly stressful situations when husbands score high on social status indicators and why it is that wives do not try to become self-sufficient in these cases.

The second question, concerned with combinations of distinctive coping behaviors or factors generated by a factor analysis, can be examined with cluster analysis techniques (Miller & Olson, 1976; Tyron & Bailey, 1970). Here, the emphasis would be on the construction of profiles to identify the range and frequency of various combinations of coping mechanisms. Now that we have made advances in reliably identifying through factor analysis what some of the structures of coping behavior are, we can expect greater use of data analysis techniques based on clustering principles to assist in locating repertoires of coping.

The third question, concerning sequences of coping activities, can be examined only after we have time-ordered data and would be pursued with techniques developed for those kinds of data, such as the stochastic methods mentioned above. It will be particularly important here to distinguish search processes and success or failure sequences. That is, early responses may in some instances be unsuccessful, so that family members "grope" before they cope. In other instances, we may find that whatever coping behaviors are exhibited do not have their intended effects or that all such behaviors are linked in a series of repeated successes. Furthermore, particular sequences may be more successful than others for specifiable periods of time. If so, we would have not only a better understanding of the ways coping is "played out" over time but also a tool for educational and therapeutic purposes, useful for helping to maximize family functioning as the situation changes. This mode of thinking has already made an impact on studies of divorce adjustment (Kaslow, 1981; Salts, 1979). It seems equally applicable to other topics in the family stress and problem-solving areas.

CONCLUSION

The study of family stress, crisis, and coping presently has considerable momentum, as this volume attests. Several family scholars and teams of scholars are actively involved in research and theory development which promises to yield quantum leaps in our understanding of the processes involved. By contrast, the study of family problem solving is currently in the doldrums.[7] This difference in attention can be explained several ways. On the one hand, the first generation of family problem solving researchers has moved to other career agendas and has not sustained its effort long enough to train or inspire a critical core of disciples. On the other hand, the study of family stress-crisis-coping has drama on its side. The kinds of issues of concern to these researchers remain practical because they are matters of broad social concern.

The first task required to integrate the SCC and PS streams of work is the identification of conceptual overlaps and variables whose range is truncated by an exclusive focus on problems or crises. It has been suggested here, for example, that problems and crises may differ mainly in the degree of stress or disruptiveness associated with them. In terms of structural properties, the PS stream has been most productive in drawing attention to the macro (cultural and societal) and the micro (family role organization) levels. SCC theory and research has extended its own concern to the meso level of community and social networks. No theory of family behavior is going to be complete unless all three levels are adequately represented.

The family must also remain the primary analytic unit. This means that much of the recent SCC work will need to be rethought in terms of the patterns of interaction which characterize the family as a group or system. The concept of stress, for example, is too readily captured by psychological and biophysical imagery and not often or well examined in sociological terms. Since interaction is not only patterned but also fluid, the integrated theory will need to examine processes at two levels. One level is the short-term process of information exchange as families cope with or attempt to solve the various difficulties they face or create. The other level of process involves the effects of prior experience with situations of a similar or comparable nature. Such experiences socialize family members or create dispositions to respond in ways which are not random.

Once progress is made in identifying overlapping concepts and variables, attention may turn to a search for essentially equivalent propositions in SCC and PS theory or to general propositions from which more specific ones can be derived for studying crisis coping and problem solving. An illustrative candidate here concerns the notion of adaptability or openness to change. The traditions of SCC and PS theory have both maintained the idea that families which are not extremely rigid in their roles, rules, or paradigms can meet the difficulties posed by problems and crises better than families which are rigid in these senses. This is but one idea upon which a common vision might be constructed for these two domains of research interest.

The struggle for a useful if not reigning conceptual framework or orienting image which does justice to the complexity of family behavior has been a continual part of the history of the field. While the search for an overarching framework which can deal equally well with SCC and PS is worthwhile, we expect no resolution in the immediate future. Different frameworks remain useful for different purposes and our commitments as social scientists, conditioned by our intellectual ecologies, affect the choices we make. The substantive concerns of this paper, however, suggest that a kind of dexterity is in order. The usual dichotomies between structural and interactional, macro and micro, developmental and historical, objective and subjective, functional and dysfunctional, or external and internal control no longer seem to serve us well when they are used to drawing battle lines between adversary positions. What we can do, then, is to become more aware of our assumptions and agendas as we work toward integrating concepts, propositions, and theories in the areas of SCC and PS.

This same dexterity seems imperative as we begin to think of research strategies. The strong suspicion here is that we need to supplement reports of crisis-coping and problem-solving behaviors with more observations, concurrent reports with the retrospective and prospective, single-occasion with multiple-occasion studies, situation-specific concerns with the trans-situational, and naturalistic with simulated designs. Our review of the limitations of behavior count and factor analysis also suggests the need to make a greater use of the data analysis techniques which will illuminate sequences and repertoires of behavior and interaction.

All of these hopes have an admittedly arid ring to them. Most have been expressed before in different contexts. Although momentum is currently on the side of those who are troubled by the family's ability to cope with the crises and stresses of the modern world, one expects problem solving behavior to continue to be relevant, and for the two streams of research to become increasingly integrated in the years ahead.

NOTES

1. Tallman (1970, p. 95) reflects the tone of the PS approach by arguing that problem solving "applies only to those situations which provide new or modified conditions so that solutions are not immediately apparent." He makes the point that this definition is intended to distinguish problem solving from decision making or the more general class of behaviors (means) chosen to achieve goals. Hence, much of the vast literature on family decision making is presumably considered irrelevant to PS. Notice that Tallman's definition does not rule out coping with stress or crisis, however, unless those behaviors were to occur in a ritualistic fashion, that is unless the required action is "immediately apparent."

2. Burr (1973, pp. 199-203) comes close to providing an appropriate measure. He defines "stressor event" (and "hardship" as well) in terms of the amount of change an event produces in the family and he defines "crisis" in terms of the amount of disruptiveness, severity, incapacity, or disorganization that occurs as a result of a stressor event. His proposition linking the two essentially states that the amount of change positively influences the amount of disruptiveness. This proposition seems testable and not merely an analytical definition. The difficulty arises in establishing criteria for disruptiveness, severity, and so on. Who is to judge how disruptive a change is? Presumably, the family itself is the judge, because its definition of the situation matters most. A situation is not a crisis if the family does not define it as such. Hence, we have a proposition that essentially states the following: The more serious or severe or disruptive the family defines changes in its structure as being, the more serious, severe or disruptive (or crisis-like) the situation "actually" is. This proposition is *not* testable, and therefore is most usefully seen as an analytical definition. The analyst, in effect, says that he will define the situation however his research subjects define it.

3. Consider divorce, for example. We would treat a particular divorce as a crisis, following the ABCX model, if the event or experience had been sufficiently stressful (thus being a stressor event), if the affected persons lacked the resources to cope with that stress (for some period of time), and if those persons defined it as a crisis themselves. These conditions provide us with criteria for deciding whether or not a given divorce is to be fruitfully analyzed as a crisis, but they do not tell us anything about what caused the divorce to occur in the first place. Furthermore, they do not tell us why the divorce may have been stressful, why coping

resources may have been insufficient, or why the affected persons may have interpreted the divorce as a crisis. For these reasons, the ABCX model has limited explanatory power and would more usefully be treated as a definition.

4. Included in this model are such interaction variables as the amount of verbal and nonverbal communication, the amount of conflict and the degree to which it is issue-oriented, the amount of support and of creativity and the elaborateness of language codes. Other interaction variables included refer to the distribution and normativity of interaction, which encompass such ideas as the centralization and legitimacy of power, the extent to which leadership is coordinative (as opposed to being directive), and the degree to which the interaction proceeds in accordance with selected criteria of rationality (Klein & Hill, 1979, pp. 520-523).

5. One interesting study which places the individual in a community context of helping networks has been recently published by Warren (1981). Although the family unit figures into this study in only a marginal way, the volume contains many insights which family scholars may wish to extract.

6. Hill (1981) has pointed out in personal communication that early research in the SCC tradition was often more sensitive to the issues concerning process than recent research has been. So, for example, some families have been described as thriving in the aftermath of severe crises even though they lack the key resources of integration and adaptability (Hill, 1949).

7. As of this writing, only three research projects in addition to those cited in Klein and Hill (1979) are known to have been conducted on PS, and no new initiatives are apparently under way. The data from the three studies were collected in the early-to-mid 1970s, and they have not yet been published (Tallman et al., 1981; Thomas, Rollins, Peterson & Galligan, 1981; and Aldous, 1981).

REFERENCES

Aldous, J. A framework for the analysis of family problem solving. In J. Aldous, T. Condon, R. Hill, M. Straus, & I. Tallman (Eds.), *Family problem solving: A symposium on theoretical, methodological, and substantive concerns.* Hinsdale, IL: The Dryden Press, 1971.
Aldous, J. The search for alternatives: Parental behaviors and children's original problem solutions. *Journal of Marriage and the Family,* 1975, *37,* 711-722.
Aldous, J. Personal communication, 1981.
Aldous, J., Condon, T., Hill, R., Straus, M., & Tallman, I. (Eds.), *Family problem solving: A symposium on theoretical, methodological, and substantive concerns.* Hinsdale, IL: The Dryden Press, 1971.
Angell, R. C. *The family encounters the depression.* New York: Charles Scribner, 1936.
Bales, R. F. *Interaction process analysis.* Cambridge, MA: Addison-Wesley, 1950.
Bales, R. F., & Cohen, S. P. *SYMLOG: A system for the multiple level observation of groups.* New York: The Free Press, 1979.
Bee, H. L. Socialization for problem solving. In J. Aldous, T. Condon, R. Hill, M. Straus, & I. Tallman (Eds.), *Family problem solving: A symposium on theoretical, methodological, and substantive concerns.* Hinsdale, IL: The Dryden Press, 1971.
Boss, P. G., McCubbin, H. I., & Lester, G. R. The corporate executive wife's coping patterns in response to routine husband-father absence. *Family Process,* 1979, *18,* 79-86.
Burr, W. R. *Theory construction and the sociology of the family.* New York: Wiley, 1973.
Chambers, D. W. Coping with stress. In S. S. Boundy & N. J. Reynolds (Eds.), *Current concepts in dental hygiene.* St. Louis, MO: Mosby, 1979, 155-168.
Craddock, A. E. Marital problem-solving as a function of couples' marital power and marital value systems. *Journal of Marriage and the Family,* 1980, *42,* 185-196.
Day, R. D., & Raschke, H. J. The development of a general theory of crisis and recovery

and its applicability for divorce adjustment. Paper presented at National Council on Family Relations Annual Meeting, Portland, Oregon, October, 1980.
Filsinger, E. E., & Lewis, R. A. *Assessing marriage: New behavioral approaches.* Beverly Hills, CA: Sage Publications, 1981.
Geismar, L. L., & Ayres, B. *Patterns of change in problem families.* St. Paul, MN: Family Centered Project, 1959.
Gottman, J. M. *Marital interaction: Experimental investigations.* New York: Academic Press, 1979.
Goulet, D. *The uncertain promise: Value conflicts in technology transfer.* New York: IDOC/ North America, 1977.
Hansen, D. A., & Hill, R. Families under stress. In H. T. Christensen (Ed.), *Handbook of marriage and the family.* Chicago: Rand McNally, 1964, 782-819.
Hansen, D. A., & Johnson, V. A. Rethinking family stress theory: Definitional aspects. In W. Burr, R. Hill, F. I. Nye, and I Reiss (Eds.), *Contemporary theories about the family,* Vol. 1, New York: The Free Press, 1979.
Hill, R. *Families under stress.* New York: Harper & Row, 1949.
Hill, R. Generic features of families under stress. *Social Casework,* 1958, *39,* 139-150.
Hill, R. Personal communication, 1981.
Hill, R., & Hansen, D. A. The family in disaster. In G. Baker & D. Chapman (Eds.), *Man and society in disaster.* New York: Basic Books, 1962.
Kaslow, F. W. Divorce and divorce therapy. In A. S. Gurman & D. P. Kniskern (Eds.), *Handbook of family therapy.* New York: Brunner/Mazel, 1981, 662-696.
Klein, D. M., & Hill, R. Determinants of family problem solving effectiveness. In W. Burr, R. Hill, F. I. Nye, & I. Reiss (Eds.), *Contemporary theories about the family,* Vol. I. New York: Free Press, 1979, 493-548.
Kutash, I. L., Schlesinger, L. B., & Associates (Eds.), *Handbook on stress and anxiety: Contemporary knowledge, theory and treatment.* San Francisco: Jossey-Bass, 1980.
Lipman-Blumen, J. A crisis framework applied to macrosociological family changes: Marriage, divorce, and occupational trends associated with World War II. *Journal of Marriage and the Family,* 1975, *37,* 889-902.
Maynard, P., Maynard, N., McCubbin, H. I., & Shao, D. Family life and the police profession: Coping patterns wives employ in managing job stress and the family environment. *Family Relations,* 1980, *29,* 495-501.
McCubbin, H. I. Integrating coping behavior in family stress theory. *Journal of Marriage and the Family,* 1979, *41,* 237-244.
McCubbin, H. I., Boss, P. G., Wilson, L. R., & Lester, G. R. Developing family invulnerability to stress: Coping patterns and strategies wives employ. In J. Trost (Ed.), *The Family and Change.* Uppsala, Sweden: International Library, 1980.
McCubbin, H. I., Dahl, B. B., Lester, G. R., Benson, D., & Robertson, M. L. Coping repertoires of families adapting to prolonged war-induced separations. *Journal of Marriage and the Family,* 1976, *38,* 461-471.
McCubbin, H. I., Joy, C. B., Cauble, A. E., Comeau, J. K., Patterson, J. M., & Needle, R. H. Family stress and coping: A decade review. *Journal of Marriage and the Family,* 1980, *42,* 855-871.
McCubbin, H. I., & Patterson, J. M. Broadening the scope of family strengths: An emphasis on family coping and social support. In N. Stinnett, J. DeFrain, K. King, P. Knaub, & G. Rowe (Eds.), *Family strengths, 3.* Lincoln: University of Nebraska Press, 1981.
McCubbin, H. I., & Patterson, J. M. Family stress and adaptation to crises: A double ABCX model of family behavior. Paper presented at National Council on Family Relations Annual Meeting, Milwaukee, WI, October, 1981. To be published in D. H. Olson & B. C. Miller (Eds.), *Family Stress Review Yearbook,* Beverly Hills, CA: Sage Publications, in press.
Miller, B. C., & Olson, D. H. *Cluster analysis as a method for defining types of marriage interaction.* Paper presented at National Council on Family Relations Annual Meeting, New York, October, 1976.

Nunnally, J. C. *Psychometric theory.* New York: McGraw-Hill, 1967.
Patterson, J., & McCubbin, H. Gender roles and coping. *Journal of Marriage and the Family,* in press.
Pearlin, L. I., & Schooler, C. The structure of coping. *Journal of Health and Social Behavior,* 1978, *19,* 2-21.
Puryear, D. A. *Helping people in crisis.* San Francisco: Jossey-Bass, 1979.
Raush, H. L., Barry, W. A., Hertel, R. K., & Swain, M. A. *Communication, Conflict, and Marriage.* San Francisco: Jossey-Bass, 1974.
Reiss, D. Varieties of consensual experience I: A theory for relating family interaction to individual thinking. *Family Process,* 1971, *10,* 1-28.
Reiss, D. *The family's construction of reality.* Cambridge, MA: Harvard University Press, 1981.
Reiss, D., & Oliveri, M. E. Family paradigm and family coping: A proposal to linking the family's intrinsic adaptive capacities to its responses to stress. *Family Relations,* 1980, *29,* 431-444.
Salts, C. J. Divorce process: Integration of theory. *Journal of Divorce,* 1979, *2,* 233-240.
Selye, H. The stress concept today. In I. L. Kutash, L. B. Schlesinger, & Associates (Eds.), *Handbook on stress and anxiety: Contemporary knowledge, theory, and treatment.* San Francisco: Jossey-Bass, 1980, 127-143.
Simmons, R., Klein, S., & Thornton, K. The family member's decision to be a kidney transplant donor. *Journal of Comparative Family Studies,* 1973, *4,* 88-115.
Straus, M. A. Communication, creativity, and problem-solving ability of middle- and working-class families in three societies. *American Journal of Sociology,* 1968, *73,* 417-430.
Tallman, I. Adaptability: A problem solving approach to assessing childrearing practices. *Child Development,* 1961, *32,* 651-668.
Tallman, I. The family as a small problem solving group. *Journal of Marriage and the Family,* 1970, *32,* 94-104.
Tallman, I. Social structure and socialization for change. Paper presented at National Council on Family Relations Annual Meeting, Portland, Oregon, October, 1972.
Tallman, I., Klein, D. M., Cohen, R., Ihinger, M., Marotz, R., Torsiello, P., & Troost, K. *A taxonomy of group problems and implications for group problem solving.* Minneapolis: Minnesota Family Study Center Technical Report #3, 1974.
Tallman, I., Marotz-Baden, R., & Pindas, P. *Socialization for social change: A comparative study of parent-adolescent relations in Mexico and the United States.* Unpublished manuscript. 1981.
Tallman, I., & Miller, G. Class differences in family problem solving: The effects of verbal ability, hierarchical structure, and role expectations. *Sociometry,* 1974, *37,* 13-37.
Thomas, D., Rollins, B., Peterson, G., & Galligan, R. Personal communication with Thomas and Galligan, 1981.
Tryon, R. C., & Bailey, D. E. *Cluster analysis.* New York: McGraw-Hill, 1970.
Warren, D. I. *Helping networks.* Notre Dame, IN: University of Notre Dame Press, 1981.
Weick, K. E. Group processes, family processes, and problem solving. In J. Aldous, T. Condon, R. Hill, M. Straus, & I. Tallman (Eds.), *Family problem solving: A symposium on theoretical methodological and substantive concerns.* Hinsdale, IL: The Dryden Press, 1971.

Chapter 5

Individual Coping Efforts and Family Studies: Conceptual and Methodological Issues

Elizabeth G. Menaghan

Like stress before it, "coping" is rapidly becoming an enormously popular and increasingly ambiguous concept in a wide variety of disciplines concerned with families. There are increasing efforts to describe and assess coping variables, to determine their precursors and correlates, to document their effectiveness, and to recommend intervention techniques to "help people cope" with the stresses they encounter. In this review, I attempt to complement recent reviews of family-level problem solving and coping styles (Hansen & Johnson, 1979; Klein & Hill, 1979; McCubbin, Joy, Cauble, Comeau, Patterson, & Needle, 1980) by focusing on the coping efforts of individuals, and seek to evaluate current findings in this area.

Whether at the level of families or individuals, the general question to be considered is a multifaceted one: how and under what conditions are what sorts of coping variables effective in modifying relationships between stress and outcomes? To address this question, we must first specify more carefully the meaning of stress, coping, and outcomes.

CONCEPTUAL ISSUES

Stress, Coping and Outcomes

Three broad variable sets—characteristics of the environment or situation, person characteristics and resources, and environmental

Elizabeth G. Menaghan is Assistant Professor, Department of Sociology, Ohio State University, Columbus, Ohio.

appraisal or definition—recur in most definitions of stress and coping. In stress research, for example, the usual stress definition essentially posits some mismatch—actual or perceived—between environment and person: environmental demands tax or exceed the adaptive capacities or resources of the person, and/or environmental opportunities do not permit the satisfaction of individual needs. In the family literature, Hill's (1949) definition of crisis as a product of event characteristics, family resources, and family appraisals can be seen as a specification of this more general model.

Like the concept of stress, coping is a term that has been used at differing levels of generality and abstraction. It seems useful to distinguish three basic sets of coping variables, which we may label resources, styles, and efforts. *Resources* are *generalized attitudes and skills* which can be considered advantageous: attitudes about self (esteem, ego strength); attitudes about the world (sense of coherence, belief in mastery); intellectual skills (cognitive flexibility and complexity, analytic abilities, knowledge); and interpersonal skills (communicating skills, competence and ease in interpersonal interaction). *Coping styles* are generalized coping strategies, defined as *typical, habitual preferences* for ways of approaching problems: for example, a tendency to withdraw from other people, versus a tendency to move closer to them; denial of difficulties, versus dwelling on them; to be active versus reactive; to blame others rather than oneself. Such coping style typologies, by definition, assume some cross-situational, relatively stable problem solving tendencies in individuals. *Coping efforts* are *specific actions* (covert or overt) taken in *specific situations,* which are intended to reduce a given problem or stress (e.g., appraise the problem, express or inhibit emotions, begin a new activity, ask for help, refuse to think about it, etc.). Situational specificity, of course, can vary in degree: studies may examine strategies specific to a single role or relationship (Pearlin & Schooler, 1978), a single event—reaction to an exam (Morris & Engle, 1981) or a reprimand at work (Andrews, Tennart, Hewson, & Vaillant, 1978), or recurrent experiences such as a spouse's business trips (Boss, McCubbin, & Lester, 1979).

Implicit in the concept of coping at all levels is the notion of effectiveness: to cope is to manage stress successfully, and coping responses are presumed to reduce distress and/or improve one's situation. Empirical assessments of coping effectiveness have used a wide array of possible outcome criteria. Some studies (e.g., Berman & Turk, 1981; McCubbin, Dahl, Lester, Benson, & Robertson, 1976) focus on perceived effectiveness—respondents' claims that this or that strategy was helpful to them in some way. Such testimonies, of course, stand in an uncertain relationship to actual effects. Videka (1979), for example, found that participants in Mended Hearts self-help groups considered the group very helpful to them, but they could generally not be distinguished from similar nonparticipating heart surgery patients on a wide net of social and psychological measures. Averill (1973) similarly reported essential independence in laboratory stress studies between what respondents found helpful and what improved their physiological or self-reported response. For example, most respondents preferred self-administration of shocks and preferred having information about shock timing; but these conditions did not reduce negative response, at least in the studies Averill reviewed.

Other studies go beyond this and attempt some measure of observed effectiveness. A typical criterion is the reduction of feelings of distress or depressive affect (e.g., Pearlin & Schooler, 1978). This, of course, does not capture the implied expectation that coping might actually reduce problems or lead to some optimal solution; but only a few studies have looked at problem reduction over time (Menaghan, 1981b). One might also consider changes in the stressed individual's own quality of role performance; assess the functioning of some larger group (e.g., the family system); consider the acceptability of solutions to others; or examine the psychological well-being of involved others, such as the individual's spouse, co-worker, or child. For each of these, one may also distinguish short-range and long-range effects. The same coping resources, style or action may have opposing effects on differing indicators: for example, Stern and Pascale (1979) found that heart attack patients who denied the seriousness of their illness were overtly less anxious and depressed, and more likely to resume their role responsibilities, but their wives, were more prone to depression. Similarly, the same response positively associated with short-term well-being (e.g., maintaining hope that one's missing-in-action husband will be found) may be negatively associated with well-being if it persists years afterward (Boss, 1980). Thus, one's conclusions about the effectiveness of coping may vary depending on one's choice of outcome criteria and time frame in which effects are examined.

Substantive Questions

As stated earlier, the general question posed is to specify the conditions under which coping variables are effective in modifying the relationships between stress and outcomes. This broad question embraces many specific questions which could be profitably pursued. One may first try to understand *what sorts of people, under what conditions, use certain coping strategies.* Much of the recent work in both individual and family coping has conceptualized patterns of coping in terms of generalized styles of responding which are relatively invariant across situations and relatively stable over time within individuals or within families. Empirically, the extent of both situational invariance and temporal stability remain relatively unexplored questions. How different are any one individual's approaches to parental versus marital problems, or to either versus occupational or economic problems, for example? How diverse are a family's strategies for dealing with health problems, a delinquent child, and a shrinking paycheck?

Related to issues of usage is the question of *linkages among the coping* resources, styles or efforts *of individual family members* and the resources, styles or efforts *of the family* as an interacting and problem-solving group. Klein and Hill (1979), for example, argue that characteristics of individual members influence both cultural orientations and group structured properties, with these in turn shaping problem-solving interactions. On the other hand, Reiss (1981) reports essential independence between individuals' tolerance of ambiguity and locus of control and their conceptual close relations at the family level.

Linked to this question are *the relationships among the coping tendencies of individual family members.* Are spouses, for example, likely to complement one another's styles, or to seek a shared way of managing difficulties? Are particular combinations of coping efforts—such as wives wishing to talk things out and ventilate feelings while husbands prefer suppression of feelings and withdrawal from interaction—particularly problematic, as Cook (1982) suggests?

For any individual or family, we may also explore *the interconnections* between the three categories of coping variables—*resources, styles, and efforts*—as well as their relative stability. Coping resources are generally considered fairly stable characteristics which shape problem solving preferences or styles; and these, in turn, are thought to influence specific efforts, which are seen as the least stable and most situationally influenced of the three categories. These presumed patterns of association and stability, however, are seldom empirically examined.

Finally, a critical question is *how effective,* according to some criteria, *coping styles or efforts may be.* And just as we noted that the problem invariance and stability of usage predictors were open questions, so may we ask how problem-specific or probleminvariant any conclusions about effectiveness may be. For example, a recent analysis (Menaghan, 1981b) finds selective inattention to marital problems related to greater marital distress and not directly related in either direction to later marital problems; would this conclusion hold for the use of selective inattention for parental or health problems as well?

Obviously, this set of questions cannot all be explored in this relatively brief paper. I shall focus here on (a) correlates of usage and relationships among the three categories of coping variables; (b) evidence for effectiveness; and (c) taxonomies of coping variables, particularly as individual and family-level coping typologies might parallel one another.

The present discussion relies on a broad model for ordering situations, stress, coping, and outcomes (Figure 1). The overall structural arrangements and value-orientations of the society are expected to influence the events, situations, and role conditions individuals encounter, as well as the individual characteristics, resources, and attitudes they are likely to possess. The latter may in turn influence generalized coping styles; and situations, resources and generalized coping styles jointly influence one's appraisal of one's situation. Both one's generalized styles and one's appraisal of the situation at hand may influence the specific coping efforts made. The final outcomes of the process are influenced both by the objective characteristics of the situation and by the specific coping efforts made (in possible interaction). While not the focus of discussion

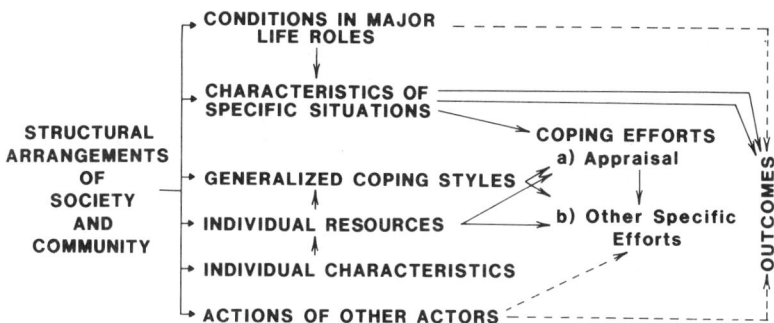

FIGURE 1: The context of coping variables: Societal precursors, situations and outcomes

here, it seems apparent that any complete accounting of the outcomes would have to take into account the impact of the actions and perceptions of other actors, and, when narrowing in on any single event or situation, on the conditions the individual faces in other major life arenas. I shall focus here on the central coping variables and on their effect on outcomes.

COPING: THE RESEARCH EVIDENCE

Correlates of Usage and Interrelations Among Variables

Predictors of one's coping resources have generally utilized demographics and situational variables. For example, George (1980) notes that one's financial resources, good health and education can furnish skills and aids for dealing with difficulty. In particular, education appears to foster a cognitive complexity that facilitates realistic stress perception and problem-solving skills. Worden and Sobel (1978) find that socio-economic status is positively related to greater ego strength among their sample of cancer patients. Similarly, higher education and more autonomous occupations seem to increase intellectual flexibility for both men and women (Kohn & Schooler, 1978; Miller, Kohn, Schooler, & Miller, 1979).

Some research has linked these general resources with coping styles and coping efforts. Worden and Sobel (1978), for example, show that their general measure of ego strength predicts the greater use of a coping style associated with less distress (problem redefinition and the lesser uses of several coping styles associated with greater distress (fatalistic acceptance of problems, blaming others, and suppressing emotions). Similarly, Pearlin, Lieberman, Menaghan, & Mullan (1981) report that individuals with higher self-esteem and a more internal sense of mastery used more effective strategies for coping with economic problems.

All of these linkages are cross-sectional, and certainly do not establish the direction of association. Some researchers (e.g., Shalit, 1977) have suggested that these linkages may be particularly strong in ambiguous situations, where the problem itself does not powerfully "press" for particular responses. Similarly, at the family level, Klein and Hill (1979) argue that in the face of uncertainty, the best predictor of initial attempts to solve a problem may be the family's established interaction preferences; and Reiss (1981) also argues that the very ambiguous nature of his laboratory task brings out problem-solving efforts that flow from a family's conception of itself and its social world.

Evidence for Effectiveness

Coping resources: Beliefs, attitudes, and skills. The most studied personal resource variables are one's attitudes and beliefs about one's self and one's world. Particularly frequent are measures of locus of control. The model of autonomous individuals who hold their fates in their own hands, as Diaz-Buerrero (1979) and Antonovsky (1979) have noted, is the culturally preferred stance in the West, and it is not surprising that measures of mastery and control are quite popular. Their meaning, however, is often ambiguous. Most locus of control measures seem to combine views of world and of self. In answering whether I can control what happens to me, a "yes" seems to imply a view of the world as predictable, comprehensive, and lawful. External scores are more ambiguous: I may feel I have little leverage because the world is chaotic and/or incomprehensible (*no one* can control what happens), or because, although I understand its order and ways of working, I have concluded that I, as an individual, am excluded from real power in it (others may control what happens, but I cannot). These two meanings seem quite distinct.

One's view of the world and of one's own influence on it may vary tremendously from one role to another and even within roles from one relationship to another. Certainly, areas of life are frequently discussed as if there is objective variation in how much influence is possible (marriage and family life, for example, often being seen as permitting greater personal shaping than the occupational sphere); and it is reasonable to expect that people's perceived extent of control may similarly vary by life arena. Similarly, they may see little coherence in the world taken as a whole, but much more in their own occupational, community or family setting. Nevertheless, the argument is made that general measures of coherence and mastery do predict better outcomes, in part because they encourage a more rational, optimistic problem-solving stance (cf. Lefcourt, 1976).

Similar questions can be raised about the generality of "general" interpersonal skills. For example, Wampler and Sprenkle (1980), discussing "marital improvement" techniques, claim that learning how to communicate in an "open" style—with high self-disclosure, high receptivity to partner's disclosure, and "speaking for self"—gives one a resource which will powerfully aid in the resolution of interpersonal conflict. Linden and Feuerstein (1981) also discuss the liability of "social incompetence," which seems to be a mixture of "inappropriate" *behaviors* when in distressing social situations, increased *anxiety* when in those situations, and a "pessimistic cognitive set" or *belief* that one doesn't handle interpersonal encounters very well. However, the generality of this variable across relationships has not been demonstrated; it seems likely that the ease and skill with which one negotiates problems varies for the pairs and subgroups one is part of. If this is so, relationship-specific measures may be more appropriate in assessing effectiveness.

It seems difficult to argue against notions that more positive and potent views of the self, more orderly conceptions of the world, more skills in information-gathering and analysis, and greater interpersonal ease and skills are better than their opposites. Nevertheless, it is interesting that demonstrations of their effectiveness, and explorations of their influence on coping styles and efforts, are still fairly meager.

Generalized coping styles. Coping styles, like personal resources, are considered to be general and relatively stable qualities of individuals which they bring to situations, in contrast to more situationally variable coping efforts. In practice, this distinction is hard to maintain, since some researchers reach their conclusions about general style by empirically generalizing across specific situations (Vaillant, 1976; Worden & Sobel, 1978). Others ask respondents to report their "usual" tendencies directly. Typically, the categories used reflect a psychoanalytic scheme of defense mechanisms such as denial, displacement, and anticipation. While some studies look at these separately, others (e.g., Andrews et al., 1978; Frydman, 1981) follow Vaillant (1976) in hierarchizing such styles as more or less "mature" and deriving an overall "maturity of coping style" score from specific responses to specific situations, or from endorsements of various responses to hypothetical vignettes.

Judgements of coping styles as more or less mature are somewhat different than measures of effectiveness. Some of these theorists implicitly or explicitly reject empirical assessments of effectiveness in judging the adequacy of coping. In this view, efforts or styles may fail to overcome problems; nevertheless, some styles are preferable to others because they are intrinsically better or more mature approaches.

What are the *criteria* by which a mature style is identified? Vaillant derived his hierarchy in part from theoretical concerns and in part from age trends in relative usage. The use of "immature" styles, like acting out, and denial through fantasy, decreased from late adolescence to middle age, while the use of "mature" styles (sublimation, altruism, anticipation, and suppression) increased. (Several of the intermediate approaches, notably intellectualization, accounted for a fairly constant proportion of responses over time.) Haan's (1977) categorization of ego processes as reflecting either an adaptive ("coping") or maladaptive ("defense") mode depends on their flexibility, future-orientation, relative freedom from reality distortion, complexity, allowance for gratification of impulses, and expression of affect. Antonovsky (1979) also proposes criteria for evaluating the overall maturity of coping styles; he stresses rationality (i.e., accuracy and objectivity of appraisal); flexibility (i.e., creating contingent plans and tactics and being willing to consider them); and farsightedness (i.e., anticipation of the long-range as well as immediate responses to actions envisaged). This clearly overlaps with Haan's typology, and with Buehler and Hogan's (1980) dimensions of long-range/short-range orientation and comprehensive versus piecemeal approach to problems.

Again, these theoretical preferences for some styles over others do not necessarily imply that they have been demonstrably more effective than their opposites, in all or even most situations. Apparent denial (less rational and more "distorted" assessments which minimize the seriousness of one's situation) is an example: Rosentiel and Roth (1981) find it associated with better outcomes, and at the family level, Hansen and Johnson (1979) argue that misperceptions may make it easier to cope with problems, in part through fostering illusions of competence or control. However, there is some evidence that more mature coping styles, as judged by the above criteria, are more effective. Vaillant (1976), for example, found his overall summary score correlated with better career, interpersonal and psychological functioning, as well as with higher marital enjoyment and greater subjective happiness.

Specific coping efforts. Although individuals may actually try a sequence of specific efforts in response to any given problem, data about such sequences are sparse. Some recent studies (e.g., Folkman & Lazarus, 1980) have tried to develop a time frame of coping efforts by using closely spaced repeated measures. Others (e.g., Alonzo, 1980a, 1980b) have relied on detailed retrospective questioning to reconstruct the sequence of coping actions. More typically, investigators have obtained an overall report of what people have done, thought, or felt, how often or how extensively they did so, and/or how helpful certain possible actions were to them. There is wide variation in how effectiveness has been measured.

One recurring problem is the failure to assess usage and perceived helpfulness separately. Horowitz (1978), however, attempted to capture this difference. He presented respondents with 33 possible responses to life events and asked them, first, to identify which they had done, and of those, to identify those that were very helpful. There were large variations in usage and helpfulness reports: for example, in a sample of people facing bereavement, 46 percent tried to find new interests, and 69 percent tried to look at their situation as realistically as possible, but not a single respondent thought either of these very helpful. The exact figures, of course, are less important than the general lack of association between helpfulness and usage: analysis utilizing only helpfulness ratings, or only usage, would reach very different conclusions.

Part of the problem is the ambiguity involved in a rating of "not helpful." We have no way of knowing whether strategies judged less helpful were tried and found wanting, avoided because they were judged unlikely to be helpful, or used extensively despite their perceived ineffectiveness. Thus, the relationship between patterns used and either perceived helpfulness or observed effectiveness cannot be ascertained. Such data may, however, suggest how perceived helpfulness ratings compare with other outcome measures. For example, Berman and Turk (1981) report that respondents with lower life satisfaction and worse mood state considered "engaging in social activities" and "trying to increase autonomy" less helpful, and "expressing their negative feelings" more helpful, than more positive respondents; considering home and family activities less helpful was an additional predictor of negative life satisfaction.

Similar helpfulness ratings characterize a series of studies carried out by McCubbin and a variety of collaborators (Boss, McCubbin, & Lester, 1979; McCubbin, 1976; McCubbin, Dahl, Lester, Benson, & Robertson, 1976; McCubbin & Shao, 1980). All used wives as respondents, and explored the impact on them of various aspects of their husbands' work lives; and all assessed coping with measures that asked the wives to rate how helpful (not at all, minimally, very) they found each of a list of possible behaviors to be to them, rather than how often they performed such behaviors.

McCubbin and his colleagues also report some associations between these measures of perceived helpfulness and other outcome variables selected to reflect the psychological functioning and role performance of the respondent wives and their children. Wives who perceived tension-management behaviors as more helpful reported more symptoms; wives who rated relying on religion and the past as helpful reported more role adjustment problems; but no helpfulness ratings predicted children's difficulties. In a related analysis, Maynard et al. (1980) relate helpfulness ratings to wives' descriptions of their family organization: Wives who considered self-reliant strategies helpful also characterized their families as more expressive, more independent but also more cohesive; wives who found conscientious togetherness efforts helpful characterized their families as less conflictual but also less independent; and wives who found social interaction outside the family helpful characterized their families as less rigidly organized. The causal ordering here, and the relationship of such variables to usage of coping patterns as distinct from perceived helpfulness, are important questions for future research.

Even when usage is assessed separately from perceived helpfulness, the non-parallel nature of the coping efforts assessed makes it difficult to generalize about effectiveness. Folkman and Lazarus (1980), in repeated measurements of a sample of 100 white, middle-aged, non-poor respondents, asked for usage or non-usage of 68 coping efforts intended to tap the relative focus on problem-resolving (P) and emotional management (E) efforts. While other researchers (e.g., Anderson, 1977) had seen these as alternative approaches and reported them to be negatively correlated, Folkman and Lazarus reported a positive association (r about .44) in their data. They have not yet reported information about the effectiveness of such efforts.

Pearlin and Schooler (1978) also used a variant of the problem- versus emotion-focused classification in discussing the specific coping efforts in four major role areas of occupation, economic life, marriage, and parenting. They classified the 19 coping efforts as three independent factors: (a) action to alter the situation, (b) reinterpretation of the problem, and (c) efforts to manage negative emotions (e.g., emotional ventilation). They assessed their effectiveness in reducing role-related distress. Even though all of their items were initially culled from open-ended interviews concerning how people dealt with their role problems, eight of the 19 strategies (e.g., advice seeking, selective ignoring, passive forebearance, emotional discharge) were related to *greater* role distress at any given level of strain. It was the *lesser* use of such efforts, along with the greater use of others (e.g., negotiation in marriage and optimistic comparisons in both marriage and parenting) that predicted lower distress.

In a subsequent analysis restricted to the marital role, Menaghan (1981b) extended the criteria for effectiveness to include changes in the extent of problems reported four years later. Here, both negotiations and optimistic comparisons reduced later problems with initial problem level, distress and a variety of demographic and contextual controls held constant, but selective ignoring and passive forebearance had no direct impact on later problems.

Colletta and Gregg's (1981) study of 64 black adolescent mothers follows Pearlin's categorization of coping responses as those that modify the situation, those that modify the meaning of the situation, and those that manage the resulting stress. However, they view problem and emotion-focused coping as two ends of a single continuum, with direct action high and all other types low. With self-esteem and available social supports held constant, this overall measure of active coping was related to lower emotional distress in their sample.

Interactions and effectiveness. For all levels of coping variables, an emerging issue (Felton, 1980; Jenkins, 1979; LaRocco, House, & French, 1980) is how effectiveness should be measured and what the form of the relationship should be. The basic question is whether the impact of coping varies systematically at different levels of situational stressfulness. House (1980) has developed a parallel argument about the relationships between social supports, situations, and outcomes: To the extent that support (or coping) has largely main effects, everyone would benefit from enhancing those levels; but if it has primarily buffering effects, enhancement "will be of significant value to people experiencing moderate to high levels of stress, but of lesser, or even no, value to people experiencing little or no stress" (p. 37).

Actually, House is discussing only one possible form of such interaction. It could be that a given coping variable has a greater impact in low-stress situations but is increasingly impotent as troubles mount; or even that coping efforts are maximally effective at some moderate level of stress, and less so at both extremely high and extremely low levels of stress—at high levels because they are not enough, and at low levels because they are not necessary.

As Figure 2 shows, if interaction is present, our conclusions about its form may vary depending on the particular range of stressfulness we have sampled. Within the extreme low end of stressfulness, we would find that more of some coping effort is beneficial at all levels but has greater impact at lower levels of stress (box a); within the extreme high range of stressfulness, coping seems counterproductive (box b). Within the moderate range of stressfulness, coping may appear to have no effect at low stress but some negative effect at higher stress levels (box c), or its effect may seem restricted to lower levels of stress (box d). Joining box c and d (box e), we might conclude that coping enhances outcome at low

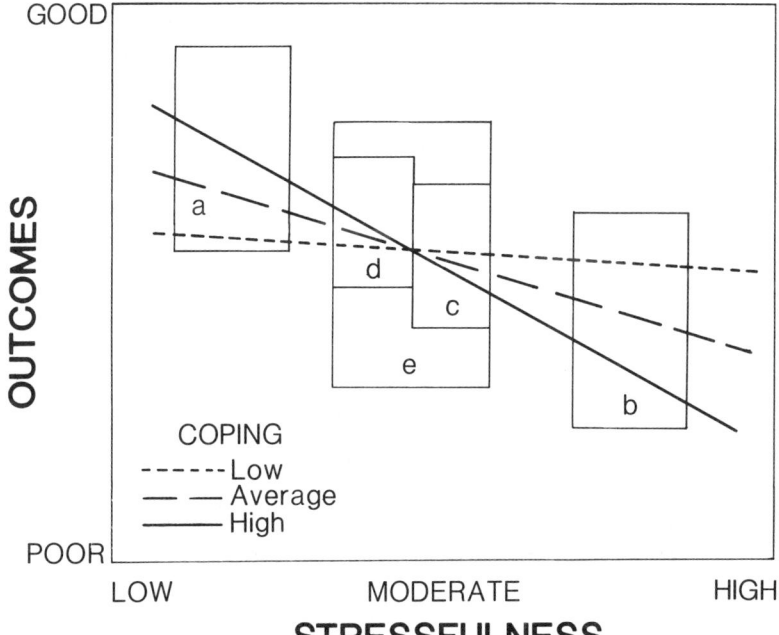

Box a: Coping effect at all stress levels; effect greatest at higher levels of stress.
Box b: Coping effect at all stress levels; effect greatest at lower levels of stress.
Box c: Coping effect not present at all stress levels; effect limited to high stress.
Box d: Coping effect not present at all stress levels; effect limited to low stress.
Box e: Reversal of effect: positive at low stress, negative at high stress.

FIGURE 2: Interactions between situational stressfulness and coping efforts in explaining outcomes: Variations in observed relationships within different ranges on the stress continuum

levels of stress, is insignificant in the middle range, and exacerbates the situation at high levels of stress. Thus, any interpretation of findings of interaction must consider at what point on the broad continuum of stressfulness one has sampled.

The effectiveness of coping strategies may also vary for people in different situations or life stages. For example, Menaghan (1981b) found that the effect of several marital coping efforts in reducing later problems was stronger for those in higher social classes. Variations in effectiveness for men and women, while not yet reported, also seem intuitively plausible.

There has been very little analysis aimed at identifying the optimum range of situations for specific coping variables, or in assessing the presence or form of interactions. We may find that most if not all of the variables discussed here operate in the same direction and to the same degree for all levels of situational stressfulness, and this would be no reason to exclude them from the pantheon of coping variables. But future research and theory could profitably look more rigorously and systematically for non-additive relationships, and try to explain their nature, as Pearlin et al. (1981) and Menaghan (1982) have recently attempted.

Taxonomies of Coping Variables

As the studies reviewed here make clear, there is a long list of "coping" variables assessed in the literature. Actually, there is much conceptual overlapping, and it seems useful to articulate key dimensions, and to explore how such dimensions of individual coping might parallel taxonomies of interpersonal and family-level coping.

The categories of coping resources, styles and efforts have clear parallels at the individual and family level. Individual resources include overall views of self and world, cognitive and analytic skills, and interpersonal skills. Reiss and Oliveri (1980) emphasize that a family's "abiding conception of the social world in which it lives" similarly constitutes a resource which influences both routines and specific efforts to deal with events and tasks. And just as the individual level stresses a sense of mastery or control, so do Reiss and Oliveri emphasize the degree to which family members believe that the social world in which they live is ordered by a coherent set of principles which they can discover and master through exploration and interpretation. The individual level had stressed intrapersonal analytic skills and cognitive flexibility—essentially problem-solving competency. At the family level, Klein and Hill (1979) emphasize homogeneity of such competencies, i.e., the extent to which particular problem-solving skills and overall problem-solving skills are evenly distributed among family members. Finally, concern with individual interpersonal skills as a generalized resource is echoed by a family level concern for established conflict-resolution strategies of the group, patterns of boundary maintenance, positional and personal norms governing leadership, and extent to which families effectively mine the knowledge and skills of their members.

Similarly, the notion of relatively stable preferences among possible ways of approaching problems, labeled here coping styles, occurs at both individual and family-level views of coping. For example, Reiss and Oliveri argue that families have characteristic positions on the dimensions of configuration (ability to perceive/tendency to search for pattern and organization), coordination (degree of information exchange), and closure (openness to new information and ability to tolerate uncertainty and delay). Olson, Sprenkle, and Russell (1979) argue that families establish preferred family styles of relative separateness/connectedness and relative structural rigidity/randomness, and that these in turn influence specific problem-solving efforts of families.

Finally, the idea of problem-specific coping efforts—actions intended to resolve particular problems or manage particular dilemmas—also occurs at both individual and family levels.

Nevertheless, of course, there seem to be obvious differences between individual and family coping. Klein and Hill comment that, in contrast to the reflective thinking and individual decision making of one person, family-level coping necessarily involves exchange of perspectives and efforts at coordination of decisions and actions, an interpersonal activity demanding more persuasive and empathic skills than does an individual's efforts to manage problems.

Without minimizing such differences, there still seems to be a certain parallelism of individual and family-level coping possibilities if we conceptualize these at the level of general adaptive tasks facing all those in stress. For example, Moos (1977) posited four such tasks that must be simultaneously addressed:

1. preserving a reasonable emotional balance;
2. preserving a satisfactory self-image, with a sense of competence and mastery;

3. preserving relationships with family and friends; and
4. preparing for an uncertain future.

Haan (1977), discussing what individuals must do to cope with stress, argues one needs at minimum to (a) regulate affect (manage tension); (b) focus attention and interpretively simplify the problem; and (c) engage in cognitive processing or problem-solving efforts. In their studies of wives, McCubbin and his colleagues repeatedly emphasize (a) efforts at tension release; (b) efforts to increase independence and resources; (c) efforts to develop or maintain interpersonal supports; and (d) efforts to use the norms of some collective group to guide their own actions and interpretations. Fockman & Lazarus (1980) also stress problem appraisal, emotion-management efforts, and problem-solving efforts; and Pearlin and Schooler (1978) similarly see direct action, perceptual or interpretive strategies, and tension-managing strategies as three prongs of individual coping efforts.

I would argue that an implicit typology of coping strategies flows from the notion of stress itself. Recall that stress can be defined as a mismatch or discrepancy between environmental demands and individual or family resources or capacities; or as a mismatch between environmental opportunities and individual or family needs, goals, or preferences. Efforts at stress reduction, then, must try to alter one of the four elements involved: environmental demands; environmental opportunities; self or family capacities or resources; or self or family needs, goals, or preferences (Table 1). At the family level, concern with the overall integration or cohesion of the family, or efforts to increase self-reliance of individual family members, sometimes considered without parallel at the individual level, are seen as problem-resolution efforts aimed at increasing resources, analogous to individual efforts to obtain more education or increase efficiency. Similarly, individual interpretive/appraisal efforts are echoed by family-level redefinitions of the situation. Table 1 sketches further suggestive examples.

It is important to note that these need not be alternative strategies: individuals or families may simultaneously be trying to reduce stress through change in any of the four elements.

At the same time, stress is presumably an unpleasant, anxiety-arousing, and tension-producing experience; and efforts at problem-resolution are probably ordinarily preceded by or accompanied by efforts to avoid being overwhelmed by negative effect. Haan (1979)

TABLE 1: A TAXONOMY OF COPING EFFORTS BY FOCUS OF ACTION

KINDS OF COPING EFFORTS	EXAMPLES	
	INDIVIDUAL	FAMILY

I. PROBLEM RESOLUTION EFFORTS
A. Direct Action
  1) On Environment/Situation
     (reduce demands or increase opportunities)
	– add/subtract roles
	– negotiate role demands
		– negotiate role demands with other institutions

2) On Self or Family Group (increase capacities, resources or reduce goals, preferences)	– increase efficiency – seek education, advice – postpone goals – obtain support, aid of others	– increase self-reliance – negotiate new consensus re goals, role expectations – increase coordination, cohesiveness, integration

B. Interpretive/Appraisal
   1) Of Environment/Situation
     (change view of demands on)
	– redefine role expectations
	– use temporal or peer comparisons
	– selective ignoring
		– negotiate new "definition of the situation"

2) Of Self or Family Group (change view of capacities or goals)	– alter view of capacities – alter beliefs about preferences, needs	– develop new "family definitions"
II. EMOTION MANAGEMENT EFFORTS		
1) Expression/Release	– "let off steam" – escape	
2) Suppression/Restraint	– acknowledge but control	
3) Diversion/Substitution/Displacement	– seek pleasurable experiences	– joint participation in cohesive building activities – shared rituals

has pointed out that there is a rather small and fairly exhaustive set of possibilities; these are listed on Table 1. Again, it seems important to avoid the assumption in some research that one either manages emotions or resolves problems; the temporal ordering and interrelationships among these approaches remains an important question for empirical analysis.

While the particular examples in Table 1 are not very developed here, it is hoped that the utility of the direct action/interpretive appraisal/emotion management triad and the four manipulative elements of stress to organize a wide range of individual and family level coping efforts is apparent.

RECOMMENDATIONS FOR THE FUTURE

Given the recency of sustained work in this area, it seems wise to recall Reiss and Oliveri's (1980) warning about premature conclusions and "rushing to judgement" on slender evidence. Rather than attempting to construct generalizations on still meager evidence, it seems appropriate to outline some general recommendations for future work which might enhance its yield.

Research Design

Many of the studies reviewed have small samples assessed at a single time point, and use measures and concepts unique to that study. Small scale exploratory studies may, as Hill (1981) argues, "generate more discoveries per hour expended than large scale quantitative verification or experimentally designed studies in laboratories"; but if there is no comparability among such studies, the generalizability of individual discoveries remains uncertain. Larger samples with multiple assessment points and repeated measures of outcome variables as well as problem severity and coping efforts would also improve the quality of this research by making it possible to explore the complex pathways of plausible effects. Lazarus is intensively studying a subsample of a larger population, an innovative approach which can yield a great deal of background information as well as furnishing a comparative pool for normative levels of many variables. Similarly, the cooperative ventures of McCubbin and his colleagues, and the use of Pearlin's coping measures by other researchers, are two ways to increase the possibility of generalization.

Whether borrowed or created *de novo,* coping measures ideally should assess usage as well as perceived helpfulness, and permit some gradation in such reports rather than binary (yes/no) choices. The stability over time, and the interrelationships among levels of coping variables, and among variables at a single level, are empirical questions that need to be examined, and one's measures and designs should permit such analysis.

Analysis and Discussion

For many of the studies reviewed, it was difficult to determine exactly how scores were assigned, the basic distributions of variables, or any sense of summary univariate and bivariate statistics. Multivariate assessments of coping as well as situational variables as predictors of outcomes were rare, even when the reported data collection efforts suggested that information was available for more adequate analyses. When multiple regression methods were used, researchers seldom examined non-linear or non-additive forms of the relations.

Future studies would be more useful if they would consistently report basic statistics as well as selected interrelationships, test multivariate models whenever appropriate, and examine the data for indications of non-additivity and non-linearity.

Conceptualization

Much of the confusion in the coping literature reflects not so much problems of samples or techniques as a lack of specific theoretical models. For example, the conflicting emotion-focused versus problem-focused coping correlations reported here suggest a need for more specificity in our questions. Under what conditions, such as high anxiety, would we expect both forms of coping to occur, or to occur in sequence; under what other conditions are they likely to be alternatives? Should generalized coping strategies have a greater impact on specific coping efforts when the situation is ambiguous rather than clear? Theories of coping thus far are not particularly helpful in illuminating such questions. Thus, greater conceptual and theoretical development are essential future tasks.

The Interface Between Levels of Coping Variables

Several of the key questions initially raised about coping—the association and possible conflict among the individual coping styles and efforts of individual family members, and the process by which individual coping strategies may shape family-level measures—although not addressed here, remain important unanswered questions for future research.

At the same time, further study of correlates of particular patterns, linkages between resources, styles and efforts, and the use of multiple criteria of effectiveness are needed to strengthen our confidence in the generalizations beginning to emerge.

In some ways, current knowledge resembles the many blind men, each basing his description of an elephant on the part within his grasp. Interpreting the different levels of coping, and relating them to individual and family functioning, remains an immense challenge for the future.

REFERENCES

Alonzo, A. Acute illness behavior: A conceptual exploration and specification. *Social Science and Medicine*, 1980, *14A*, 515-526. (a)

Alonzo, A. The mobile coronary care unit and the decision to seek medical care during acute episodes of coronary artery disease. *Medical Care*, 1980, *18*(3), 297-318. (b)

Andrews, G., Tennant, C., Hewson, D., & Vaillant, G. Life event stress, social support, coping style and risk of psychological impairment. *Journal of Nervous and Mental Disease*, 1978, *166*(5), 307-316.

Anderson, C. R. Locus of control, coping behaviors and performance in a stress setting: A longitudinal study. *Journal of Applied Psychology*, 1977, *62*(4), 446-451.

Antonovsky, A. *Health, stress, and coping*. San Francisco: Jossey-Bass, 1979.

Averill, J. R. Personal control over aversive stimuli and its relationship to stress. *Psychological Bulletin*, 1973, *80*(4), 386-403.

Barrios, B. A., & Shigitomi, C. C. Coping-skills training for the management of anxiety: A critical review. *Behavior Therapy*, 1979, *10*(4), 491-522.

Berman, W. H., & Turk, D. C. Adaptation to divorce: Problems and coping strategies. *Journal of Marriage and the Family*, 1981, *43*(1), 179-189.

Boss, P. G. The relationship of psychological father presence, wife's personal qualities and wife/family dysfunction in families of missing fathers. *Journal of Marriage and the Family*, 1980, *42*(3), 541-550.

Boss, P. G., McCubbin, H. I., & Lester, G. The corporate executive wife's coping patterns in response to routine husband-father absence. *Family Process*, 1979, *18*, 79-86.

Buehler, C. A., & Hogan, M. J. Managerial behavior and stress in families headed by divorced women: A proposed framework. *Family Relations*, 1980, *29*, 525-532.

Burke, R. J., & Wier, T. Patterns in husbands' and wives' coping behaviors. *Psychological Reports*, 1979, *44*(3, Pt. 1), 951-956.

Caplan, G. Mastery of stress: Psychosocial aspects. *American Journal of Psychiatry*, 1981, *138*(4), 413-420.

Coelho, G. V., Hamburg, D. A., & Adams, J. E. (Eds.), *Coping and adaptation*. New York: Basic Books, 1974.

Cohen, J., & Lazarus, R. Active coping processes, coping dispositions, and recovery from surgery. *Psychosomatic Medicine*, 1973, *35*, 375-389.

Colleta, N. D., & Gregg, C. H. Adolescent mothers' vulnerability to stress. *Journal of Nervous and Mental Disease*, 1981, *169*(1), 50-54.

Cook, J. *Adjustment of the death of a child: Gender differences in responses and outcomes in the first years.* Unpublished doctoral dissertation, Department of Sociology, The Ohio State University, 1982.

Diaz-Guerrero, R. The development of coping style. *Human Development*, 1979, *22*, 320-331.

Dill, D., Feld, E., Merten, J., Beukeme, S., & Belle, D. The impact of the environment on the coping efforts of low-income mothers. *Family Relations*, 1980, *29*, 503-510.

Edwards, D., & Kelly, J. G. Coping and adaptation: A longitudinal study. *American Journal of Community Psychology*, 1980, *8*(2), 203-215.

Ekehammar, B. Interactionism in personality from a historical perspective. *Psychological Bulletin*, 1974, *81*(12), 1026-1048.

Felton, B. J., Brown, P., Lehman, S., & Liberatos, P. The coping functions of sex-role attitudes during marital disruption. *Journal of Health and Social Behavior*, 1980, *21*, 240-248.

Folkman, S., & Lazarus, R. S. An analysis of coping in a middle-aged community sample. *Journal of Health and Social Behavior*, 1980, *21*(3), 219-239.

Friedrich, W. N. Predictors of the coping behavior of mothers of handicapped children. *Journal of Consulting and Clinical Psychology*, 1979, *47*(6), 1140-1141.

Frydman, M. I. Social support, life events and psychiatric symptoms: A study of direct, conditional and interaction effects. *Social Psychiatry*, 1981, *16*, 69-78.

Gal, R., & Lazarus, R. S. The role of activity in anticipating and confronting stressful situations. *Journal of Human Stress*, 1975, *1*(4), 4-20.

George, L. K. *Role transitions in later life.* Belmont, CA: Wadsworth Publishing Company, 1980.

Haan, N. *Coping and defending: Processes of self-environment organization.* New York: Academic Press, 1977.

Hansen, D. S., & Johnson, V. A. Rethinking family stress theory: Definitional aspects. In W. Burr, R. Hill, F. Nye, & I. Reiss (Eds.), *Contemporary theories about the family* (Vol. 1). New York: The Free Press, 1979.

Harrison, A., & Minor, J. H. Interrole conflict, coping strategies, and satisfaction among black working wives. *Journal of Marriage and the Family*, 1978, *40*(4), 799-805.

Heim, E., Moser, A., & Adler, R. Defense mechanisms and coping behavior in terminal illness: An overview. *Psychotherapy and Psychosomatics*, 1978, *30*(1), 1-17.

Hill, R. *Families under stress.* New York: Harper & Row, 1949.

Hill, R. Whither family research in the 1980's: Continuities, emergents, constraints, and new horizons. *Journal of Marriage and the Family*, 1981, *43*(2), 255-258.

Holmes, T. H., & Rahe, R. H. The social readjustment rating scale. *Journal of Psychosomatic Research*, 1967, *11*, 213-218.

Horowitz, M. *The coping inventory.* Informal presentation at meeting on Measurement Issues in Coping Research, University of California at San Francisco, March 1978.

House, J. S. *Work, stress, and social support.* Reading, MA: Addison-Wesley, 1981.

House, J. S., & Wells, J. A. Occupational stress, social support and health. In A. McLean, G. Black, & M. Colligan (Eds.), *Reducing occupational stress: Proceedings of a conference*, New York Hospital-Cornell Medical Center, 1977.

Janis, I. L., & Mann, L. Emergency decision-making: A theoretical analysis of responses to disaster warning. *Journal of Human Stress*, 1971, *3*(2), 35-48.

Jenkins, C. D. Psychosocial modifiers of response to stress. *Journal of Human Stress*, 1977, *5*(4), 3-15.

Klein, D. M., & Hill, R. Determinants of family problem-solving effectiveness. In W. R. Burr, R. Hill, F. Nye, & I. Reiss (Eds.), *Contemporary theories about the family* (Vol. 1). New York: The Free Press, 1979.

Kobasa, S. C. Stressful life events, personality and health: An inquiry into hardiness. *Journal of Personality and Social Psychology*, 1979, *37*, 1-11.
Kohn, M., & Schooler, C. The reciprocal effects of the substantive complexity of work and intellectual flexibility: A longitudinal assessment. *American Journal of Sociology*, 1978, *84*, 24-52.
LaRocco, J. M., House, J. S., & French, J. R. P., Jr. Social support, occupational stress, and health. *Journal of Health and Social Behavior*, 1980, *21*(3), 202-218.
Lazarus, R. *The ways of coping questionnaire*. Informal presentation at meeting on Measurement Issues in Coping Research, March, 1978.
Lefcourt, H. M. *Locus of control: Current trends in theory and research*. New York: John Wiley & Sons, 1976.
Lieberman, M. A., & Borman, L. I. *Self-help groups for coping with crises*. San Francisco: Jossey-Bass, 1979.
Lieberman, M. A., & Jourash, H. Effects of change groups on the elderly. In M. A. Lieberman & L. I. Borman (Eds.), *Self-help groups for coping and crisis*. San Francisco: Jossey-Bass, 1979.
Linden, W., & Feuerstein, M. Essential hypertension and social coping behavior. *Journal of Human Stress*, 1981, *7*(1), 28-34.
Looney, J. G., Harding, R. K., Blotcky, M. J., & Barnhart, F. D. Psychiatrists' transition from training to career: Stress and mastery. *American Journal of Psychiatry*, 1980, *137*(1), 32-36.
Maynard, P., Maynard, N., McCubbin, H. I., & Shao, D. Family life and the police profession: Coping patterns wives employ in managing job stress and the family environment. *Family Relations*, 1980, *29*, 495-502.
McCubbin, H. I. Integrating coping behavior in family stress theory. *Journal of Marriage and the Family*, 1979, *41*(2), 237-244.
McCubbin, H. I., Dahl, B. G., Lester, G. D., Benson, D., & Robertson, M. Coping repertoires of families adapting to prolonged war-induced separation. *Journal of Marriage and the Family*, 1976, *38*, 461-471.
McCubbin, H. I., Joy, C. B., Cauble, A. E., Comeau, J. K., Patterson, J. M., & Needle, R. H. Family stress and coping: A decade review. *Journal of Marriage and the Family*, 1980, *42*(4), 855-871.
Menaghan, E. G. *Marital coping strategies: Variations in effectiveness*. Paper presented at National Council on Family Relations Annual Meeting, Milwaukee, Wisconsin, October 1981.
Menaghan, E. Assessing the impact of family transitions on marital experience: Problems and prospects. In H. I. McCubbin, A. E. Cauble, & J. M. Patterson (Eds.), *Family stress, coping and social support*. Springfield, IL: Charles C. Thomas, 1982. (a)
Menaghan, E. *Marital stress and family transitions: A panel analysis*. Unpublished paper, The Ohio State University, 1982. (b)
Miller, J., Schooler, C., Kohn, M. L., & Miller, K. A. Women and work: The psychological effects of occupational conditions. *American Journal of Sociology*, 1979, *85*, 66-94.
Moos, R. *Coping with physical illness*. New York: Plenum Press, 1977.
Morris, L. W., & Engle, W. B. Assessing various coping strategies and their effects on test performance and anxiety. *Journal of Clinical Psychology*, 1981, *37*(1), 165-171.
Neugarten, B. N. Time, age and the life cycle. *American Journal of Psychiatry*, 1979, *136*, 887-894.
Newman, B. M. Coping and adaptation in adolescence. *Human Development*, 1979, *22*(4), 255-262.
Newman, J. E., & Beehr, T. A. Personal and organizational strategies for handling job stress: A review of research and opinion. *Personnel Psychology*, 1979, *32*(1), 1-43.
Olson, D. H., Sprenkle, D. H., & Russell, C. S. Circumplex model of marital and family types, and clinical applications. *Family Process*, 1979, *18*, 3-28.
Pearlin, L. I., & Schooler, C. The structure of coping. *Journal of Health and Social Behavior*, 1978, *19*, 2-21.

Pearlin, L. I., Lieberman, M. S., Menaghan, E. G., & Mullan, J. T. The stress process. *Journal of Health and Social Behavior*, 1981, *22*, 337-356.

Rabkin, J. G., & Streuning, E. L. Life events, stress, and illness. *Science*, 1976, *194*, 1013-1020.

Reiss, D., & Oliveri, M. E. Family paradigm and family coping: A proposal for linking the family's intrinsic adaptive capacities to its responses to stress. *Family Relations*, 1980, *29*, 431-444.

Rich, A. R., & Schroeder, H. E. Research issues in assertiveness training. *Psychological Bulletin*, 1976, *83*, 1081-1096.

Rosenstiel, A. K., & Roth, S. Relationship between cognitive activity and adjustment in four spinal-cord injured individuals: A longitudinal investigation. *Journal of Human Stress*, 1981, *7*(1), 35-43.

Shalit, B. Structural ambiguity and limits to coping. *Journal of Human Stress*, 1977, *3*(4), 32-45.

Shanan, J., De-Nour, A. K., & Garty, I. Effects of prolonged stress on coping style in terminal renal failure patients. *Journal of Human Stress*, 1976, *2*(4), 19-27.

Skinner, D. A. Dual-career family stress and coping: A literature review. *Family Relations*, 1980, *29*, 473-482.

Stern, M. J., & Pascale, L. Psychosocial adaptation to post-myocardial infarction: The spouse's dilemma. *Journal of Psychosomatic Research*, 1979, *23*(1), 83-87.

Stewart, A. J. A longitudinal study of coping styles in self-defining and socially defined women. *Journal of Consulting and Clinical Psychology*, 1978, *46*(5), 1079-1084.

Suls, J., & Mullen, B. Life events, perceived control and illness: The role of uncertainty. *Journal of Human Stress*, 1981, *17*(2), 30-34.

Vaillant, G. E. Natural history of male psychological health: Vol. 5. The relation of choice of ego mechanisms of defense to adult adjustment. *Archives of General Psychiatry*, 1976, *33*, 535-545.

Videka, L. M. Psychosocial adaptation in a medical self-help group. In M. A. Lieberman & L. I. Borman (Eds.), *Self-help groups for coping with crises*. San Francisco: Jossey-Bass, 1979.

Wampler, K. S., & Sprenkle, D. H. The Minnesota couple communication program: A follow-up study. *Journal of Marriage and the Family*, 1980, *42*(3), 577-584.

Warheit, G. J. Life events, coping, stress, and depressive symptomatology. *American Journal of Psychiatry*, 1979, *136*, 502-507.

Worden, J. W., & Sobel, H. J. Ego strength and psychosocial adaptation to cancer. *Psychosomatic Medicine*, 1978, *40*(8), 585-592.

Zeitlin, S. Assessing coping behavior. *American Journal of Orthopsychiatry*, 1980, *50*(1), 139-144.

Chapter 6

Social Support and Family Stress

Marc Pilisuk
Susan Hillier Parks

INTRODUCTION

One of the major breakthroughs in contemporary understanding of the family came through the work of the family system theorists (Haley, 1968; Minuchin & Montalvo, 1967; Tharp, 1963). These pioneers in the appreciation of family dynamics introduced a departure from the view that psychotherapy was essentially an operation performed upon the minds of single individuals. Rather, individuals were enacting, in their thoughts, feelings, and behavior, the dynamic balancing roles permissible within a system of familial exchanges. Once such a system of exchanges had been applied to the pathology-inducing family it became useful to apply the system concept to the normal family, a view which enabled us to give more recognition to the importance of familial role expectations in the understanding of individual functioning. Now we are facing the need for a still more radical departure. The actual functional family or living unit in the 1980s exhibits more diverse forms, has less stability, and is more greatly affected by its own connections, or lack thereof, with community supports than in previous generations. If it made limited sense to treat an individual and then send that individual back to a pathology-inducing family, it makes limited sense to treat the family and send it back to a dysfunctional community. It is worthwhile, therefore, to ask what have we actually spawned in contem-

---

Marc Pilisuk is Professor and Susan Hillier Parks is Post-graduate Research Associate, Department of Applied Behavioral Sciences, University of California, Davis, California.

Work on this project was sponsored by Grant #3617 from the Experiment Station, University of California, Davis. The authors express appreciation to Guy Whitlow and Paula Heady for assistance in preparing the manuscript.

© 1983 by The Haworth Press, Inc. All rights reserved.

porary varieties of family; and what forms of nurturance are needed so that families or family-type groupings can provide environments in which a better quality of life may be found.

In this chapter we wish to review, briefly, some of the evidence relating supporting ties of the type associated with family life to the maintenance of physical and emotional well-being. We will then examine changes in the nuclear and the extended family, not as a general review but as a source of information for one particular question, i.e., who lacks the supportive familial ties that may contribute to health maintenance and what alternative sources have been found?

SOURCES OF SOCIAL SUPPORT

We have defined social support as a set of exchanges which provide the individual with material and physical assistance, social contact and emotional sharing, as well as the sense that one is the continuing object of concern by others (Pilisuk & Parks, 1981). Where people choose to go for these necessary exchanges depends upon their personal circumstances and individual characteristics, and varies with culture and availability of resources. The traditional expectation of the family as the central source of social support has given way to examinations of other sources of supportive exchange (Cantor, 1979; Gartner & Reissman, 1977; Litwak & Szelenyi, 1969; Pilisuk, in press; Pilisuk & Parks, 1980). The sources include friends and work associates, neighbors, community agencies and general quality of the community, in addition to extended and immediate kin.

THE STRESS-ILLNESS CYCLE

The contemporary history of medicine shows a gradual decline in the incidence of lethal, infectious illness, and a concomitant increase in the occurrence of stress-related illness. The range of stress-linked maladies include cancer, heart ailments, depression, accidents, suicide, homicide, cirrhosis of the liver, hypertension, and stomach ulcer. But even disorders with a likely genetic factor in their origins, such as schizophrenia, and disorders with known bacterial causation, such as tuberculosis, are known to occur with increased likelihood under highly stressful conditions. This fact prompted Lazarus (1975) to suggest that we look more closely at the stress factor in every disease state rather than at the distinction between stress-induced and infection-induced illness.

For every study indicating the effects of stress on health breakdown, there is another indicating that individuals who are part of a socially supportive network of continuing interpersonal ties achieve a measure of protection or immunity from these same disorders. The evidence for this latter conclusion has been painstakingly assembled in a number of reviews of the epidemiological and experimental literature (Cassel, 1976; Cassel & Tyroler, 1961; Cobb, 1976; Pilisuk & Froland, 1978). While social support is an amorphous and multifaceted concept, it appears, nonetheless, to be the construct best able to bring order to a variety of studies showing the buffering effect against illness provided by marriage, church or organizational affiliation, community cohesiveness, or the presence of a confidant.

Conversely, the effects of divorce, bereavement, separation, social dislocation, and marginality have been associated with the widest range of health breakdowns (Berkman & Syme, 1979; Bunch, 1972; Nuckolls, Cassel, & Kaplan, 1972; Orford, 1975). A currently circulating hypothesis holds that long-term exposure to stressful conditions reduces the resistance of the host individual to breakdown in whichever biological or psychological system the person is most susceptible. However, involvement in a continuing supportive network appears to serve as a buffer increasing the level of immunological protection (Pilisuk, in press).

DEFICIENCIES IN SUPPORT FROM KIN

Kinship, in former times through the nuclear family, the extended family, or clan bonds, provided the main source in which supportive functions were assumed to occur. Such ties have remained surprisingly durable. Massive migrations from other continents to North America and from the rural areas to the cities were disruptive to some of these bonds. But the cord of family ties has shown great elasticity. More children still live in families with two parents than any other arrangement (Visher & Visher, 1979). Most adults live in communities in which they maintain one or more contacts with a living parent or other close relative (Sussman, 1965; Troll, 1971). And most elderly people are able to name at least one living relative who lives close by and would care for them (Kulys & Tobin, 1980). The extended family has retained its functional form in urban as well as in rural America (Litwak, 1960a, Litwak, 1960b; Litwak & Szelenyi, 1969; Skolnik, 1973; Sussman & Burchinal, 1962). A particular form of three-generation family involving both fictive and real kin has continued to thrive in the black community (Stack, 1974). In the Chicano community, extended family ties have remained particularly strong (Sena-Rivera, 1979). The extended family in the United States obviously survives. But how adequate are its supportive functions, given the complexity and stress of modern lifestyles?

The earlier pattern of geographic mobility resulting from a search for a more fruitful or less oppressive environment often had one familial envoy explore the new setting and then send for others of the immediate and the extended family. Professional mobility, however, introduces the concept of marketability in which one leaves, at any time, to pursue the offer promising the best career advancement. Multiple career lines within the extended family, and even within the nuclear family, add a major strain toward separation and a reduction in the supportive exchanges provided by kin.

SUPPORT NEEDS OF CHILDREN

One perspective on the adequacy of familial support may be gleaned from an examination of the supportive needs of children. While most children still reside in a nuclear family household with two parents, a large and perhaps growing number, estimated at 17% of all children under 18 years of age, live with a single parent and an added 13% live in reconstituted families (Colvin, Greenwood, & Hansen, 1981; Visher & Visher, 1979). The changing role of women, often abetted by economic necessity, has brought larger numbers of women into the work force. Forty-three percent of married mothers with children under age six now work outside of the home and more than two million children between seven and thirteen return from school to households with no adult present (Langway, Lord, Reese, Ellis, Maitland, Gelman, & Whitman, 1980). While studies show that children of working mothers can fare quite well (Hoffman, 1974), adequate resources for the child's care must be available (Lambert, Rothschild, Allard, & Green, 1972). Problems do appear, however, with inadequate adult support. In poorer environments the development of the female adolescent, for example, tends to be adversely affected by the mothers' employment (Burke & Weir, 1978). Such poverty is not uncommon among working mothers, and 51% of the women in single-parent families live below the poverty line (Verzaro & Hennon, 1980). Additionally, of seven million children with parents working outside the home, public licensed day care facilities are available for only 1.6 million. Faced with inadequate public child care, the extended family is often called upon to give more to the developing child at the very time when fewer of its adult female members are available in either a geographic, an economic, or a psychological sense.

The social supports brought about through association with the family unit as a whole appear to be critical to the family system well-being. An available parent or sibling in town at the time of childbirth can provide the trusted relief necessary to avoid the isolation and post partum depression of the mother, which is frequently observed during the infant's first three months. When the infant presents unusual difficulties in handling, it is the social support received by the mother that appears critical to development of the crucial bonding relationship between mother and infant (Crockenberg, 1980). In another study, socioeconomic stress in the absence of adequate material support accounted for more than one-third of the variance in predictions of child abuse and maltreatment (Garbarino, 1976). Contact with grandparents is apparently a factor in the child's development of pro-social behavior (Bryant, 1981). Conversely, school attendance is adversely affected by lack of supportive ties in the home (Boardman, 1975).

In examining each of those functions, we find that the issue is not so much whether the nuclear or extended family continues to survive. Rather the issue emerges as one in which the surviving forms of family life show a wide range in their ability to provide the needed supports during the prenatal or early childhood periods. It is the *range* of difference in the availability of supportiveness provided by kinship ties which gives reason for concern.

The deficit side of nurturance within families has attracted the attention of some researchers in an effort to examine just what forms of support are or are not being provided by family ties. Bronfenbrenner (1974) noted the high degree of estrangement prevalent between children and adults. The lives of couples, as well as single parents, are for many adults no longer able to accommodate the tasks of parenting. For example, in one study, paternal interaction with 1-year old infants occurred only 2.7 times per day with an average duration of 37 seconds (Bronfenbrenner, 1974). In developing a theory of shared function, Hawkes (1978) reported on the large nebulous area of socialization activities left to be divided between the family and the formal institutions in which the child participates.

These and other examinations of the supportive needs of dependent children and their frequently stressed parents show an area in which many kinship structures, despite their persistence, lack the supportive resources for effective socialization (Broeck, 1974; Bronfenbrenner, 1977; Cochran & Brassard, 1979). Similar gaps in nurturant functions appear in an examination of the needs of the elderly.

SUPPORT NEEDS OF THE ELDERLY

Whether because supportive public services have been insufficient or because of cultural traditions, the evidence continues to suggest that family ties are extremely important in the lives of the elderly. Family help, particularly at times of acute illness, and important exchanges of services provide evidence that bonds of kinship ties are not easy to erase (Cantor, 1979; Rosenmayr & Kockeis, 1970; Shanas, 1979; Troll et al., 1979). Spouses are the most frequently mentioned source of assistance with household tasks for elderly persons who are ill or homebound (Shanas, 1979). Adult children, living either with their parents or outside the home, provide the next greatest amount of such assistance and are the largest category of assistance for elderly women.

These ties to kin become particularly important in times of crisis. When elderly adults were asked to designate who would be responsible for them in a crisis, 86% named a close relative (Kulys & Tobin, 1980). This becomes significant when coupled with the information that approximately 10% of elderly are without a geographically or emotionally proximate relative (Shanas, 1979). Of further significance, in one study a substantial minority of elderly were unsure whether the individual they named as being responsible in times of crisis would actually come through. In some cases, they named someone who was annoyed by the choice or who expressed disinterest in the role (Kulys & Tobin, 1980). Since network size typically declines with age (Kahn & Antonucci, 1980; Stueve & Fischer, 1978), the problem of support for the elderly partner who is a caretaker of an ill spouse is a formidable one (Fengler & Goodrich, 1979). A large number of the elderly, particularly men, succumb within months of the death of their spouse (Parkes, 1972). That finding is even more striking when considered in relation to studies that indicate the value of a single confidant or supportive tie in mitigating the stressful effects of bereavement (Lowenthal, 1968).

SUPPORT NEEDS OF THE FAMILY

Family size and social roles are both factors selectively limiting the support available for family members all along the age continuum. The number of elderly has risen rapidly, and so also has the number of very old and surviving frail elderly. Adults who are themselves retired and growing older have increasingly found that they have a responsibility for care of an elderly parent. Persons who were of childbearing age during the Great Depression tended to limit the size of their families, and the population had a higher incidence of never-married persons (Treas, 1977). Therefore, there are presently fewer kin available in the pool of caretakers. From the pool, more of the offspring are past middle age and more of the women are committed to careers and work outside the home. Too large a number of frail elderly live in unsatisfactory institutional settings or alone in inexpensive and isolated single room occupancy hotels.

Among the elderly, as among children, there is substantial subset of individuals with needs for supportive assistance from families that are not being met either by kinship networks, by friendship networks, or by association with formal service organizations. In developed countries there has been a gradual transition to formal bureaucratic institutions of functions once thought to be unique to the family. Longer life, higher education, and better standards of living contribute to the definition of needs so that broader needs for support have become necessities (Rosenmayr, 1977). The number of social services provided is legion, but their adequacy in meeting the economic, social and health needs of individuals is questionable. The conclusion that some people are falling through the cracks in their supportive systems may be assumed by the extremely large use of psychoactive drugs by older adults (Brecher, 1972; Green, 1978), and by the fact that one-fourth of all suicides in the U. S. are by persons aged 65 or older (Butler, 1975). These indicators for the elderly are matched by conditions in the young family. The high incidence of child abuse and delinquency provide striking examples.

SUPPORT NEEDS UNDER CONDITIONS OF HIGH STRESS

The very old and the very young are perhaps the most obvious casualties of an inadequate network of supportive affiliation. However, there are other life transition times and other disruptive life circumstances which tax the resources of the typical kin network. Marital separation is one example, and a common one. Two percent of all U.S. marriages terminate each year, and the actual number of divorces in a given year has reached a figure of half the number of marriages (Bloom, Asher & White, 1978). The human costs are noted by the finding that marital separations have been associated with higher rates of alcoholism, traffic accidents, admission to psychiatric facilities, homicides and disease mortality generally (Bloom et al., 1978). The adverse effects upon supportive care for children have been noted, as have the reciprocal effects that problem children may have upon their divorced parents (Hetherington, Cox, & Cox, 1977).

Stresses upon the nuclear family which culminate in marital disruption for some, exist at a somewhat lower threshold within a larger number of nuclear family households and individuals. Many of the contributing tensions are the product of such persistent environmental stressors as job loss, unemployment, underemployment, discrimination, stressful working conditions, natural disaster, and excessive social conflict.

The concept of *endemic stress* has been coined by Fried (in press) to describe the pervasive social strains affecting larger numbers of persons through interactive mechanisms. The amount of social support available to most individuals may be adequate to help individuals through the range of short-term hassles and pressures. Yet these same sources may prove inadequate to deal with needs that require intensive support over an extended time period. The management of illness provides an example of the limits of social support. Sickness of short duration is typically met by a mobilization of the immediate family. Chronic illness, however, frequently requires a greater economic and psychological sacrifice than many kin are ready to provide (Moos, 1977).

Just as there are limits to the resources of familial support, so also is there a division in the chosen size of the available network of close family ties. A substantial number of individuals, unmarried by choice, have accommodated with fair success to their life demands. Such people, however, do best if they are young, educated, well-employed, attractive, and healthy. Their adjustment depends upon their market value and as a group they are at high risk following stressful life events because of their low level of familial support.

AN HYPOTHESIS ON THE NEED FOR BOTH STRONG AND WEAK TIES

It is our thesis first that most people have maintained ties with their kin but that these ties, on the whole, are less frequent and less intimate than in generations past. Second, the need for supportive ties has remained and voluntary supportive relationships have become important to many people largely as an aid to problems caused by mobility, life transition, and personal autonomous development. By and large these ties, despite some important exceptions, prove transitory.

The need for community is inconsistent with both the myths and the realities of autonomous, competitive individual achievement fostered by the socioeconomic order. Our media cultivate the image, for women as well as for men, of the lone hero. The automated and specialized workplace has been exempted by management and by labor unions as a place which esteems the value of each contributing cooperator to a mutually valued task. Hence, the workplace, like the school environment, becomes a source for only the more transient forms of support. For most men the absence of a companion outside of one's spouse has become a reality. Lacking a network of self-validating relationships, sex, or more likely the pursuit of sex, has become a filler against anomic loneliness. This appears more the prototype of all interactions—its supportive value lies in the encounter, not in the enduring relationship. Feelings of the moment become more a cherished value because the continued feelings of relatedness, while present, are less deep and less secure.

Competitive industrial development has changed roles within the family. When men held dominant and exclusive roles in the non-house workforce, the assigned but often unappreciated role left to women was that of builder of supportive familial networks. Post-college and professional mobility introduced the era of the portable nuclear family, with the woman's role becoming one of coping with moves made for the good of the company of the husband's career. The industrial system has now made openings for many women to leave the role of family caregiver and to join men in the role of the lone worker, pursuing an often ephemeral success. This social perspective brings us back to our original question: who among us in this society lacks the necessary supportive familial ties that may contribute to health maintenance?

It seems quite obvious that those who are the recipients of nurturant care provided primarily by full-time homemakers are more likely to be in need. Elderly parents or dependent children (or husbands) are prime candidates. The women who now work outside of the home and also try to maintain the former role of supportive caretaker are another group for whom the available supportive resources are often too skimpy.

SUPPORTIVE FUNCTIONS OF STRONG AND WEAK TIES

Caplan (1974) and Frank (1979) are among the psychiatrists and social critics who have taken a dim view of *gemeinschaft* protection available in modern industrial society. The small dense network with frequent interaction is viewed as the main social form capable of protecting individuals from the confusing feedback and the disorder of modern life. The argument has been made by some social theorists that the complexity against which Caplan would have us protected is the very vitality of urban life, the very connection of the individual to the mainstreams of civilization (Sennet, 1970a). In fact, the examples of isolated middle class suburban families are viewed from this theory as being oppressive and restrictive to their members (Sennet, 1970b). But Caplan's emphasis upon primary groups effectively makes a point when he examines the functions they provide for the individual. Such functions include consistent communication, clear expectations, supportive assistance with tasks, evaluation of day-to-day behavior and rewards for daily behavior (Caplan, 1974). He might also have added continuity of relationships over time, and assistance in coping with the threats to self-esteem incurred by the larger environment.

Several studies pointing to the presence of familial ties as buffers against health breakdown suggest that a small, densely interconnected network of intimate ties remains critical to individual well-being (Cassel & Tyroler, 1961; Lasch, 1978; Phillips, 1975; Stout, Morrow, Brand, & Wolf, 1964). The idea that such ties, however important, may be insufficient for certain types of psychosocial transition has been highlighted by Granovetter (1973). Job loss is an example of the circumstances for which the dense, kinship dominated network can typically provide consolation but not reassurance or assistance in the location of a new job. There are just too few jobs available on family farms or other family businesses. To branch out, to get a track on more opportunities requires a more disparate network. Bereavement provides still another example. The family can be consoling. Where its assistance is hampered by psychological or physical distance, a small supportive mutual help group can be of great value. But for eventual movement into new areas of commitment, whether it be finding new colleagues or a new spouse, the larger network of weaker ties may also be critical (Parkes, 1972).

Hirsch's (1980) finding that *low* density of family-friendship networks is related to *more* favorable coping surely supports the weak ties viewpoint. The subjects in his study were middle-aged women who were either re-entry students or widows. Of five categories of supportive exchanges studied, cognitive guidance (i.e., advice, explanation and information) emerged as the most critical form of support. It appears that coping with the stress of the transition typically requires a set of associations that go beyond a small close circle of familial supports. Coser (1975) has made a similar point in his discussion of the values of role complexity. While initial solace may have been offered by a few close ties, the women in the Hirsch study apparently needed something else to assist their coping with a transition in role. Our conclusion must be that social support is more than a single quality and may require a variety of sources, including but not restricted to the family, to meet the diversity of individual needs.

SOCIAL SUPPORT: THE EXTRA-FAMILIAL CONTEXT

The importance of this support has been observed in health consequences to persons lacking adequate support. The continuity and vitality of the nuclear and the immediate extended family remains the single most important social factor in continuity of supportive relationships. But the supportive needs of family members often exceed the capacities of small kin groups. This is, in part, a reflection of societal pressures, internalized within the individual, and/or individual success in the broader society. The family is affected in two ways. Not only are its members in need of more diverse forms of support, but its members are more often preoccupied with pursuits which compete with the support they can offer to other members of their immediate family. In consequence, the family is pressed. It is less certain as a source of satisfaction and more frequently disrupted. With familial support less sufficient, it becomes necessary to view the diverse forms of nonfamilial support that have arisen not only as supports to the individual but as needed supports to relieve the strains and demands placed upon the family.

Modern industrial societies have given rise to a traditional set of human service institutions supplanting the family in a number of important functions relevant to the health, education, and welfare of family members and of individuals bereft of their families. Human services organizations in the U. S. have rarely enjoyed a level of fiscal support equal to the task. However, as both resources and functions have expanded, so apparently has the need. This fact has given rise to current arguments regarding the proper role for bureaucratized human services.

A concern has increased over the past decade with the identification of natural helping systems within the community. The search has led to a reexamination of the strength of familial ties. It has led also to the uncovering of non-kin support networks.

In almost all subpopulations where supportive needs have surpassed familial resources we have witnessed the phenomenon of voluntary groups explicitly created to provide support for their members. Among the forms most widely studied are the self-help or mutual help groups. These groups of individuals may be linked by a common characteristic, such as single parenthood, a recent mastectomy, birth of a first child, or an alcoholic family member. Each group provides a measure of emotional sharing and social support. Several major studies of such groups have taken place (Gartner & Reissman, 1977; Katz & Bender, 1976), and a scheme for classifying voluntary support groups has been developed (Pilisuk & Parks, 1980).

One form of mutual help grouping is the intentional extended family, a voluntary linkage typically spanning generations of several nuclear families. It is designed to provide many of the supportive needs which the kin-based extended family has served (Kuster-Ginsburg, 1970; Newcomber, 1972; Pringle, 1974).

Informal supportive relationships have also been found in the presence of natural neighborhood helpers (Collins & Pancoast, 1976). These individuals play an important role in the informally organized provisions for care of children, of visiting and providing other forms of assistance to homebound elders, and of serving as trusted sources of advice and referral.

The increase in such informal supportive associations testifies to their need. Many of these groupings have faced difficulties, often from the same societal pressures that placed some limitations on the utility of the family as a support system. Hence mobility, individualistic and competitive career goals, and fears of making emotional commitments have contributed to discontinuities even in those support groups that have been designed for continuing rather than transitional purposes.

In view of the widespread recognition that both the family and the informal supportive associations are performing vital functions that could not be easily replaced by professional assistance, the job for the professional helper has been to respect and sometimes to augment the naturally occurring systems of social support. This has taken several forms. Perhaps the most dramatic has been the involvement of the extended family and of other community ties in the process of family therapy (Bowen, 1966; Reuveni, 1975; Speck & Attneave, 1973). A second form of assistance has come in the sensitive relating of formal bureaucratic services to informal networks of assistance (Froland, Brodsky, Olson, & Stewart, 1979; Pilisuk, D'Onofrio, & Chandler, 1981).

Figure 1 shows the pattern of variation in the supportive contexts available to the nuclear family and to family members. The intact family well connected to its circle of extended kin and to the community is represented by Diagram 1. A recently separated individual or family member in such circumstances (Diagram 2) will have the

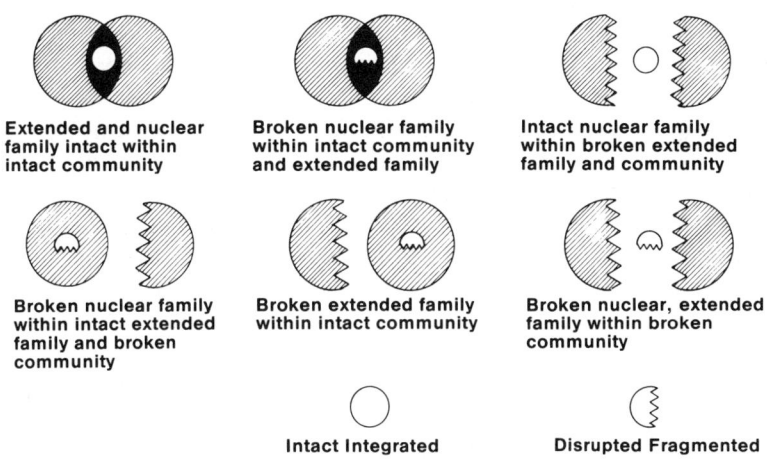

FIGURE 1: Familial and community resources for support of the nuclear family

range of supports necessary to deal with stressful circumstances. The third diagram represents the newly relocated nuclear family in a strange environment. Its potential for necessary support will depend upon the reweaving of social ties. Diagrams 4, 5, and 6 all show the disrupted nuclear family or isolated individual under circumstances of inadequate support either from the extended family, from the community, or from both. The supportive assistance needed by formal or informal service providers will vary with the nature of the deficit.

Table 1 offers a more detailed view of specific forms of supportive assistance and their likely sources. The importance of kinship ties is clearly seen in the number of important support functions they provide. However, it is also clear that ties outside of the kinship circle are primary for some functions. Moreover, when one considers both the primary source of support and the backup needed when that source is unavailable, the importance of strong community ties and effective community services is obvious.

A supportive community is important as a supplement for kinship ties, and sometimes as replacement for them. Five forms may be identified:

1. institutionalized support systems for dependent populations
2. organized channels for natural helping
3. reciprocal help groups
4. network and family-oriented therapeutic interventions
5. supportive organization of work and school settings.

Given this analysis, one would anticipate a more supportive and health promoting environment in a community which establishes such supportive programs as day health care, work site child care, friendly visitor, or meals on wheels programs—all to meet needs of populations with known dependencies.

Organized channels for informal helping include such programs as big brother, big sister and foster grandparent arrangements as well as special contact arrangements like the widow-to-widow program. Consultation with natural neighborhood helpers can enlarge their visibility and their resources.

Mutual help groups provide still another form of community supports, particularly important because their self-help emphasis can build confidence. In the formal social support system, roles are sometimes rigid. Beyond the resources of the family, individuals in

TABLE 1: Primary and Back-Up Sources for Different Supportive Needs

	Nuclear Family	Extended Family	Neighbors	Friends, work, school assoc.	Mutual help assoc.	Natural helpers	Hired service workers	Professional helpers	Agencies
Immediate Emergency Aid	X		X			X			
Intimate Emotional Sharing	X			X	X				
Financial Aid	X	X						X	
Illness, Short-term (chores & personal care)	X	X					X		
Illness, Chronic & Long-term Disability (chores & personal care)	X	X					X		
Feeling of Being Loved	X	X		X					
Advice and Support for Role Transitions	X			X		X	X		
Support for Special Problems					X	X	X	X	X
Social Contact	X	X	X	X					
Affirmation of Competence				X	X			X	
Affirmation of Belongingness	X	X		X	X				

151

mutual help groups have a chance to gain recognition for their capacity as supportive resources to others. Alcoholics Anonymous, parenting groups, and kidney dialysis groups are examples. The intentional extended family, whether loosely affiliated or in common residence, can be a major factor in developing multipurpose cross-generational ties, particularly when real kin are geographically dispersed.

Strong community supports should also include the availability of therapeutic practitioners geared to make use of the kinship and community network whether in crisis intervention, in the recapturing of latent long-term ties or in developing new relations. A variety of family therapies and community mental health interventions contribute to this.

It appears necessary to rethink some of the relationships between the individual and the bureaucracy. The bureaucratic setting, whether in school, at work or in the marketplace, must take on a dual task if it is to operate consistently with the supportive needs of its participants. The first of these is to allow individuals the amount and flexibility of time to honor their commitments to the familial and friendship networks in which most of supportive interactions transpire. The second task of the bureaucracy is to make available those opportunities for the alleviation of stress, for the formation of supportive friendships and for the inclusion of the family as are commensurate with supportive needs.

SUMMARY AND DISCUSSION

The question of how best to characterize the sense of connectedness in modern society was addressed in one study of social networks by Wellman (1979). He refuted the hypothesis that the densely knit community of old had survived or that individuals were living essentially an anomic existence and that the primary community had been lost. Rather, the finding was that the community has been liberated. Most of its members do, or can find, some close ties. Supportive relationships do occur, but they are not given in form or substance by the structure of kinship. Rather, with kinship as one base, the opportunities for other forms of supportive association must be grasped. More than ever before the family, to provide adequate social support, particularly in times of stress, needs to be embedded in a supportive community.

The nuclear and extended family remains a psychological base of enduring social support for most individuals. It is not available or suitable as a complete source for most individuals and is virtually absent as a source for a smaller number. With fewer individuals serving as full-time caregivers, children and older people have felt the major brunt of inadequate support, although many others feel the sparsity of familial support during periods of sustained stress.

Sustained stress with inadequate support results in an array of breakdowns in physical and psychological health. Two sources of social support that may complement family ties are the informal network of friends or voluntary supportive groups and formal agency services. A community setting furnishing opportunities for these additional supports provides the context necessary for families to find the resources to meet the supportive needs of their members. Other non-kinship forms of informal support have come into being, and human services have increasingly viewed their role as network building. The implication from all of this for future research is that we still have much to learn in just what types of supportive relationships will be of value in the prevention of just what types of pathogenic family circumstances. The danger lies in an emphasis upon segmented special supportive services to the exclusion of inquiry into the cultural and economic values that relegate continued caring relationships to a lesser place than they deserve.

REFERENCES

Berkman, L., & Syme, S. L. Social networks, host resistance, and mortality: A nine-year follow-up study of Alameda County residents. *American Journal of Epidemiology,* 1979, *109* (2), 186-204.
Bloom, B., Asher, S., & White, S. Marital disruption as a stressor: A review and analysis. *Psychological Bulletin,* 1978, *85* (6), 867-894.
Boardman, V. School absences, illness and family competence. In B. Caplan & J. Cassel (Eds.), *Family and health: An epidemiologic approach.* Chapel Hill, NC: University of North Carolina, Institute for Research in Social Sciences, 1975.
Bowen, M. The use of family therapy in clinical practice. *Comparative Psychiatry,* 1966, *5* (7), 365-374.
Brecher, E. M. *Licit and illicit drugs.* Boston: Little, Brown, 1972.
Broeck, E. T. The extended family center. *Children Today,* 1974, *3,* 2-6.
Bronfenbrenner, U. The origins of alienation. *Scientific Monthly,* 1974, *231,* 53-61.
Bronfenbrenner, U. Toward an experimental ecology of human development. *American Psychologist,* 1977, *32,* 513-531.
Bryant, B. K. *Developmental perspectives on sources of support and psychological wellbeing.* Department of Applied Behavioral Sciences, University of California, Davis, 1981.
Bunch, J. Recent bereavement in relation to suicide. *Journal of Psychosomatic Research,* 1972, *16,* 361-366.
Burke, R. J., & Weir, T. Maternal employment status social support on adolescents' wellbeing. *Psychological Reports,* 1978, *42,* 1159-1170.

Butler, R. N. *Why survive? Being old in America.* New York: Harper & Row, 1975.
Cantor, M. H. Neighbors and friends: An overlooked resource in the informal support system. *Research on Aging,* 1979, *1,* 434-463.
Cassel, J. The contribution of the social environment to host resistance. *American Journal of Epidemiology,* 1976, *104,* 107-123.
Cassel, J., & Tyroler, H. A. Epidemiological studies of culture change: Health status and recency of industrialization. *Archives of Environmental Health,* 1961, *3,* 25-33.
Caplan, G. *Support systems and community mental health: Lectures on concept development.* New York: Behavioral Publications, 1974.
Cobb, S. Social support as a moderator of life stress. *Psychosomatic Medicine,* 1976, *38,* 300-314.
Cochran, M. M., & Brassard, J. A. Child development and personal social networks. *Child Development,* 1979, *59*(3), 601-616.
Collins, A., & Pancoast, D. *Natural helping systems.* Washington, DC: National Association of Social Workers, 1976.
Colvin, B. K., Greenwood, B. B., & Hansen, S. A look at today's families. *Tips and Topics in Home Economics,* Spring 1981.
Coser, R. L. The complexity of roles as a seedbed of individual autonomy. In L. A. Coser (Ed.), *The idea of social structure: Papers in honor of Robert K. Merton.* New York: Harcourt, Brace, Jovanovich, 1975.
Crockenberg, S. Infant irritability, mother responsiveness, and social support influences on the security of infant-mother attachment. *Child Development,* in press.
Fengler, A. P., & Goodrich, N. Wives of elderly disabled men: The hidden patients. *The Gerontologist,* 1979, *19*(2), 175-183.
Frank, J. Mental health in a fragmented society. *American Journal of Orthopsychiatry,* 1979, *49*(3), 397-408.
Fried, M. Endemic stress. *American Journal of Orthopsychiatry,* in press.
Froland, C., Brodsky, G., Olson, M., & Stewart, L. Social support and social adjustment: Implications for mental health professionals. *Community Mental Health Journal,* 1979, *15*(2), 82-93.
Garbarino, J. A preliminary study of some ecological correlates of child abuse: The impact of socioeconomic stress on mothers. *Child Development,* 1976, *47,* 178-185.
Gartner, A., & Reissman, F. *Self-help in the human services.* San Francisco: Jossey-Bass, 1977.
Granovetter, M. S. The strength of weak ties. *American Journal of Sociology,* 1973, *78,* 1360-1372.
Green, B. The politics of psychoactive drug use in old age. *The Gerontologist,* 1978, *18*(6), 525-530.
Haley, J., & Hoffman, L. *Techniques of family therapy.* New York: Basic Books, 1968.
Hawkes, G. R. Who will rear our children? *The Family Coordinator,* April 1978, 159-166.
Hetherington, E. M., Cox, M., & Cox, R. The aftermath of divorce. In J. H. Stephens, Jr., & M. Mathews (Eds.), *Mother-child father-child relations.* Washington, DC: National Association for the Education of Young Children, 1977.
Hirsch, B. J. Natural support systems and coping with major life changes. *American Journal of Community Psychology,* 1980, *8*(2), 159-172.
Hoffman, L. W. Effects on the child. In L. W. Hoffman & F. Nye (Eds.), *Working Mothers.* San Francisco: Jossey-Bass, 1974.
Kahn, A., & Antonucci, T. C. *Convoys of social support: A life-course approach.* Ann Arbor, Michigan: Institute for Social Research, 1980.
Katz, H. A., & Bender, E. L. *The strength in us: Self-help groups in the modern world.* New York: Franklin-Watts, 1976.
Kulys, R., & Tobin, S. S. Older people and their "responsible others." *Social Work,* 1980, *25*(2), 138-145.
Kuster-Ginsberg, C. *Family by choice: A "Gross Familie."* Talk delivered to Offentililches forum mit der Evangelischen Studentengemeinde, Dusseldorf, November 1970.

Lambert, B. G., Rothschild, B. F., Allard, R., & Green, L. B. *Adolescence: Transition from childhood to maturity.* Monterey, CA: Brooks, Cole, 1972.
Langway, L., Lord, M., Reese, M., Ellis, P., Maitland, T., Gelman, E., & Whitman, L. The superwoman squeeze. *Newsweek,* May 19, 1980, 72.
Lasch, C. *The culture of narcissism: American life in an age of diminishing expectations.* New York: W. W. Norton, 1978.
Lazarus, R. S. The self-regulation of emotion. In L. Levi (Ed.), *Emotions - Their parameters and measurement.* New York: Ravel Publishing, 1975.
Litwak, E. Geographic mobility and extended family cohesion. *American Sociological Review,* 1960, *25*:385-394. (a)
Litwak, E. Occupational mobility and extended family cohesion. *American Sociological Review,* 1960, *25,* 9-21. (b)
Litwak, E., & Szelenyi, I. Primary group structures and their functions: Kin, neighbors, and friends. *American Sociological Review,* 1969, *34,* 465-474.
Minuchin, S., Montalvo, B. *Families of the slums: An exploration of their structure and treatment.* New York: Basic Books, 1967.
Newcomber, D. The family of the future? A kinship model. *Social Action,* 1972, *39*(4), 25-30.
Nuckolls, K. B., Cassel, J., & Kaplan, B. Psychosocial assets, life crisis and the prognosis of pregnancy. *American Journal of Epidemiology,* 1972, *95,* 431-441.
Orford, J. Alcoholism and marriage: The argument against specialism. *Journal of Studies on Alcohol,* 1975, *36*(11), 18-24.
Parkes, C. M. *Bereavement: Studies of grief in adult life.* New York: International Universities Press, 1972.
Phillips, R. L. Role of lifestyle and dietary habits in risk of cancer among Seventh Day Adventists. *Cancer Research,* 1975, *34,* 3513-3522.
Pilisuk, M. Delivery of social support: The social innoculation. *American Journal of Orthopsychiatry,* in press.
Pilisuk, M., D'Onofrio, C., & Chandler, S. *Reweaving the social fabric: A model for immunizing against stressed-induced illness.* Department of Applied Behavioral Sciences, University of California, Davis, 1981.
Pilisuk, M., & Parks, S. H. Structural dimensions of social support groups. *The Journal of Psychology,* 1980, *106,* 157-177.
Pilisuk, M., & Froland, C. Kinship, social networks, social support and health. *Social Science and Medicine,* 1978, *12B,* 273-280.
Pilisuk, M., & Parks, S. H. The place of network analysis in the study of supportive social associations. *Basic and Applied Social Psychology,* 1981, *2*(2), 121-132.
Pringle, B. Family clusters as a means of reducing isolation among urbanites. *The Family Coordinator,* April 1974.
Rosenmayr, L. The family - A source of hope for the elderly? In E. Shanas & M. B. Sussman (Eds.), *Family, bureaucracy and the elderly.* Durham, NC: Duke University Press, 1977.
Rosenmayr, L., & Kockeis, E. Family relations of the elderly. In C. C. Harris (Eds.), *Readings in kinship in urban society.* New York: Pergamon Press, 1970.
Reuveni, U. Network intervention with a family in crisis. *Family Process,* 1975, *14*(2).
Sena-Rivera, J. *La Familia Hispana* as a natural support system: Strategies for prevention in mental health. In R. Valle & W. Vega (Eds.), *Hispanic natural support systems: Mental health promotion perspectives.* State of California, Department of Mental Health, 1980.
Sennett, R. The brutality of modern families. *Transaction,* 1970, *7*(11), 29-37. (a)
Sennett, R. *The uses of disorder: Personal identity and city life.* New York: Vintage, 1970. (b)
Shanas, E. The family as a social support system in old age. *The Gerontologist,* 1979, *19,* 169-174.
Skolnik, A. *The intimate environment: Exploring marriage and the family.* Boston: Little, Brown, 1972.

Speck, R., & Attneave, C. *Family networks.* New York: Pantheon, 1973.
Stack, C. *All our kin.* New York: Harper & Row, 1974.
Stout, C., Morrow, J., Brand, N., & Wolf, S. Unusually low incidence of death from myocardial infarction. *Journal of American Medical Association,* 1964, *188,* 845-855.
Stueve, A., & Fischer, C. S. *Social networks and older women.* Working Paper 292, Institute of Urban and Regional Development, University of California, Berkeley, 1978.
Sussman, M. B. Relationships of adult children with their parents in the United States. In E. Shanas & G. F. Streib (Eds.), *Social structure and the family: Generational issues.* Englewood Cliffs, NJ: Prentice-Hall, 1965.
Sussman, M. B., & Burchinal, L. Kin family network: Unheralded structure in current conceptualizations of family functioning. *Marriage and Family Living,* 1962, *24,* 320-332.
Tharp, R. Dimensions of marriage roles. *Marriage and Family Living,* 1963, *25,* 389-404.
Treas, J. Family support systems for the aged: Some social and demographic considerations. *The Gerontologist,* 1977, *17*(6), 486-491.
Troll, L. E., Miller, S., & Atchley, R. *Families in later life.* Belmont, CA: Wadsworth Publishing Co., 1979.
Troll, L. E. The family of later life: A recent review. *Journal of Marriage and the Family,* Spring 1971, *33,* 263-290.
Verzaro, M., & Hennon, C. B. Single-parent families: Myth and reality. *Journal of Home Economics,* 1980, *72*(3), 32-36.
Visher, E. B., & Visher, J. S. *Stepfamilies: A guide to working with stepparents and stepchildren.* New York: Brunner/Mazel, 1979.
Wellman, B. The community question: The intimate networks of East Yonkers. *American Journal of Sociology,* 1979, *84*(5), 1201-1231.

Chapter 7

Contribution of Personality Research to an Understanding of Stress and Aging

Paul T. Costa, Jr.
Robert R. McCrae

In recent years, a number of investigators with interests in history, society, the family, and aging have begun to define a field of research on aging and the family (Glick, 1977; Hareven, 1978; Neugarten, 1968; Shanas, 1979, 1980; Sussman, 1976). In particular, with her 1971 review and more recent volume (Troll, Miller, & Atchley, 1979), Lillian Troll clarified a number of issues in both disciplines, and called attention to significant research issues which needed to be empirically addressed. Our aim in this chapter is similar, if much more limited: we hope to review briefly what is known about aging and family stress, drawing on both the gerontological and family studies literatures, and to review some of our own work on personality, stress, and aging. We will then discuss the implications of these findings for future research on aging and the family.

STRESS, AGING AND THE FAMILY

The Family

Troll (Troll et al., 1979) documents a number of misconceptions which students of the family commonly share about aging and the family. Both sociologists and laymen in contemporary America use the word "family" most frequently to refer to the nuclear family

---

Paul T. Costa, Jr. is Chief of the Section on Stress and Coping and Robert R. McCrae is Senior Staff Fellow at the Gerontology Research Center, National Institute on Aging, National Institute of Health, Baltimore, Maryland.

unit of a married couple with independent children. Perhaps because of this linguistic tradition, the impression has been created that family bonds are destroyed or greatly weakened when children leave the home and parents age. Older individuals are often depicted as being deserted by their children and isolated from their families. Although the true extended family, with multiple generations living in the same house is rare today, studies clearly show that family ties continue to be strong, both emotionally and behaviorally, across the life span.

Thus, Shanas, Townsend, Wedderburn, Friis, Milhy, & Stehouver (1968) report that 84% of individuals over 65 live within one hour's traveling time from at least one child. Hill (Hill, Foot, Aldous, Carlson, & MacDonald, 1970) reported that 40 to 70% of adult children in a Minneapolis sample saw their parents weekly. Older individuals frequently receive help from their children, and just as frequently give it, particularly in the form of money and child care (Riley & Foner, 1968). Finally, a number of studies have shown that positive emotional feelings tend to characterize the parent-child bond at all ages. Troll concluded that "it seems that parents remain important to their children throughout the life of the child" (p. 94); and Cumming and Henry (1961) found that among adults over 50, attachment to children exceeded feelings toward siblings and even spouse. In short, most older people are actively involved in their family life and value it highly (Seelbach & Hansen, 1980); and they in turn are highly valued by their families (Bengston & Cutler, 1976).

Is Aging Stressful?

Aging is widely feared and often misunderstood in this culture, especially by the young. The litany of "D"'s is often thought to characterize the elderly: decline, disease, dementia, depression, disengagement, death. The popular belief that old age is a period of particular stress, therefore, is understandable; but the facts do not necessarily bear it out.

If stress is conceived in terms of major life changes, then the most stressful period of life is young adulthood, when the individual is involved in marriage, beginning a career, and raising children. Grandparents and parents often die in this period; and death of friends or spouse, while rare, seem to be particularly traumatic when they do occur. By comparison, most older people lead relatively uneventful lives, free from the pressures of raising a family or making a career.

The stresses which older persons face are more likely to be chronic than acute life changes. For a significant portion of the elderly, limited financial resources pose a continuing stress, particularly since there is little they can do to change their economic circumstances. Declining health and the threat of physical or mental incapacity are also widely felt stresses. In short, with age there is not a general increase in the amount of stress, but there is a change in the nature of the stresses encountered.

These same considerations apply to the more specific area of family stress. Research has repeatedly shown that some events which make major changes in the family are not regarded as stressful by the majority of people. The "empty nest," the period in which children have left home, is a major turning point in the life of the family. From a role-theoretical point of view, it entails massive changes, particularly for the woman who has not developed a career outside the home. Yet several studies (Lowenthal & Chiriboga, 1972) have documented that this change is accepted with a minimum of stress or distress; and some show small improvements in sense of well-being during this period. Since the empty nest is often accompanied by more freedom, privacy, and economic resources, these changes are not really surprising.

Retirement also has been shown to be less stressful than had been supposed. It was once believed that health deteriorated rapidly after retirement, suggesting that the stress of perceived uselessness led to higher mortality. But when health status before retirement is taken into account (as it must be, since retirement is often determined by health status), there are no noticeable differences in mortality (Haynes, McMichael, & Tyroler, 1977). Similarly, studies of the psychological well-being of retired individuals show little change in life satisfaction or morale as a result of retirement (Sheppard, 1976).

It is only when illness, disability, and death enter that the period of "old age" (Neugarten & Hagestad, 1976) becomes a source of stress to the family. Widowhood, extensively studied by Lopata (1973), is a common occurrence for aging women. Because they marry younger and live longer than men, about half the women in America over age 65 are widows (Troll et al., 1979). Most widowed men remarry; but the disproportion of their numbers means that far fewer widowed women will ever marry again. Thus, in addition to loss, they face the prospect of continued singlehood. Loss of spouse is generally rated as the most stressful normative life event (Holmes & Rahe, 1967), and bereavement may be characterized by depression, preoccupation with thoughts of the spouse, somatic complaints and somewhat greater rates of mortality. Responses, however, show considerable individual variation. Lopata (1973) reports that 48% of widows believe they have gotten over their husband's death within one year, whereas another 20% did not believe they ever would. Fewer studies have been made of the effects of widowhood on men, and Troll reports that there is controversy in the literature about whether men or women suffer more from widowhood.

Most older people are not incapacitated, either mentally or physically, and only one in twenty must be institutionalized. But for those who do suffer from these limitations, a considerable stress can be placed on the family. The adult child may be faced in these circumstances with financial burdens, and may be required to devote time and effort to maintaining the parent's health, safety, and home. The decision to move the parent into the child's home, or to institutionalize, is often painful (Tobin & Lieberman, 1978); and viewing the patient's physical or mental deterioration may also be distressing. These same issues, of course, are equally distressing to the parent, who may resent the enforced dependency on his or her children, and fear the necessity of institutionalization. The great majority of older people prefer to remain in their own homes, and moving in with their children has little appeal (Troll et al., 1979). Health and finances are major factors in the quality of relationship between parents and their adult children (Johnson & Bursk, 1977; Robinson & Thurner, 1979), and a number of authors (e.g., Clark & Anderson, 1967), have concluded that feelings between the generations are best when both parties are independent and able to run their own lives.

However, despite these potential problems, few families respond to these problems with rejection or neglect. Families have resources for meeting crises (Hill, 1949), and, as Troll points out, attachment between the generations continues throughout life.

Stress in the Context of the Family

"Stress" is one of the most often used and least understood terms of contemporary social science. Among the most basic of confusions is the use of "stress" to mean (a) the external circumstance or event; (b) the psychological reactions of frustration, anxiety, or distress which follow the individual's perception of the event; and (c) a particular physiological response (Selye, 1950). For the present discussion, we will ignore the physiological definition, and reject the equation of stress with distress; in fact, we will take particular pains to separate these two, since research which fails to separate them is often guilty of circularity (McCubbin, Joy, Cauble, Comeau, Patterson, & Needle, 1980).

Maintaining the distinction between the objective stress and the subjective distress is often difficult, however, As Lazarus, Averill, & Opton (1974) make clear, an event is stressful only in relation to an individual. What is stressful to one family may not be to another, a circumstance which Hill (1949) makes axiomatic in his classic model of stress in the family. The normative approach, in which an external event is designated as a "stress" by the investigator, is therefore somewhat artificial, and will in some instances be incorrect. However, given the difficulties of research under any other set of assumptions, this simplification should probably be employed.

The difficulties of defining and measuring stress and its effects in the individual pale beside the formidable problems of defining and measuring family stress. Since the time of Burgess (1926), the family has been conceived by sociologists as an organic unit, a total greater than, and different from, the sum of its parts. It is this family unit with which the theorists of family stress have concerned themselves. Hill's ABCX model (1949; 1958) has dominated the field in conceptualizing a family crisis (X) as an event (A) interacting with the resources of the family (B) and the family's perception of the event (C).

This concept has intuitive appeal, and has been the basis of a good deal of theorizing (Burr, 1973; Hansen, 1965; McCubbin, 1979; Reiss & Oliveri, 1980), but it has proven exceedingly hard to operationalize. Sociological data is normally obtained by interviewing individuals, who may be viewed as parts of a family or couple. But as Troll observes in the case of couples, "Such an approach can be treacherous if it assumes . . . that either member can speak for the couple itself" (p. 17). Much of the best empirical work in this field, such as the effects of the Depression (Elder, 1976) or war separation (McCubbin, Dahl, Lester, Benson, & Robertson, 1976) on family members has analyzed chiefly responses of the individual. This literature might better be styled the study of the effects of stress on *family members,* rather than on the *family* (McCubbin et al., 1980).

Research on family stress in the Hill tradition is difficult because a highly subjective (family defined) view of stress is used, and because it is not clear how to observe or measure effects on the family, other than by asking family members. Because of this, a number of writers, including Troll (1971) and McCubbin et al. (1980) in decade reviews, have pointed out that there is a paucity of relevant research on which to evaluate these theories; and that the theories themselves often encourage tautologous research findings.

Since research on family stress has been so heavily focused on the responses of individuals, our studies of stress, coping, and personality in the individual may be of some interest. In fact, research on individuals which ignores some of the findings of recent years may be in danger of adopting erroneous conclusions. Conversely, the introduction of concepts and measures from personality research may illuminate research on family stress, and allow sociologically-oriented investigators to proceed to the challenge of conceptualizing and measuring responses to stress of the family as an organic unit.

PERSONALITY, STRESS AND COPING

There is increasing recognition that stress cannot be understood without some consideration of the characteristics of the individuals under stress. Personality traits influence the stressful events people encounter, the perception of them as stressful, the choice of coping mechanisms, and the outcomes of psychological distress and dissatisfaction. Recent research in personality has refocused attention on the power and pervasiveness of personality dispositions, and their implications for understanding stress are beginning to be understood. This chapter provides an opportunity to consider in some depth the possible influences of personality on stress and aging in the family context. Since many researchers in this area are sociologically oriented, it may be useful to review briefly what is meant by personality, and what is now known about its relation to stress and to the family.

A Model of Personality

Although it is conceptualized in widely differing ways, personality is usually measured in the form of traits. Trait models, therefore, represent the form of personality theory most accessible to empirical research. Since the writings of Allport (1937), traits have been defined as enduring dispositions which exert a consistent and pervasive influence on thoughts, feelings, and behaviors. It is recognized that many other variables, including mood, situation, role requirements, and abilities also influence behavior, so that traits may be a modest or even poor predictor of any single instance of behavior. On the other hand, when a wide range of behaviors is considered in the aggregate, a clear pattern will often emerge. It is on the basis of this pattern that we characterize a person as "anxious" or "assertive" or "imaginative." It should also be recalled that personality traits are continuous, more or less normally distributed variables. When we speak of a person as "anxious" we really mean that he or she is located in the upper end of the distribution of anxiety and "extravert" is someone above average on the dimension of introversion-extraversion.

Allport and Odbert (1936) listed 18,000 trait names in the English language, and psychologists have proposed hundreds of scales for the measurement of traits. However, there is a growing consensus that most of these traits can profitably be grouped into a much smaller number of trait domains, each of which consists of a set of related traits. The NEO (Neuroticism-Extraversion-Openness) model is a conceptual organization of traits into three such domains. *Neuroticism* includes the traits of anxiety, hostility, depression, self-consciousness, impulsiveness, and vulnerability. *Extraversion* includes warmth, gregariousness, assertiveness, activity, excitement seeking, and position emotions. *Openness to experience* can be seen in the areas of fantasy, aesthetics, feelings, actions, ideas, and values. The NEO Inventory was developed to measure these eighteen traits, and factor analyses have shown that the traits do group themselves into the hypothesized domains (Costa & McCrae, 1980a). Moreover, a great deal of the research using older instruments can also be understood by this approach. Neuroticism, for example, is also measured by scales from the MMPI, particularly the Hypochondriosis, Hysteria and Depression scales; by low ego strength, guilt-proneness, low self-control and tenseness scales of the Personality Factor Questionnaire (16PF); by low scores on the emotional stability, objectivity, friendliness, and personality relations scales of the Guilford-Zimmerman Temperament Survey; and by the Neuroticism scale of the Eysenck Personality Inventory. Extraversion and openness also encompass a variety of concepts and measures in the literature. By recognizing these three groups of traits, we can organize the literature more effectively. A schematic representation of the NEO model is offered in Figure 1.

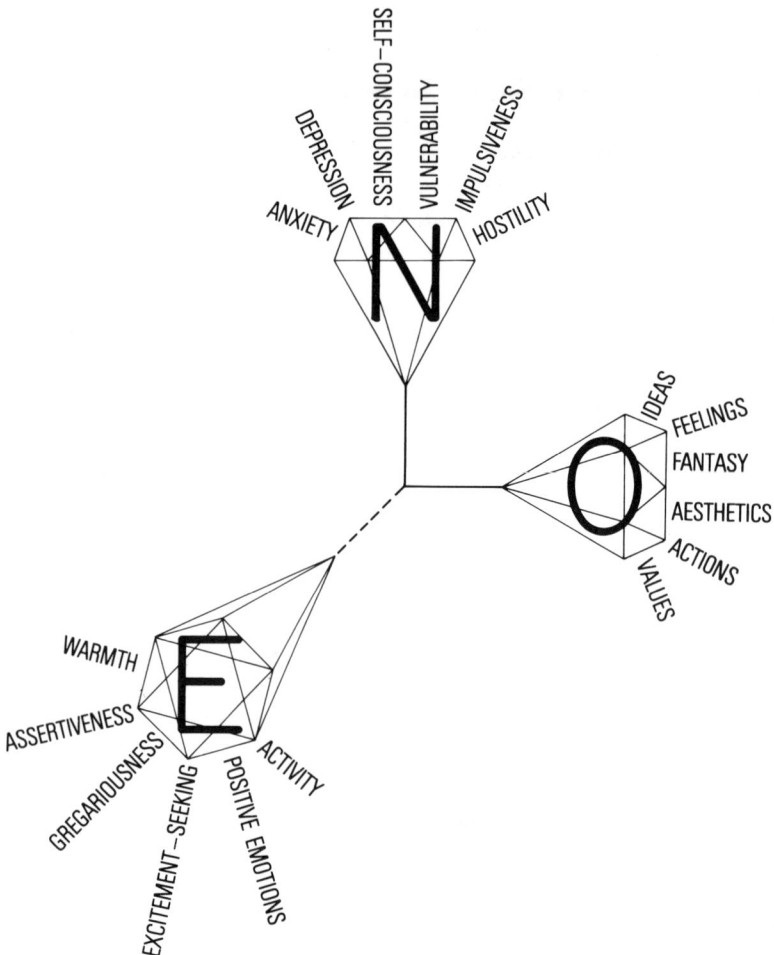

FIGURE 1. Schematic representation of the 18-facet neuroticism-extraversion-openness (NEO) model of personality traits.

Personality and Aging

Trait psychologists have always conceived of traits as enduring dispositions, but until recently it was not known just how enduring they were. As long as college students were the subjects of study, the question was both unresolvable and relatively unimportant. But when personality theorists began to examine the full adult life span, an answer became both possible and necessary. Theories of adult development (Erikson, 1951; Gould, 1972; Levinson, Darrow, Klein, Levinson, & McKee, 1976) had suggested that regular changes in some aspects of personality should occur, and popular stereotypes portrayed the elderly as withdrawn, cranky, or depressed; but an accurate description of personality across the life span awaited data obtained from longitudinal studies conducted over a period of several years.

There are two major questions involved in assessing the stability of personality dispositions. The first concerns the mean level of the disposition in groups of aging individuals. Do all (or most) people become, say, more introverted or hypochondriacal with advancing age? Are there regular and pronounced declines in some aspects of personality, as there are in certain kinds of memory (Arenberg & Robertson-Tchabo, 1977)? The answer, based on a number of longitudinal studies, is a clear "no" (Costa & McCrae, 1978, 1980a; Douglas & Arenberg, 1978; Siegler, George, & Okun, 1979). Only a few traits, such as activity level, show any regular change with age, and these changes are very small. It is especially noteworthy that there is no longitudinal evidence for changes in sociability or emotional instability. Stereotypes of older individuals who are withdrawn or hostile may be based on the highly visible but untypical older persons who are found in nursing homes. Many of these individuals are suffering from senile dementia, an organic condition which apparently does alter personality. Among individuals in good neurological health, aging does not appear to have a predictable effect on the level of personality dispositions.

The stability of group means does not imply that each individual will show a consistent personality throughout adulthood. Some may be increasing on a trait while others are decreasing. Knowing the stability of means tells us nothing about the stability of the rank ordering of individuals. Only retest correlations (or stability coefficients) can provide this information. Longitudinal studies from California (Block, 1981), Massachusetts (Costa & McCrae, 1977), Minnesota (Leon, Gillum, Gillum, & Gouze, 1980), North Carolina (Siegler et al., 1979) and Maryland (Costa, McCrae, & Arenberg, 1980), concur in finding high levels of retest stability for a wide range of personality traits over intervals of from eight to thirty years. In the last-mentioned study, equally high levels of stability (correlations ranging from .59 to .87 over 12 years) were found for young, middle, and older men. Although no study has yet followed a group of individuals across the full adult life span, it appears that the individual who is extraverted in youth will probably be extraverted in old age; and that the older person who is closed to experience was probably equally closed as a young adult. As will become clear later, it is particularly noteworthy to researchers in the fields of stress and coping that neuroticism is also highly stable. An individual manifesting signs of anxiety, depression, or hostility probably has a lengthy history of these symptoms, and will probably continue to show them in the years ahead.

Stress, Distress, and Personality

Personality is relevant to the study of family stress and aging because it is closely related to stress and the responses to stress which the individual makes. Even if we adopt the most objective definition of stress, we find a role for personality variables. Clearly defined life events such as career change or advancement, or separation or divorce, have been shown to be influenced in some degree by characteristics of the individual (Costa & McCrae, 1980a). It is not surprising that suicide rates should be higher among less well-adjusted individuals, but one large-scale study (Keehn, Goldberg, & Reese, 1974) even offers evidence that neurotic individuals are more likely to be the victims of homicide! People provoke a certain amount of the stress they encounter in life.

Second, there is beginning to be some evidence that personality influences the choice of coping mechanisms which individuals will choose to use in response to stressful events. In two studies carried out at the Gerontology Research Center on coping with the stresses of middle and later life (McCrae & Costa, in preparation), individuals high in neuroticism were shown to be more likely to use such relatively ineffective mechanisms as hostile reactions, wishful thinking, self-blame, and withdrawal from others. Extraversion was associated with rational action, perseverance, and active distraction. Open individuals were more likely to use humor to cope with stress, whereas closed individuals more often relied on faith in God. Of course, the nature of the situation was the primary determinant of the specific coping response—few individuals, no matter how open, used humor to cope with death of a loved one. But over the course of a lifetime, the small but pervasive influence of personality should have a major cumulative effect on the selection of coping mechanisms, and thus the success of coping efforts.

But there is a third and more direct way in which personality influences the outcome of encounters with stress. In most research on stress in humans, the outcome variable is some subjective state of the individual. Psychological well-being (Bradburn, 1969), morale (Lawton, 1972), and numerous indicators of mental health (Dohrenwend, Oksenberg, Shrout, & Dohrenwend, in press) have been used to assess the impact of stresses like unemployment, relocation, and divorce. But all of these criteria are also related to the personality disposition of neuroticism (Costa & McCrae, 1980b). At any given time, the person high in neuroticism is more likely to report being unhappy, lonely, frustrated or distressed—regardless of the presence or absence of objectively verifiable external stress.

Many researchers have been concerned with physical illness, rather than mental distress, as the outcome of stress (Holmes & Rahe, 1967). In much of this literature, physical health has been assessed through self-reports of symptoms. Yet there is a growing body of evidence that self-reported health is heavily influenced by neuroticism (Costa & McCrae, 1980c; Tessler & Mechanic, 1978). Individuals high in neuroticism are more likely to complain of physical symptoms, just as they are to report emotional problems. Thus, unless it is based on hard evidence (such as mortality or documented myocardial infarction), physical health as a criterion is likely to be influenced by the personality disposition of neuroticism.

The three kinds of effects of personality on stress and responses to it are illustrated in Figure 2.

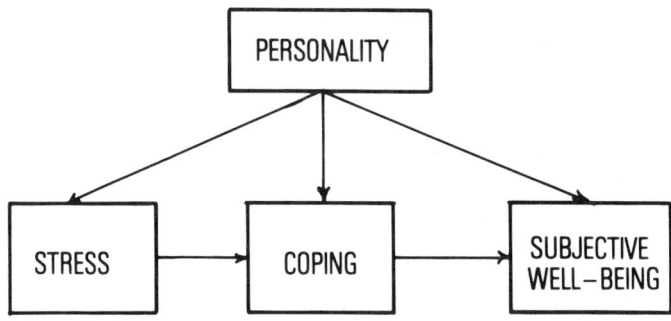

FIGURE 2. The influences of neuroticism on stress and its consequences.

Implications for the Study of Stress

The close association of enduring personality dispositions with stress and the responses to it has the most profound consequences for the interpretation of data on stress and coping. When an individual reports that he or she is distressed, the researcher is likely to attribute it to the harmful effects of some stressful condition or event. But it is equally possible that the distress is long-standing; a chronic condition related to an underlying personality disposition, not recent stress. If the researcher asks the subject directly about the source of discomfort, the subject is almost certain to respond with some life circumstance which he or she believes is responsible. Research on attribution (Jones & Nisbett, 1971) shows that individuals more often attribute their moods and actions to circumstances than to their own dispositions, and this would seem to be particularly likely in the case of unpleasant moods.

The effect of this bias is most likely to be found in the impressions of clinicians. Older individuals who happen to be high in neuroticism may complain that they feel depressed, lonely and isolated. Perhaps on the advice of their physician, they may be referred to a counselor or therapist. When asked why they feel depressed, they may cite the neglect of their children; the common belief that children neglect their elder parents may make this seem like a plausible explanation for the distress they feel. On the basis of many such cases, the clinician may form the idea that older people really are neglected, and that this is a cause of much suffering. This interpretation may be wrong on both counts. First, as Troll argues, the "professionals who work with older people . . . are perhaps in the worst position to judge. Their view of the situation is biased by the fact that . . . the older people they see are disproportionately alienated and neglected" (p. 99). Second, the alienation which their clients report may not be a result of neglect at all; instead, it may be simply the latest manifestation of long-term neuroticism. If these persons' children spent more time with them, they might complain just as bitterly that their children were interfering in their lives.

For the researcher, failure to take personality into account will have more subtle influences. Consider the studies of widowhood. We know from the work of Lopata (1973) that some individuals adjust more quickly and satisfactorily than others to the loss of a spouse. One year later some individuals will be higher in measures of psychological well-being and lower in measures of psychosomatic complaints than others. The researcher may want to find out why, and may be convinced that coping efforts or social supports hold the answer. Perhaps the investigator will ask a question such as: "When you were faced with this problem, did you tend to withdraw from others and try to deal with the problem yourself?" On finding that those who answered the question in the affirmative were less well-adjusted to the loss, the reseacher would probably conclude that withdrawal led to poor adjustment and that coping through seeking help and support was effective in minimizing the stress of widowhood.

But our research shows that coping mechanisms may be as much as outcome of personality as a predictor of adjustment to stress. In this example, an alternative explanation would be that neuroticism led to the use of withdrawal, and also to the poor adjustment in bereavement, but that there was no direct link between the coping behavior and the outcome.

The implication for research on stress is very clear. Somehow, the researcher must take into account and control for the potential confounding effects of neuroticism. Perhaps the best way to do this is by using a strictly predictive design, in which individuals are measured before the stressful event and after. Differences between the two measurements can then be attributed to the event, or to coping efforts, social supports, or other circumstances outside the personality of the individual. Since this design can rarely be followed (because stressful events cannot normally be predicted), the second alternative is to measure neuroticism and other personality variables, and use them as statistical controls in the analysis of the data. Even better, the researcher could combine these strategies to see how, and how effectively, individuals of varying personality characteristics cope with stress.

SUGGESTIONS FOR THE STUDY OF FAMILY STRESS

We have argued that some knowledge and consideration of personality dispositions is essential for students of family stress. Personality is an enduring and pervasive influence on the lives of family members, and it conditions the likelihood of stress and the individual's responses to it. To the extent that studies of family stress remain studies of stress in family members, these facts make it necessary to control for individual differences in personality when interpreting data.

But what of the researcher who wishes to deal with the family as a superorganic unit; who wishes to speak of the *family's* perceptions of stress, or the *family's* response to it? As has been noted, this is not an easy task. Some level of observation and analysis must be devised which integrates and transcends the information obtained from individual members.

Consider the concept of "authoritarian" vs. "equalitarian" families (Byrne, 1965). It should be possible to classify families on the basis of the kinds of decision-making procedures they employ: are decisions made by one family member and enforced on the others, or does everyone have some voice? Perhaps family members would concur in their description of this aspect of the family; or perhaps naturalistic observations or laboratory simulations could be used to measure this dimension of family organization. It would then be possible to record the responses of authoritarian and equalitarian families to stressful events (such as major illness or the addition of an aged parent to the household). The differences observed might be a function of the structure of the family.

We say *might* be, because there are powerful alternative hypotheses. We know, for example, that individuals who are closed to experience tend to score high on measures of traditional family ideology (Costa & McCrae, 1978). We do not yet know whether closed individuals are able to translate these ideological preferences into practice. If so, then measuring the decision-making process of the family might be an indirect method of measuring the personality of family members; and the differences between authoritarian and equalitarian families in response to stress might be reducible to the differences between closed and open individuals.

It is not our intention to be reductionistic; we have neither the evidence nor the inclination to maintain that families are nothing but the sum of the personalities of the members. But we do suggest that this issue can only be fruitfully resolved by research which attempts to study both levels simultaneously (Handel, 1967). Studies which show that characteristics of the family influence responses to stress *above and beyond* that which can be explained by characteristics of individual family members would make a powerful contribution to the fields of both stress and family studies. Indeed, the studies of how individuals with distinctive personalities interact over the life span in this most intimate of contexts is one of the least explored and most exciting topics for research in family studies.

REFERENCES

Allport, G. W. *Personality: A psychological interpretation.* New York: Henry Holt, 1937.
Allport, G. W., & Odbert, H. S. Trait names: A psycho-lexical study. *Psychological Monographs,* 1936, *47,* No. 211, 1-171.
Arenberg, D., & Robertson-Tchabo, E. A. Learning and memory. In J. E. Birren & K. W. Schaie (Eds.), *Handbook of the psychology of aging.* New York: Van Nostrand Reinhold, 1977.
Benston, V. L., & Cutler, N. E. Generations and intergenerational relations: Perspectives on age groups and social change. In R. H. Binstock & E. Shanas (Eds.), *Handbook of aging and the social sciences.* New York: Van Nostrand Reinhold, 1976.
Block, J. Some enduring and consequential structures of personality. In A. I. Rabin (Ed.), *Further explorations in personality.* New York: Wiley-Interscience, 1981.
Bradburn, N. M. *The structure of psychological well-being.* Chicago: Aldine, 1969.
Burgess, E. E. The family as a unity of interacting personalities. *Family,* 1926, *7,* 3-9.
Burr, W. R. *Theory construction and the sociology of the family.* New York: Wiley, 1973.
Byrne, D. Parental antecedents of authoritarianism. *Journal of Personality and Social Psychology,* 1965, *1,* 369-373.
Clark, M., & Anderson, B. G. *Culture and aging.* Springfield, IL: Charles C. Thomas, 1967.
Costa, P. T., Jr., & McCrae, R. R. Age differences in personality structure revisited: Studies in validity, stability, and change. *Aging and Human Development,* 1977, *8,* 261-275.
Costa, P. T., Jr., & McCrae, R. R. Objective personality assessment. In M. Storandt, I. C. Siegler, & M. F. Elias (Eds.), *The clinical psychology of aging.* New York: Plenum Press, 1978.
Costa, P. T., Jr., & McCrae, R. R. Still stable after all these years: Personality as a key to some issues in adulthood and old age. In P. B. Baltes & O. G. Brim (Eds.), *Life-span development and behavior,* Vol. III. New York: Academic Press, 1980. (a)
Costa, P. T., Jr., & McCrae, R. R. The influence of extraversion and neuroticism on subjective well-being: Happy and unhappy people. *Journal of Behavioral Medicine,* 1980, *3,* 245-257. (b)
Costa, P. T., Jr., McCrae, R. R., & Arenberg, D. Enduring dispositions in adult males. *Journal of Personality and Social Psychology,* 1980, *38,* 793-800.
Cumming, E., & Henry, W. *Growing old.* New York: Basic Books, 1961.
Dohrenwend, B. P., Oksenberg, L., Shrout, P. E., Dohrenwend, B. S., & Cook, D. What brief psychiatric screening scales measure. In S. Sudman (Ed.), *Proceedings of the third biennial conference on health survey research methods.* Bethesda, MD: NCHS, in press.
Douglas, K., & Arenberg, D. Age changes, cohort differences, and cultural change on the Guilford-Zimmerman temperament survey. *Journal of Gerontology,* 1978, *33,* 737-747.
Elder, G. H. *Children of the great Depression.* Chicago: University of Chicago Press, 1974.
Erikson, E. H. *Childhood and society.* New York: W. W. Norton, 1950.
Glick, P. C. Updating the life cycle of the family. *Journal of Marriage and the Family,* 1977, *39,* 5-13.
Gould, R. L. *Transformations.* New York: Simon & Schuster, 1978.
Handel, G. Psychological study of whole families. In G. Handel (Ed.), *The psychological interior of the family: A sourcebook for the study of whole families.* Chicago: Aldine, 1967.
Hansen, D. A. Personal and positional influence in formal groups: Propositions and theory for research on family vulnerability to stress. In M. B. Sussman (Ed.), *Sourcebook in marriage and the family,* 3rd ed. Boston: Houghton Mifflin, 1968.
Haraven, T. K. (Ed.), *Transitions: The family and the life course in historical perspective.* New York: Academic Press.

Haynes, S. G., McMichael, A. J., & Tyroler, H. A. The relationship of normal, involuntary retirement to early mortality among U.S. rubber workers. *Social Science and Medicine,* 1977, *11,* 105-114.
Hill, R. *Families under stress.* New York: Harper & Row, 1949.
Hill, R. Social stresses on the family. In M. Sussman (Ed.), *Sourcebook on marriage and the family,* 3rd ed. Boston: Houghton Mifflin, 1959.
Hill, R., Foote, N., Aldous, J., Carlson, R., & MacDonald, R. *Family development in three generations.* Cambridge, MA: Schenkman, 1970.
Holmes, T. H., & Rahe, R. H. The social readjustment rating scale. *Journal of Psychosomatic Research,* 1967, *11,* 213-218.
Johnson, E. S., & Bursk, B. J. Relationships between the elderly and their adult children. *The Gerontologist,* 1977, *17,* 90-96.
Jones, E. E., & Nisbett, R. E. *The actor and the observer: Divergent perceptions of the causes of behavior.* New York: General Learning Press, 1971.
Keehn, R. J., Goldberg, I. D., & Beebe, G. W. Twenty-four year mortality follow-up of army veterans with disability separations for psychoneurosis in 1944. *Psychosomatic Medicine,* 1974, *36,* 27-46.
Lawton, M. P. The dimensions of morale. In D. P. Kent, R. Kastenbaum, & S. Sherwood (Eds.), *Research, planning and action for the elderly.* New York: Behavioral Publications, 1972.
Lazarus, R. S., Averill, J. R., & Opton, E. M., Jr. The psychology of coping: Issues of research and assessment. In G. V. Coelho, D. A. Hamburg, & J. E. Adams (Eds.), *Coping and adaptation.* New York Basic Books, 1974.
Leon, G. R., Gillum, B., Gillum, R., & Gouze, M. Personality stability and change over a 30-year period - middle age to old age. *Journal of Consulting and Clinical Psychology,* 1979, *47,* 517-524.
Levinson, D. J., Darrow, C. N., Klein, E. B., Levinson, M. H., & McKee, B. *The seasons of a man's life.* New York: Alfred A. Knopf, 1978.
Lopata, H. Z. *Widowhood in an American city.* Cambridge, MA: Schenkman, 1973.
Lowenthal, M. F., & Chiriboga, D. Transition to the empty nest: Crisis, challenge, or relief? *Archives of General Psychiatry,* 1972, *26,* 8-14.
McCrae, R. R., & Costa, P. T., Jr. Personality traits and coping responses. In preparation.
McCubbin, H. I. Integrating coping behavior in family stress theory. *Journal of Marriage and the Family,* 1979, *40,* 237-244.
McCubbin, H. I., Dahl, B. B., Lester, G. R., Benson, D., & Robertson, M. L. Coping repertories of families adapting to prolonged war-induced separations. *Journal of Marriage and the Family,* 1976, *38,* 461-471.
McCubbin, H. I., Joy, C. B., Cauble, E. A., Comeau, J. K., Patterson, J. M., & Needle, R. H. Family stress and coping. A decade of review. *Journal of Marriage and the Family,* 1980, *41,* 855-871.
Neugarten, B. L. (Ed.), *Middle age and aging.* Chicago: University of Chicago Press, 1968.
Neugarten, B. L., & Hagestad, G. O. Age and the life course. In R. H. Binstock & E. Shanas (Eds.), *Handbook of aging and the social sciences.* New York: Van Nostrand Reinhold, 1976.
Reiss, D., & Oliveri, M. E. Family paradigm and family coping: A proposal for linking the family's intrinsic adaptive capacities to its responses to stress. *Family Relations,* 1980, *29,* 431-444.
Riley, M. W., & Foner, A. Aging and society, Vol. I. *An inventory of research findings.* New York: Russell Sage, 1968.
Robinson, B., & Thurner, M. Taking care of aged parents: A family cycle transition. *The Gerontologist,* 1979, *19,* 586-593.
Seelbach, W. C., & Hansen, C. J. Satisfaction with family relations among the elderly. *Family Relations,* 1980, *29,* 9-15.
Selye, H. *The physiology and pathology of exposure to stress.* Montreal: Acta, 1950.

Shanas, E. The family as a social support system in old age. *The Gerontologist*, 1979, *19*, 169-174.

Shanas, E. Older people and their families: The new pioneers. *Journal of Marriage and the Family*, 1980, *41*, 9-15.

Shanas, E., Townsend, P., Wedderburn, D., Friis, H., Milhhoj, P., & Stehouver, J. *Older people in three industrial societies.* New York: Atherton Press, 1968.

Sheppard, H. L. Work and retirement. In R. H. Binstock & E. Shanas (Eds.), *Handbook of aging and the social sciences.* New York: Van Nostrand Reinhold, 1976.

Siegler, I. C., George, L. K., & Okun, M. A. A cross-sequential analysis of adult personality. *Developmental Psychology*, 1979, *15*, 350-351.

Sussman, M. B. The family life of old people. In R. H. Binstock & E. Shanas (Eds.), *Handbook of aging and the social sciences.* New York: Van Nostrand Reinhold, 1976.

Tessler, R., & Mechanic, D. Psychological distress and perceived health status. *Journal of Health and Social Behavior*, 1978, *19*, 254-262.

Tobin, S. S., & Lieberman, M. A. *Last home for the aged.* San Francisco: Jossey-Bass, 1978.

Troll, L. E. The family of later life: A decade review. *Journal of Marriage and the Family*, 1971, *33*, 263-290.

Troll, L. E., Miller, S. J., & Atchley, R. C. *Families in later life.* Belmont, CA: Wadsworth, 1979.

Chapter 8

Family Divorce and Separation: Theory and Research

Stephen W. White
Kitty Mika

As the average annual increase in the divorce rate rose from five percent to eight percent from 1963 to 1976, a concomitant rise in interest in separation and divorce as an area of study for the social sciences has occurred. Other than the classic studies by Goode (1949, 1956) and Locke (1951), there was little attention paid to the antecedents, consequences, and family adaptations of divorce in the era prior to 1960. As the demographic evidence of the magnitude of the problem accumulated (see Norton & Glick, 1979), epidemiological evidence revealed that a surprisingly wide variety of physical and emotional disorders were associated with the status of being separated or divorced (Bloom, Asher & White, 1978). Because of this evidence there was, during the decade of the 1970s, a tremendous increase in the number of studies examining separation and divorce, its impact on men and women, and the adaptation made by men and women to a life change that it is presently estimated will affect between one-third and one-half of currently married couples (Glick & Norton, 1978; Norton & Glick, 1979).

The purpose of this chapter is not an attempt to review the growing literature, for analytic reviews are already available (Bloom et

---

Stephen W. White is a Clinical Psychologist at the Children's Hospital in Denver, Colorado. Kitty Mika is a Psychologist with the Counseling Services, University of Colorado, Boulder, Colorado.

The authors wish to thank Bernard L. Bloom for his guidance and encouragement and also wish to acknowledge the assistance provided through the facilities of the Center for Family Studies, Box 345, Department of Psychology, University of Colorado, Boulder, Colorado, 80309. Requests for reprints should be addressed to the senior author at the Center for Family Studies.

al., 1978; Kelly, in press; Kitson & Raschke, 1981; Levinger & Moles, 1979; Price-Bonham & Balswick, 1980; Wallerstein & Kelly, 1980) as are comprehensive bibliographies (Sell, 1980). Instead, its purpose is to identify and review critically research approaches that have characterized recent investigations, to examine theoretical premises that provide the foundation for current research, and to suggest integrations of theory and transitions in design that seem particularly appropriate at this time.

CURRENT METHODOLOGY IN SEPARATION AND DIVORCE

As noted, the interest in separation and divorce research produced a plethora of investigations in the 1970s and a large number of these reports have now been published. Kitson and Raschke (1981), in their comprehensive critique of this research, have discussed the variations in design most prominent in the research to date.

In an attempt to examine systematically the diversity of design variations, it is useful to point out some basic, structural methodological similarities shared by certain investigations. First, there is a group of clinical investigations that are characterized by planned efforts to provide post-divorce intervention services with relatively lenient controls in sampling, design, and methodology. The Wallerstein and Kelly (1980) Martin County study provides the most representative and well known example. Second, there is a larger group of studies examining adjustment consequences for men and/or women of separation and/or divorce at either one or more points in time, often using samples derived from court records (White & Bloom, 1981), but also using convenience samples like Parents Without Partners groups (Berman & Turk, 1981). Third, there is the work, primarily and best represented by Hetherington, Cox and Cox (1976; 1977), who longitudinally compared a carefully selected sample of divorced families with a well matched cohort of intact families. Their study is particularly noteworthy for its methodological cohesion and strict sample control. Fourth, there are studies aimed at defining and analyzing efforts at intervention with separated and/or divorced persons (Bloom & Caldwell, 1981; Bloom & Hodges, 1981; Bloom, Hodges & Caldwell, in press). This preventive intervention program contrasts with most clinical investigations in that it is preventive and not remedial and provides for control groups and objective data collection. Fifth, there is a wide range of epidemiological studies using unobtrusive data (i.e., data immune to contamination from the process of collection) to identify correlates between marital disruption, other life events, and various psychiatric and physical disease morbidity rates (Webb, Campbell, Schwartz, & Sechest, 1966). These epidemiological studies have linked separated and divorced persons of both sexes with increased incidence of inpatient (Backrach, 1973; Bloom, 1975; Redick & Johnson, 1974) and outpatient (Bloom, 1975; Redick & Johnson, 1974) psychiatric admissions as well as an increased vulnerability to physical illness (National Center for Health Statistics, 1970b), suicide (Gove, 1972; Herman, 1977), and increased mortality rates from specific diseases (National Center for Health Statistics, 1970a). See Bloom et al. (1978) for a complete review.

The benefits of clinical investigations, such as the one by Wallerstein and Kelly (1980), without strict sample control or stringent methodological criteria, have recently been discussed (Bloom, 1981) in terms of their relevance, their ability to provide focus and direction for other investigators, and for the interest they have generated in the field of marital disruption. The inherent lack of generalizability is obvious; the necessity for such research, especially in the infancy of marital disruption research cannot, however, be disrupted.

Studies that have concentrated on the identification of problems faced by persons undergoing marital disruption and on factors associated with adjustment to those problems are the largest single methodological prototype in divorce and separation research. Some have focused solely on men (White & Bloom, 1981) but, more frequently, the subjects have been women (Granvold, Redler, & Schellie, 1979; Herman, 1977) or men and women (Chiriboga & Cutler, 1977; Chiriboga, Roberts, & Stein, 1978; Kitson & Sussman, 1977). Most of this genre of studies have focused on the already divorced (Berman & Turk, 1981; Spanier & Casto, 1979), or the formerly cohabiting (Mika & Bloom, 1981). These studies have employed both contemporary, one point in time ("snapshot"), and retrospective data collection methods. Beyond the basic structural differences outlined above, the designs differ based on the presence or absence (and/or length) of follow-up, on sampling procedure, on their definitions of the concept of adjustment and how it should be measured, and on the presence or absence of control groups. Most recent investigations share the utilization of public records (divorce petitions or annulment decrees) for assembling potential subjects; use a non-interventient type of data gathering (i.e., not offering to provide clinical, educational, or practical assistance); and attempt to relate adjustment, variously defined, to internal psychological and/or external demographic, familial, or psychosocial factors. The amount of internal methodological coherence, regarding sampling, matched control groups, subject loss, and validity and reliability of data collection tools differentiate this group of studies, not only from each other, but also more explicitly from the tightly designed work of Hetherington and her colleagues, whose two-year longitudinal study of divorced families with nonremarried parents used stringent criteria which excluded geographically mobile parents and custodial fathers. Issues that are raised by the design differences include the amount of extrapolation and generalizability of findings from one study to another, the reliability of data when strict designs are not adhered to, and the value of using more easily gathered data to stimulate new hypotheses for future investigations. Careful analysis of the recent literature (Bloom et al., 1978; Kelly, in press; Kitson & Raschke, 1981), reveals that despite the wide variation in sampling and methodology, these studies have continually identified similar problems and similar factors related to adjustment with relatively consistent variation by sex and age. Differences exist, of course, but there are presently few major points of contention in the literature on unitary problems and individual adjustment in marital disruption research that cannot be attributed to differences in sampling, geography, or methodology.

Although use of unobtrusive data was largely responsible for the identification of the potentially stressful nature of separation and divorce, its inclusion in recent literature has been minimal. As Webb et al. (1966) note, this may be regrettable:

> Today, the dominant mass of social science research is based upon interviews and questionnaires. We lament this overdependence upon a single, fallible method. Interviews and questionnaires intrude as a foreign element into the social setting they would describe, they create as well as measure attitudes, they elicit atypical roles and responses, they are limited to those who are accessible and will cooperate, and the responses obtained are produced in part by dimensions of individual differences irrelevant to the topic at hand.

> But the principal objection is that they are used alone. No research method is without bias. Interview and questionnaires must be supplemented by methods testing the same social variables but having different methodological weaknesses. In sampling the range of alternative approaches we examine their weaknesses, too. The flaws are serious and give insight into why we do depend so much upon the interview. But the issue is not choosing among individual methods. Rather it is the necessity for a multiple operationism, a collection of methods combined to avoid sharing the same weaknesses . . . . (pp. 1-2)

Their monograph examines other measures, unobtrusive in that they neither require the cooperation of a subject nor have a contaminating influence on the data collected. The inclusion of their suggestions as a way to improve data collection methods in marital disruption research is certainly timely and advisable. Hetherington et al. (1976, 1977) provide the best available model for the application of "multiple operationism" in marital disruption research.

The logical progression from (a) clinical investigations that generate hypotheses, to (b) pilot studies that expand them, to (c) tightly controlled investigations that test the hypotheses is well under way in divorce and separation research. The application of this knowledge in the form of preventive intervention programs with measurable outcomes has also begun. Yet despite the considerable progress made in the past decade, there are certain limitations inherent in the methodology of most studies in the current literature and it is timely to examine those limitations and explore suggestions for improved sampling procedures, more accurate designs, and improved data analyses, and more careful definitions and assessment of concepts like adjustment.

Sampling Issues

The limitations on our ability to generalize from the findings of the research on marital disruption due to sampling inconsistencies are generally acknowledged by most investigators. Sample representativeness is usually questionable particularly when "convenience" samples like Parents Without Partners groups or persons seeking marital counseling are utilized. As the number of studies focusing on the population of maritally disrupted persons increases, so does awareness of the problems confronted in accurately and randomly sampling from this population. The problems are especially acute where researchers have focused on the separated rather than the divorced, and when it is acknowledged that "voluntary" participation in research is usually, by its nature, self-selecting. Clearly, then, some sampling difficulties do seem to be inherent in the population being studied. Despite its shortcomings, a random sample from court records of persons filing for separation and divorce appears to be the best sampling technique currently available for reaching this population at any moment in time.

Within this particular sampling methodology, however, there have been significant variations in the criteria utilized for eligibility in each study, and it is essential to attend to these variations when comparing the results of different investigations. There have been variations from study to study in how long potential participants have been separated in order to be eligible to participate. In some investigations, the maximum allowable time since separation was six or eight months (Chiriboga et al., 1978; White & Bloom, 1981) while in others some participants were separated as long as two years (Spanier & Casto, 1979).

In the light of findings (a) that the greatest distress probably occurs prior to the divorce (Bloom et al., 1978; Price-Bonham & Balswick, 1980); (b) that change takes place quite rapidly at the time of separation (Bloom & Caldwell, 1981); (c) that the period between separation and divorce often exceeds a year (Bloom et al., 1978); and (d) that, for a substantial proportion of separating persons, the time prior to the separation is perceived as equally difficult or more difficult than the post-separation period (Albrecht, 1980; Bloom & Caldwell, 1981; Bloom, Hodges, & Caldwell, in press; Chiriboga & Cutler, 1977); it can be concluded that important data will be lost unless separating persons are examined close to the time of the actual separation. In addition, in studies which select subjects without distinguishing between groups separated for shorter and longer periods, important data are undoubtedly masked, raising questions about the validity of comparisons with the results of other studies.

Another sampling criterion that differentiates studies is the requirement that participants be experiencing their first divorce in order to be eligible to participate (White & Bloom, 1981). Common sense suggests that a second or third divorce will be experienced differently from a first divorce, and that not making this distinction will affect the results of a study. Bloom et al. (1978) discuss the distinction, often ignored in current research, between marital status and marital history. Bloom (1975) found that persons with more disrupted marital histories, (e.g., multiple divorces) were more likely to have a prior history of psychiatric care than those persons with less disrupted marital histories. Based on these findings we can conclude that, if persons who have been previously married and divorced, and/or who have been widowed, are included in a sample, they should be distinguished, for the purpose of data analysis, from persons experiencing their first marital disruption.

Although certain restrictions on sample eligibility, like those discussed above, seem desirable, when eligibility criteria become too stringent, sample representativeness is limited. In the work of Hetherington and her colleagues (1976, 1977), for example, not only were the initial criteria for eligibility quite strict, but, as noted above, participants were dropped from the study if they remarried or moved from the area. As a consequence, it is difficult to generalize the results from this restricted sample to the population as a whole.

With regard to sampling issues and the need to make careful distinctions within a group of subjects, it is also necessary to distinguish between the separation experience of men and women. There is rapidly accumulating evidence indicating that there are significant differences between men and women in terms of their perceptions of their relationships, their reactions to separation, the extent and kind of distress they experience, the period when they experience most distress, the factors that mediate the extent of distress, and the kinds of post-separation problems they face (Bloom & Caldwell, 1981; Bloom & Hodges, 1981; Bloom, Hodges, & Caldwell, in press; Chiriboga et al., 1978; Deckert & Langelier, 1978; Hetherington et al., 1976, 1977; Kitson & Raschke, 1981; Kitson & Sussman, 1977; Mika & Bloom, 1981).

Design Issues

Investigators in the field of separation and divorce seem to be unanimous in their call for prospective cohort studies. Much of what can be learned through single-point-in-time examinations has already been accomplished. The evidence clearly indicates that the impact of separation and divorce can be long term and that adjustment is a process that changes over time (Hetherington et al., 1976, 1977; Wallerstein & Kelly, 1980). The studies by Hetherington et al. (1976, 1977), Bloom and Hodges (1981), and Bloom, Hodges, and Caldwell (in press) are, therefore, important prototypes for the new direction of well designed, cohort investigations.

Investigations in the field of stressful life events emphasize the necessity of doing prospective research in order to understand what variables mediate between the occurrence of a particular life event, like marital separation, and particular outcomes, like psychiatric illness (Goldberg & Comstock, 1976; Paykel, 1978; Rabkin & Struening, 1976). Kitson and Raschke (1981) also highlight the need to investigate the process of accommodation to separation and divorce by utilizing prospective research designs. The financial expense and time consuming nature of prospective longitudinal research in this era of fiscal restraint is an obvious restriction to the development and implementation of these designs.

Another major design issue, which is also discussed by Kitson and Raschke (1981) among others, is the need for the application of multivariate statistics to research data. Study after study has found that single variables are not significant predictors of adjustment to separation. Large samples must be acquired so that statistical techniques can be applied that will allow for the assessment of the simultaneous contribution of multiple variables and their interaction effects.

The Definition and Measurement of Adjustment

The final aspect of current methodologies to be addressed here is the concept of adjustment as it has been defined and measured in the marital disruption research. The problems of definition and measurement have not received sufficient attention in empirical investigations and recent reviews. Some investigators (Kitson & Raschke, 1981; Price-Bonham & Balswick, 1980) do, however, summarize the major problems with current conceptions of adjustment, which they find are limited by lack of attention to the definition of adjustment, and, possibly as a consequence, inconsistent measurement of the ill-defined concept.

Probably the most common approach to the issue of the definition of adjustment has been to avoid a formal definition and simply define adjustment by how it is being measured. Although some investigators have made a convincing case for the use of particular measures of adjustment, and/or have carefully validated the measures they have employed, most have bypassed the most basic issue of conceptual clarification. An additional complication is that instruments used to measure adjustment vary widely from study to study. Researchers have not systematically adapted and refined one another's measures, although some refine their own measures with continued research (Bloom & Caldwell, 1981). The measures of adjustment most commonly encountered in recent research include the assessment of the extent of experienced distress in terms of physical and emotional symptoms, and/or the use of measures of self-perceived adequacy of functioning, the assessment of the severity of problems encountered in various social and occupational roles, self-perceived difficulties in the area of self-concept and self-esteem, and self-perceived overall adequacy of functioning or sense of well-being. Occasionally, reference is made to Goode's (1956) definition (Raschke, 1977), where adjustment is viewed as the development of an identity separate from one's former spouse and from one's role as a married person, and/or as the ability to function satisfactorily in roles required by the transition to non-married life.

Weissman (1975), in a review of techniques available for the assessment of social adjustment, distinguishes between social adjustment and the presence or absence of physical and psychological symptoms. She describes symptoms as reflections of internal psychological and physical states that may or may not have a discernable impact on a person's behavior in social roles. Therefore, role functioning and extent of symptomatology must be measured separately to assess adjustment adequately. An adequate measure of social adjustment would include assessment of both instrumental and affective task behavior in a broad range of life roles (occupational, community, peer relations, parental, extended family). In addition, the assessment of interpersonal behaviors that could be evident in most or all of an individual's role functioning, like hostility or reticence with others, should be undertaken.

Underlying the usual assessment paradigm is a conception of adjustment that includes satisfactory functioning in a variety of social roles and the absence of internal states of excessive tension or anxiety. Some investigators (Bloom et al., 1978; Hetherington et al., 1976, 1977) have utilized multiple measures of adjustment and have approached the kind of detailed and comprehensive assessment of adjustment outlined by Weissman (1975). But most researchers have adopted, usually implicitly, a limited conception of adjustment and utilized as measures a small number of items focusing on one aspect of adjustment, for example, emotional reactions or overall sense of well-being (Chiriboga et al., 1978). Since stressful life events have a wide variety of effects, there appear to be no specific stressful life events related to specific disorders or diseases (Dohrenwend & Dohrenwend, 1978; Goldberg & Comstock, 1976; Rabkin & Struening, 1976). Therefore, it is essential to use multiple measures of the dependent variable to ensure adequate assessment of the range of potential ways in which problems of adjustment might be evident.

Even an approach as detailed as the one described above runs the risk of failing to include an assessment of process variables, a failure that has been noted as prevalent in the marital disruption research (Kitson & Raschke, 1981). Adjustment can be conceptualized as the process that occurs between the event of marital disruption and outcomes like the extent and severity of symptoms of physiological or psychological distress. From this perspective, the measures that investigators have been using to assess adjustment can be viewed as measures of the outcome or of the result of adjustment, adjustment being viewed as the intervening process or set of processes. In order to assess the process of adjustment and how it relates to positive and negative outcomes, prospective research designs are necessary. Our conceptualizations of adjustment may, therefore, have been limited by our research designs; progress may, in turn, depend on the expansion of design parameters.

Various models of the process of adjustment to marital disruption have been proposed (Pais & White, 1971; Vaughan, 1979) but there is a lack of empirical validation of the proposed models. Some of the variables that need to be assessed in order to understand the process of adjustment to marital disruption are described in the final section of this paper.

It seems apparent that further progress in the field of marital disruption research will depend, to some degree, on the extent to which researchers grapple with these issues of definition and measurement of the concept of adjustment. Failure to do so thus far may be due primarily to the largely descriptive and atheoretical nature of the research done in the last ten years, to an eagerness to obtain data about a problem of mushrooming proportions, and to the fiscal and temporal limitations of research design. The lack of conceptual clarity, however, also points to a failure to utilize the potentially rich sources of concepts and data which exist elsewhere in the social sciences and that are directly relevant to separation and divorce research. It is with this in mind that a discussion of some of the theoretical limitations and issues of marital disruption research follows.

THEORY

Searching the marital disruption literature for theoretical foundations or hypothetical models is a frustrating task. There is certainly an abundant number of theoretical explanations for the causes of divorce (Kitson & Raschke, 1981). Yet, despite the fact that most research is oriented towards adjustment and consequences, and not causes, there is very little theory to guide that research. Bridges have certainly been constructed linking marital disruption and stressful life events theory and research (Dohrenwend & Dohrenwend, 1974, 1978) as well as crisis theory (Caplan, 1964; Parad, 1965). Bloom, Asher, and White (1978) discuss these theoretical links and also propose four explanatory hypotheses to account for the associations found between marital disruption on the one hand and various physical and emotional disorders. First, if physically or emotionally handicapped persons marry, their pre-existing handicaps may reduce the likelihood that they will remain married. Second, physical or emotional disorders arising subsequent to marriage in either spouse may significantly reduce the likelihood that the marriage will continue. Third, the status of being married and living with one's spouse may reduce vulnerability to a wide variety of diseases or emotional disorders. Fourth, marital disruption may be a life stressor that can precipitate physical or emotional disorders in married people presumably already vulnerable to them but not yet affected (p. 869).

Incorporated in the discussion of these hypotheses, Bloom et al. (1978) have critiqued earlier hypotheses in the light of recent epidemiological data and concluded that,

> . . . competing hypotheses then reduce to two—first, marital disruption is the product of previously existing disabilities that serve to mediate entrance into and exit from various marital status categories. Second, the various marital statuses or marital status changes may produce enough stress to precipitate psychiatric or other disabilities. (p. 885)

It seems imperative, as noted above, to focus research on the mediating variables essential to understanding how the stressful life event of marital disruption sometimes does and sometimes does not precipitate distress. It is in this area that theoretical guides are conspicuously absent. A theory that may prove most useful for future hypothesis generation is family stress theory and its integration with family coping theory (McCubbin, 1979; McCubbin, Joy, Cauble, Comeau, Patterson, & Needle, 1980). McCubbin and his colleagues (1980) have reviewed the theoretical components of family stress and coping and their applications to a wide variety of normative life stresses. Ahrons (1980) has also outlined a conceptualization integrating divorce in terms of family crisis, stress, and coping.

The body of literature reviewed by McCubbin and his colleagues seems to be particularly useful in generating hypotheses at a time when, in the field of separation and divorce, there is a need to shift our emphasis to the process aspects of adjustment, that is, to the variables that mediate between stress and signs and symptoms of distress, and to the interactional (family) nature of the adjustment process. Since these are major emphases of the research on family stress and coping in other areas of family stress, much should be gained from efforts to place research on separation and divorce in that larger context.

An examination of McCubbin's analysis and Ahrons' conceptualization reveals an important focus not currently well integrated into divorce research. Attention to Burr's reformulation of Hill's ABCX theory of family coping (Burr, 1973; Hill, 1949) reveals that the current marital disruption literature attends primarily to A (the event and related hardship) and X (the crisis), ignoring the interaction between A and B (the family's crisis meeting resources) as well as C (the definition the family makes of the event) almost entirely. See McCubbin et al. (1980) for an in depth discussion of the genesis and application of this model.

In the ABCX model, what is referred to as crisis is, "the amount of incapacitatedness or disorganization in the family where resources are inadequate" (McCubbin et al., 1980). Adjustment in this literature refers not only to what characteristics and resources family members bring to situations, but also to what families do in response to a stressful event. An important distinction is made between a family's vulnerability to stress, which is defined as its ability to withstand the initial impact of the stressor, and a family's regenerative power, that is, its ability to recover once there has been some internal distress and disruption (McCubbin, 1979). In addition, there is a distinction made between reactions to stress, management of existing resources, and more active coping behaviors, such as seeking out new social supports.

It is clear from this brief description that variables that are extremely relevant to the process of adjustment to marital disruption are being distinguished and more clearly defined in other areas of family stress and coping. Other important variables emerge from the literature on family stress and coping that deserve further investigation. Among the most important is the perception of and meaning attributed to the change by family members. Included in this concept of perception (the definition which the family and its members make of the event) are the presence or absence of shared definitions, and the extent to which new roles and social expectations are either ambiguous or clear. When we begin to examine these variables as they interact with one another and affect signs and symptoms of health or distress, our understanding of the adjustment process and of vulnerability to the stress of separation and divorce should be greatly enhanced.

Failure to integrate marital disruption research into a larger framework, such as family stress and coping theory, seems to point to some basic limitations underlying most marital disruption research to date. One is an assumption that divorce and separation lead to family disintegration and thus are not "family events"; therefore, the focus on individual adjustment. A second assumption is that divorce and separation are non-normative events.

These assumptions have been challenged. Ahrons (1980), for example, argues persuasively for viewing the separation process as one of moving from a nuclear family to the establishment of a postdivorce binuclear family. If the adjustment process is successfully negotiated, the family does not dissolve; it takes on a new (binuclear) form. Price-Bonham and Balswick (1980) also refer to divorce as "an incident in the relationship of spouses rather than as an ending." Ahrons (1980) suggests that marital disruption might be viewed as a normative, though unscheduled, life transition since it will be experienced by one third to one half of the married population. She also graphs the levels of complexity inherent in reorganization in binuclear families. Any research examining these complex interrelationships will certainly demand careful attention to the methodological issues discussed above.

Another limitation in the research to date is that it has been more descriptive than explanatory, and has had a disproportionate emphasis on situational, negative correlates with a minimal emphasis on process adaptation, even in the available longitudinal investigations. Clearly, the time is ripe for focus away from descriptive, statistical reflections of individual adjustment, towards focus on adaptation within redefined family systems.

The addition of process-oriented, family coping theories are suggested as an enhancement of the concepts of adjustment and are not intended to diminish the impact on importance of other theoretical formulations that have received little research attention. Clearly one important aspect of adjustment to any stress is what attributes each individual brings to the situation. Many contemporary theories of individual personality development emphasize the importance for adult behavior of early experiences of separation and loss (Bowlby, 1969; Mahler, Pine & Borgman, 1975). Contributions which these theories can make to our understanding of individual adjustment to marital disruption have largely been ignored. Investigators who are emphasizing the importance of "lingering attachment" (Brown, Felton, Whiteman, & Manela, 1980; Kitson & Sussman, 1977; Weiss, 1975) do, however, seem to be attending to components of these variables.

SUMMARY AND CONCLUSION

As the body of research in separation and divorce grows and matures, there will be no clearer evidence of its development than the concomitant development of theory to explain past findings and guide future investigations. The benefits of recent approaches to studying marital disruption have been as varied as the designs that have been employed but the limitations of those designs are beginning to be acknowledged by most researchers in the field. Theory, perhaps based on family stress and coping theory, may prove to be a viable bridge between generations of research into this common and seriously stressful event.

Beyond the development and refinement of theory, which is an exciting and provocative focus for researchers, the issues of design and methodology are becoming increasingly more prominent as investigators have become more self-critical and more prone to constructive criticism of peers. The desirability of prospective cohort designs is recognized almost universally and the dream of longitudinal studies following large numbers of single or engaged people through the process of marriage, family, separation and divorce (or marital stability), and adjustment is shared by many scholars.

Other issues in design demand further work if the literature is to mature. Sampling, control groups, and data bases are all areas that are controversial. The issue of measurement of adjustment, how it is defined, and whether it exists outside the concept of process adaptation, is perhaps the most pressing unresolved methodological question of all. These objectives could perhaps be most productively addressed through multidisciplinary research incorporating the efforts of social scientists from a variety of institutions and including attempts to link research to applied programs and ongoing clinical and community work.

Along with persuasive arguments for integrating research on marital disruption more systematically with research on other areas of family stress and coping, a case can be made for expanding the focus of marital disruption research to include an examination of the separation process among nontraditional families, for example, unmarried cohabiting couples (Mika & Bloom, 1981). Not only has cohabitation become increasingly common, but there is also evidence that the dissolution rate of these relationships is significantly higher than the rate of marital disruption (Clayton & Voss, 1977; Glick & Norton, 1978; Trost, 1975). By examining the process of separation as it occurs for cohabitating couples, and even dating couples, the characteristics that might significantly differentiate the various forms of relationship disruption should emerge. It is certainly likely, given the similarities of the events themselves, that very similar process variables will be found to mediate between the occurrence of the separation and healthy or pathological outcomes. This suggestion is not made *pro forma*, however, but rather to acknowledge that research in marital disruption is really research in family relationships and how they change, and that family relationships in the last third of the twentieth century may differ so dramatically from family relationships in the first half of the twentieth century that they "seem to emerge from a different era, almost a different world" (Bloom et al., 1978, pp. 874-875). It is to these changes that our theory and research must be flexible enough to adapt.

REFERENCES

Ahrons, C. R. Divorce: A crisis of family transition and change. *Family Relations*, 1980, 29, 533-540.
Albrecht, S. L. Reactions and adjustments to divorce: Differences in the experiences of males and females. *Family Relations*, 1980, 29, 59-68.

Bachrach, L. L. *Marital status of discharges from psychiatric in-patient units of general hospitals, United States 1970-1971: I. Analyses by age, color and sex* (Statistical Note 82, NIMH). Washington, DC: U.S. Government Printing Office, 1973.

Berman, W. H., & Turk, D. C. Adaptation to divorce: Problems and coping strategies. *Journal of Marriage and the Family,* 1981, *43,* 179-189.

Bloom, B. L. Review of J. S. Wallerstein & J. B. Kelly, *Surviving the breakup: How children and parents cope with divorce. Contemporary Psychology,* 1981, *26,* 195-196.

Bloom, B. L., Asher, S. J., & White, S. W. Marital disruption as a stressor: A review and analysis. *Psychological Bulletin,* 1978, *85,* 867-894.

Bloom, B. L., & Caldwell, R. A. Sex differences in adjustment during the process of marital separation. *Journal of Marriage and the Family,* 1981, *43,* 693-701.

Bloom, B. L., & Hodges, W. F. The predicament of the newly separated. *Community Mental Health Journal,* 1981, *17,* 277-293.

Bloom, B. L., Hodges, W. F., & Caldwell, R. A. Marital disruption: The first eight months. In E. J. Callahan & K. A. McCluskey (Eds.), *Life-span development psychology: Nonnormative life events.* New York: Academic Press, in press.

Bowlby, J. *Attachment and loss: Vol. 1. Attachment.* New York: Basic Books, 1969.

Brown, P., Felton, B. J., Whiteman, V., & Manela, R. Attachment and distress following marital separation. *Journal of Divorce,* 1980, *3,* 303-317.

Burr, W. R. *Theory construction and the sociology of the family.* New York: John Wiley & Sons, 1973.

Caplan, G. *Principles of preventive psychiatry.* New York: Basic Books, 1964.

Chiriboga, D. A., & Cutler, L. Stress responses among divorcing men and women. *Journal of Divorce,* 1977, *1,* 95-106.

Chiriboga, D. A., Roberts, J., & Stein, J. A. Psychological well being during marital separation. *Journal of Divorce,* 1978, *2,* 21-36.

Clayton, R. R., & Voss, H. L. Shacking up: Cohabitation in the 1970's. *Journal of Marriage and the Family,* 1977, *39,* 273-283.

Deckert, P., & Langelier, R. The late divorce phenomenon: The causes and impact of ending 20-year-old or longer marriages. *Journal of Divorce,* 1978, *1,* 381-390.

Dohrenwend, B. S., & Dohrenwend, B. P. *Stressful life events: Their nature and effects.* New York: John Wiley, 1974.

Dohrenwend, B. S., & Dohrenwend, B. P. Some issues in research on stressful life events. *Journal of Nervous and Mental Disease,* 1978, *166,* 7-15.

Glick, P. G., & Norton, A. J. Marrying, divorcing, and living together in the U.S. today. *Population Bulletin,* 1978, *32,* 3-38.

Goldberg, E. L., & Comstock, G. W. Life events and subsequent illness. *American Journal of Epidemiology,* 1976, *104,* 146-158.

Goode, W. J. Problems in post-divorce adjustment. *American Sociological Review,* 1949, *14,* 394-401.

Goode, W. J. *After divorce.* New York: The Free Press, 1956.

Gove, W. R. Sex, marital status and suicide. *Journal of Health and Social Behavior,* 1972, *13,* 204-213.

Granvold, D. K., Pedler, L. M., & Schellie, S. G. A study of sex-role expectancy and female post-divorce adjustment. *Journal of Divorce,* 1979, *2,* 383-393.

Herman, S. J. Women, divorce and suicide. *Journal of Divorce,* 1977, *1,* 107-117.

Hetherington, E. M., Cox, M., & Cox R. Divorced fathers. *Family Coordinator,* 1976, *25,* 417-428.

Hetherington, E. M., Cox, M., & Cox, R. The aftermath of divorce. In J. H. Stevens, Jr. & M. Matthews (Eds.), *Mother-child, father-child relations.* Washington, D.C.: National Association for the Education of Young Children, 1977.

Hill, R. *Families under stress.* New York: Harper & Row, 1949.

Kelly, J. Divorce: The adult perspective. In B. Wolman & G. Stricker (Eds.), *Handbook of developmental psychology.* Englewood Cliffs, NJ: Prentice-Hall, in press.

Kitson, G. C., & Raschke, H. J. Divorce research: What we know; what we need to know. *Journal of Divorce*, 1981, *4*, 1-37.

Kitson, G. C., & Sussman, M. B. The impact of divorce on adults. *Conciliation Courts Review*, 1977, *15*, 20-24.

Levinger, G., & Moles, O. C. (Eds.), *Divorce and separation: Context, causes, and consequences.* New York: Basic Books, 1979.

Locke, H. J. *Predicting adjustment in marriage.* New York: Holt, Rinehart & Winston, 1951.

Mahler, M. S., Pine, F., & Bergman, A. *The psychological birth of the human infant: Symbiosis and individuation.* New York: Basic Books, 1975.

McCubbin, H. I. Integrating coping behavior in family stress theory. *Journal of Marriage and the Family*, 1979, *41*, 237-244.

McCubbin, H. I., Joy, C. B., Cauble, A. J., Comeau, J. K., Patterson, J. M., & Needle, R. H. Family stress and coping: A decade review. *Journal of Marriage and the Family*, 1980, *42*, 855-871.

Mika, K., & Bloom, B. L. Adjustment to separation among former cohabitors. *Journal of Divorce*, 1981, *4*, 45-66.

National Center of Health Statistics. *Mortality from selected causes by marital status.* (Series 20, Nos. 8A & 8B, USDHEW). Washington, DC: Government Printing Office, 1970. (a)

National Center of Health Statistics. *Selected symptoms of psychological distress:* United States (Vital and Health Statistics, Series 11, No. 37). Washington, DC: U.S. Government Printing Office, 1970. (b)

Norton, A. J., & Glick, P. G. Marital instability in America: Past, present, and future. In G. Levinger & O. C. Moles (Eds.), *Divorce and separation: Context, causes, and consequences.* New York: Basic Books, 1979.

Pais, J., & White, P. Family redefinition: A review of the literature toward a model of divorce adjustment. *Journal of Divorce*, 1979, *2*, 271-281.

Parad, H. J. (Ed.), *Crisis intervention: Selected readings.* New York: Family Service Association of America, 1965.

Paykel, E. S. Contribution of life events to causation of psychiatric illness. *Psychological Medicine*, 1978, *8*, 245-253.

Price-Bonham, S., & Balswick, J. O. The non institutions: Divorce, desertion, and remarriage. *Journal of Marriage and the Family*, 1980, *42*, 959-972.

Rabkin, J. G., & Struening, E. L. Life events, stress, and illness. *Science*, 1976, *194*, 1013-1020.

Rahe, R. H. Life change events and mental illness: An overview. *Journal of Human Stress*, 1979, *5*, 2-10.

Raschke, H. J. The role of social participation in post-separation and post-divorce adjustment. *Journal of Divorce*, 1977, *1*, 129-140.

Redick, R. W., & Johnson, C. Marital status, living arrangements and family characteristics of admissions to state and county mental hospitals and outpatient psychiatric clinics, United States, 1970. (Statistical Note 100, NIMH.) Washington, DC: U.S. Government Printing Office, 1974.

Sell, K. D. *Divorce in the 1970's.* North Carolina: K. B. Sell, 1980.

Spanier, G. B., & Casto, R. F. Adjustment to separation and divorce: An analysis of 50 case studies. *Journal of Divorce*, 1979, *2*, 241-253.

Trost, J. Married and unmarried cohabitation: The case of Sweden with some comparisons. *Journal of Marriage and the Family*, 1977, *37*, 677-682.

Vaughn, D. Uncoupling: The process of moving from one lifestyle to another. *Alternative Lifestyles*, 1979, *2*, 415-442.

Wallerstein, J. S., & Kelly, J. B. *Surviving the breakup: How children and parents cope with divorce.* New York: Basic Books, 1980.

Webb, E. J., Campbell, D. T., Schwartz, R. D., & Sechrest, L. *Unobtrusive measures: Nonreactive research in the social sciences.* Chicago: Rand McNally, 1966.

Weiss, R. S. *Marital separation.* New York: Basic Books, 1975.
White, S. W., & Bloom, B. L. Factors related to the adjustment of divorcing men. *Family Relations,* 1981, *30,* 131-141.

Chapter 9

Mundane Extreme Environmental Stress in Family Stress Theories: The Case of Black Families in White America

Marie F. Peters
Grace Massey

INTRODUCTION

Family stress theories, as McCubbin, Dahl, Lester, Benson, and Robertson (1976) have pointed out, have traditionally concentrated on variations in family vulnerability and family regenerative power. Researchers using this approach usually examine how families react to and then manage stressful events which occur as part of a family's encounter with misfortune such as sudden loss of income, death of a family member, birth of a retarded or handicapped child, loss of limb, debilitating illness, or long-term parent absence.

Many researchers (e.g., Hill, 1972) have investigated the specific coping strategies families develop as they channel family resources to adapt to the stressful event. More recently, researchers are also examining the ongoing transactions between families, the corporate structure, and the community that are designed to decrease the vulnerability of families to the effects of continuous or repeated stress, with special attention given to those situations that are routinely part of a particular occupation (see Boss, McCubbin, &

Marie F. Peters is Associate Professor, Human Development and Family Relations, University of Connecticut. Grace Massey is Director, Research for Children, Oakland, California.

This research was supported by the Minority Center at the National Institute of Mental Health, Grant Number 7 R01 MH 35785-01 MN.

© 1983 by The Haworth Press, Inc. All rights reserved. *193*

Lester, 1979). For example, military families with a family member who is regularly away on active duty assignment, or the families of a professional breadwinner whose job requires constant travel away from home for extended periods of time often have built-in support systems within the occupation, either at the corporate or the employee/community level. The support system helps them to cope with the continued or recurring stress and strain due to the absence of a family member (Boss et al., 1979).

However, there are other families who must also deal with exceptional stress and strain in their daily lives, although the circumstances causing the stress differ in important ways from the situations discussed above. There are some families whose total lives unfold within a uniquely oppressive environment. For example, large numbers of families have been uprooted *en masse* from their homelands as the result of political or religious persecution, or the ravages of war. As refugee and displaced families, they were immediately outside their own political system and many lived for years under conditions of extreme deprivation, frustration, and change in a foreign, often hostile, country. Because of their cultural identity, these families had negative status in their host society, deterring their capability to provide for basic needs. Nevertheless they maintained themselves within this oppressive environment and most managed to cope with this pervasive and non-ending stress factor in their lives. Our present theories fail to consider how these families view the stress of everyday survival under such circumstances.

The impact of this displacement on family life has been explored in several studies of European refugee families. The findings have interesting and provocative implications for theoretical literature on family stress. For example, studies of refugee families who migrated or escaped to Europe or the United States from the Soviet Union or who experienced severe bombings and intensive denazification in Germany during and after World War II reported that more families who had undergone political terrorization or war-related hardships were solidified rather than disorganized by their experiences (Geiger, 1955; Shelsky, 1963). However, Geiger (1955) also found that the resulting economic deprivation families faced had a detrimental effect on interpersonal solidarities and relationships within the family. An analysis of the continued vulnerability of these refugee families to a basic and consistent oppressive situation and their adaptation due to shared/not shared regenerative power would provide important background information for the kind of family stress analysis to be suggested in this paper. Black American families provide another example of families who live under the continuous and varying stresses of oppression. As the news media occasionally recognize, and a number of social scientists continue to document (Blaumer, 1970, 1972; Carmichael & Hamilton, 1967; Cruise, 1968; Mathis, 1971, 1978), Blacks are internally colonized by the American society (Mathis, 1978). As a result of the historical circumstances that brought Blacks into this country and their minority status, the ability of Black families to live, work, or survive in the United States is consistently and pervasively constrained. The preferences, needs, and special circumstances of the culturally different Black families are peripheral to the concerns of most Americans (Mathis, 1978; Ogbu, 1974; Peters, 1976). As a result, it is more difficult for Black families to function within this social system. Myers (1977) has explained how the added stress on the lives of Black families has had a negative psychobiological effect. He writes:

> The very fact of their (Black families') ethnicity and social status imposed upon them an extra stress load which increases their susceptibility to disruptions in daily functioning and greater risks of becoming disabled because of serious illness. (p. 1)

A noted Black psychiatrist, Chester Pierce[1] (1975) compares this situation of continuing, subliminal stressful conditions undergirding the lives of Black families in America to the isolation and stress of Eskimos in the arctic—an extreme, exotic environment. He views Blacks as living in a *mundane, extreme environment;* that is, an environment where racism and subtle oppression are ubiquitous, constant, continuing, and mundane as opposed to an occasional misfortune. This, he suggested, presents many psychosocial difficulties, with the most oppressing aspect of racism being:

> . . . that I don't believe that many Blacks can live a total hour of their conscious life without recognizing the fact of their blackness and being reminded of it in all sorts of ways . . . Every Black has to be hung up on these kinds of issues. (Pierce, 1969)

Similarly, Power (1973) pointed out in her study of the effects of school desegregation on the self-concepts of Southern children, both Black and White, that "a Black child has emotional problems that are due to the very fact of his Negroness" (p. 34).

In this perspective, Black Americans' lives are encumbered by the constant threat and actual periodic occurrences of intimidation, discrimination, or denial because of race. The stresses which Black families face—sometimes subtle, sometimes overt—are pervasive, continuous, and debilitating. Pierce (1975) has labeled this set of conditions for Black families *Mundane Extreme Environmental Stress* (MEES).

In short, Black families in America are perennial "refugee" families. Yet they vary from family to family and across life spans, both in their vulnerability to racist conditions and in their regenerative abilities and strategies. They have developed internal patterns for coping with racial oppression, strategies proven to be effective in the past, that are incorporated into their own socialization processes. As Reiss and Oliveri (1980) point out: "The question of the adaptiveness of coping strategies must take into account the family's own objective and the nature of the social community in which it lives" (p. 443). Additionally, they have access to community-based programs and shared experiences which not only buffer the potential of psychological damage that is the impact of never-changing status, but also provide perspectives, support, and leadership in addressing the illegality, inhumanity, and unfairness of discriminatory issues.

RACISM AS STRESS

Factors Contributing to Mundane Extreme Environmental Stress for Black Families

There are a number of continuing factors in American life that are especially stressful to Black Americans which require resourceful accommodation.

Employment. As a group, Blacks are in a disadvantaged position in the job market.[2] As the anthropologist Ogbu (1974, 1977) has perceptively pointed out in his comprehensive study of social class and mobility, racial stratification of Black Americans in the United States has resulted in most Blacks being expected (or assigned) to do the hardest and/or lowest paid jobs.

This is seen in the income and unemployment statistics. The median income of Black families continues to be about 69% of the income of White families, in spite of the affirmative action programs of the 1970s (Bureau of the Census, 1978; Williams, 1979). Because of America's pervasive racial stratification system, a disproportionate number of Black people have low-level jobs (Ogbu, 1977; Bureau of the Census, 1978). For example, in recent years the employment of Blacks in civil service jobs has increased more than in any other segment of the job world, and they are actually overrepresented in these jobs when compared to their percentage of the population. Yet, the civil service jobs most Blacks have are concentrated in the lower grade levels. In spite of affirmative action, in most regions of the country this situation has not improved (Gibson & Yeager, 1975).

With an unemployment rate approximately double the unemployment rate for other Americans—triple for Black youth—(NBCDI, 1980), it is assumed that many lower-level jobs will be held by Blacks and disproportionate numbers of Black people remain members of the subordinate worker group in our society. Society has effectively created an unstated (but real) job ceiling for Blacks (Ogbu, 1977). Many Blacks, then, encounter obstacles to upward mobility which are difficult, sometimes impossible, to surmount. Knowing that they are always vulnerable to being "last hired and first fired" places added stress in the lives of Black families especially during times of economic recession. Blacks in America develop coping or survival strategies that accommodate job instability and the expectation of low family income.

Education. Unfortunately, society's stabilized and limited options for Blacks are not only maintained by business, industry, and agriculture, but also by educational systems as well (Ogbu, 1977). There have been many studies which document this "programmed for failure" approach in the educational realm (Clark, 1970; Woodson, 1969). Unfortunately the education system, often viewed as the only hope by some Black parents, was never intended to give Black people the necessary skills to be successful in the competitive job market, to become upwardly mobile *en masse.* On the contrary, the education system has been utilized to certify the inequalities of the larger social system in America (Carnoy, 1972; Katz, 1972).[3] From their past experiences, Blacks expect that disappointments, adjustments, and changes will be demanded of them and their children. They understand that they must always adapt to various manifestations of racism. It is with this perspective that many Black parents socialize their children for survival.

It is our purpose in this chapter to consider and develop a perspective for incorporating the unique experience of Black families into current family stress theory. The first section contains a discussion of how general stress theories and research do not adequately account for the circumstances of Black Americans. The second section presents an augmented Hill family stress formula which incorporates the concept of Mundane Extreme Environmental Stress. This formula will allow more productive and legitimate analysis of stress and coping in Black or other racial minority families. The third section highlights select findings from a three-year study of the socialization of young children in Black families, particularly related to the observed behaviors of parents in teaching their children how to cope with the effects and stresses of racism. In the last section, one family's handling of a crisis situation is analyzed using the augmented stress formula which includes MEES.

THEORY AND RESEARCH ON BLACK FAMILIES: AN UNEXAMINED PHENOMENON

Unfortunately, studies focusing on Black families have been fragmented, diverse, and typically pejorative. Most have viewed Black families as deviant and problem-prone. Research has not been much concerned with describing and analyzing actual everyday behaviors, attitudes, and coping mechanisms of Black families within an ecological and functional perspective (Billingsley, 1968; Boykin, 1979; Mathis, 1978; Peters, 1978). For example, in an informal content analysis of the recent special issue of *Family Relations* (October, 1980) devoted to "Family Stress, Coping, and Adaptation," fifteen articles were included in the section, "Change and Stress Over the Life Span." Twelve articles covered topics which are relevant to the experiences of Black and other minority families. Yet even in areas where Black representation is higher than the average for American families—such as unemployment and divorce/separation—the three relevant articles did not indicate that Blacks were included in their sample. Results were reported in generalized terms, and apparently one must assume that their findings apply to most American families. Additionally, in this same issue, the five articles under the section, "Social Support and Intervention," did not include Black families in their discussion.

This non-inclusion of the special needs, problems, and stresses of Black families in the conceptualization of stress-related research is one example of the subtle and elusive nature of institutional racism within American culture. As an outgrowth of the prevailing negative approach implicit in the omission of Blacks from many normative studies, observations and considerations of behavior in Black families have rarely been examined within the concepts of family stress theory. Thus, there has been no recognition of the MEES Black families' experience.

An early potential for this approach and interest was probably deflected by the politically motivated issues of the 1960s which focused public attention on "poverty amidst affluence." Therefore, much of the recent research on Black families developed out of the "War on Poverty." Concepts such as "cycles of poverty" and the problems of the poor, "pathological" Black family projected by the Department of Labor's "Moynihan Report" (Moynihan, 1965) were typically incorporated into the research and writings regarding Black families (Mathis, 1978; Peters, 1978). Black families that differed from mainstream America were considered to be deviant, illegitimate, and/or deteriorating and thus pathological. This label of "deviance" contributed to the misfocusing of much of the research of the sixties and early seventies involving Black families (Mathis, 1978). As a reaction to this critical and damaging research, a number of writers and social scientists began to point to the "strengths" of Black families that allowed their survival despite poverty, racism, and discrimination. (See Aschenbrenner, 1975; Heiss, 1975; Hill, 1972; Nobles, 1976; Peters, 1978; Stack, 1974; Staples, 1976.)

This literature, we suggest, can form the basis for analysis of those coping behaviors in Black families that can be viewed as a combination of adaptation and response to the continuing stress of perpetual and pervasive racism in people with an African heritage that demands and respects family survival. By examining intra-family, inter-family, and family-community relationships, interactions, and processes, the various strategies which allow racism to be absorbed, deflected, combatted, succumbed to and/or overcome by particular Black families and individuals can be studied. By exploring the outcome of various personal or family abilities to cope with either (a) the "normal," stressful everyday situations of racism, discrimination, or personal humiliation, or (b) the sudden eruption of a racially-based crisis situation, the dynamics of family regenerative power of Black or other oppressed minorities can be better understood.

We need to know what types of families are best equipped to meet continuing and changing onslaughts of racism. We need to find out the characteristics of family organization, the factors involved, and the various ways of adjustment to the impact of racism. We need to understand actions which contribute to the reduction of negative effects of racism on Black families and their children. We need to identify how Black families foster and achieve upward mobility, maintain healthy personalities, and learn how to handle racial identity-related stresses. Further, it would be instructive to explore the course of adjustment to racial stress as new situations emerge throughout the life cycle, to describe the variety of strategies families use, and to document how families socialize and teach children to survive under continued overt and covert racial oppression.

FAMILY STRESS THEORY AND MUNDANE AND CHRONIC SOURCES OF STRESS

The conceptual framework of much stress and coping research today is based on a typology of family crisis which describes a family's reaction to or handling of a sudden or new stressful event which occurs either (a) within the family and caused by a family member, or (b) outside the family and caused by a catastrophe, such as tornado damage, economic depression, war, or father absence. The model focuses on newness, suddenness, and/or severity of crises, family vulnerability, and the family's regenerative power. A family's reaction is dependent upon the type of crisis, its duration, and which members create the crisis (Hill, 1963). This perspective, however, is conceptually limiting for it does not accommodate situations of continued, ongoing oppression such as MEES, within which periodic but unpredictable stressful events and demands for sudden change can be expected to occur. Families under MEES differ from the families whose homes, for example, are located in an area subject to periodic flooding, or from families who operate a farm in a drought-prone country, or from the family whose income is dependent upon a job in an occupational field subject to seasonal lay-offs. In these situations the stressful event is anticipated and reactions and resources can be programmed for mobilization when necessary. It is only the timing of the stressful event that is uncertain. At other times, life goes on as usual. Unless the family belongs to a racial minority the undergirding effect and influence of MEES is absent. The unique situation of Black families suggests the need for family stress theories to be conceptualized within a framework which would include recognition of two additional stress factors for minority families. There is (a) the extreme but mundane stress of omnipresent racism (MEES) described above, and there is (b) the chronic and often unpredictable (but not unanticipated) racially-caused stressful events encountered throughout the life cycle. These sources of stress, whether *mundane* or *chronic* and crisis-producing are *in addition to* the kinds of family stress which other families may occasionally encounter.

Managing Mundane Extreme Environmental Stress

The Black family structure is an arena for tensions and frustrations, but also is the domain for the resolution of frustration and tension. For Black Americans, the frustrations and tensions can be exacerbated or helped by the interface of individual family members with the world outside the family. When a Black family's home is destroyed by a hurricane, for example, the stress also includes the special problems a Black family may face in locating another desirable place to live. Will the housing counselor be fair? Will the family be referred to an undesirable Black ghetto neighborhood for housing? Will the Black family encounter hostility moving into an integrated or "White" neighborhood? An analysis of a stress situation in Black families must include recognition of the subtle influence race may have on their recovery potential. Figure 1 illustrates how racism in the form of MEES and in the form of unpredictable acts of discrimination intrude as additional stress factors in the lives of Black families.

These additional stress factors suggest that to adequately understand stress in Black families, variables need to be added to Hill's classic formula for analyzing social stresses on the family. Hill's (1963) original equation is depicted in Figure 2. According to Hill's (1963) explanation:

> The second and third determinants—family resources and definition of the event—lie within the family itself and must be seen in terms of the family's structures and values. The hardships of the event, which go to make up the first determinant,

lie outside the family and are an attribute of the event itself. (p. 306)

If the additional stress and coping strategies and resources reflective of MEES are incorporated into Hill's basic formula, it becomes more comprehensive and, of course, more applicable to the lives of Black families. Figure 3 shows an augmentation of Hill's equation. It accounts for the variety of factors involved in stress/crisis events and allows for an analysis of the dynamic of living in a mundane ex-

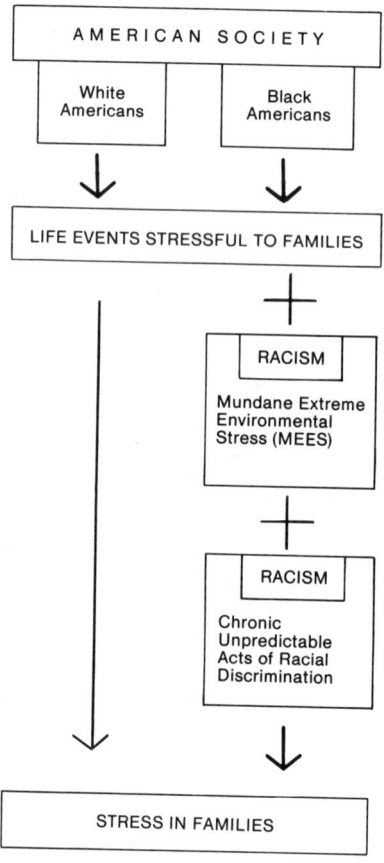

Figure 1. How racism affects Black families.

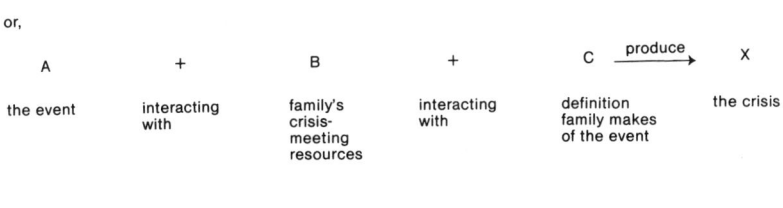

Figure 2

HILL'S EQUATION FOR ANALYZING SOCIAL STRESSES WITHIN THE FAMILY

treme environment where racism and oppression are of continuous and varying intensity.

Following Hill, in this formulation, A is the event, B is the crisis-meeting resources of the family, C is the definition of the event, and X is the crisis event. However, a new category, D, allows input related to the mundane, extreme stress of minority status (MEES), and a new category, Y, represents how Black families experiencing MEES cope with the stress/crisis event. Situations and events which influence each of the factors in the equation are also shown in this figure. For Black families, the items of C and D are especially significant, as studies are beginning to show (McAdoo, 1978; Noble, 1976; Staples, 1976; Young, 1970).

Coping with Mundane Extreme Environmental Stress

The coping strategies used by Black families, the Y factor in the augmented model, have been described by a number of researchers. Black families, Robert Staples (1976) noted, provide a sanctuary which buttresses their members from the pervasiveness of oppression and racism. Whether in the realm of strategies for survival, mutually reciprocal kin/neighbor support, or maintenance of emotional well-being, Staples suggested that factors embedded in Black values, as reflected in the family system, must be accounted for in any discussion of the stresses of Black family life. This perspective is also seen in the research of Nobles (1976) who examined the way

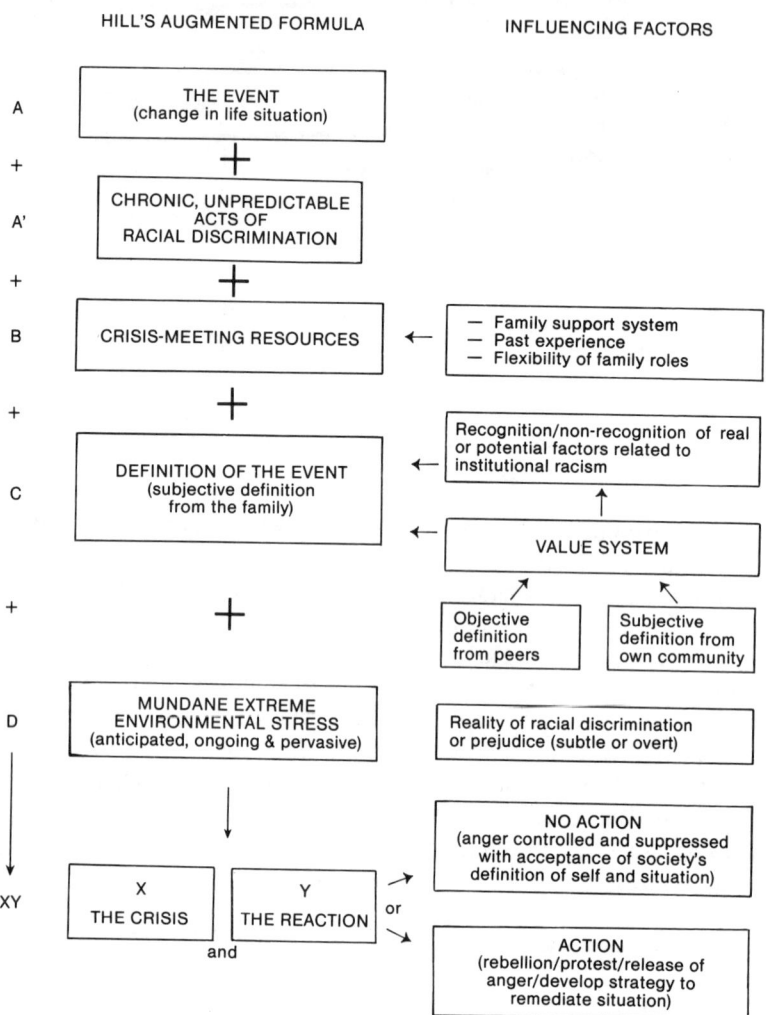

Figure 3. Formula for conceptualization of family crisis appropriate for Black American families

in which "the Black family structure and functions serve to support its members in their dealings with an overtly hostile and racist wider society" (p. 181). This has led to studies of Black family life from an ecological perspective wherein Black families are viewed as viable, functional, and interacting within a Black community encapsulated within American mainstream society (Aschenbrenner, 1975; Davison, 1978; Gay, 1975; Martin & Martin, 1978; McAdoo, 1978; Peters, 1976; Stack, 1974). Researchers have described Black family life and identified coping strategies which have allowed their survival in the given environment of MEES. This approach assumes that most Black families have developed patterns of behaviors and childrearing attitudes and practices which are appropriate to the values and constraints within their own lives. It assumes that Black parents, too, are competent, and it attempts to identify the strength, creativity, and resourcefulness Black families have found to be necessary to maintain family life and survive the "American system."

As mentioned above, a number of researchers have examined the extended family system in Black families from a functional perspective. Viewed as a resource for families whose vulnerable position in society is due to unequal access to jobs, housing, medical care, and education, the Black extended family has been shown to be a survival strategy (Hill, 1972; McAdoo, 1978; Peters, 1976; Stack, 1974) and a vehicle for upward mobility (McAdoo, 1978) as well as a culturally approved way of life (Shimkin, Shimkin, & Frate, 1978). The research of McAdoo (1980) which compared the patterns of kin-help/support systems of low-income urban Black families with middle-income suburban Black families found that in this sample population, the content of the support often varied, depending on individual family circumstances. Patterns of interaction, contact, and of mutual aid were evident in both low-income and middle-income groups and Black family structures were seen to function as stress absorbing entities.

Black parents attempt to buffer the negative messages which may be transmitted to their children from a society which perpetrates stereotypic images about Black people (McAdoo, 1980; Ogbu, 1977; Scanzoni, 1971). Evidence that parents are successful has been dramatically demonstrated in studies assessing the self-esteem of Blacks. As pointed out by Taylor (1976) in his comprehensive evaluation of studies of Black self-esteem, most Blacks, despite pervasive myths to the contrary, have "high levels of self-esteem," especially if they have been raised in the Black community and have attended predominately Black schools (Massey & Dornbusch, 1975). Few studies have explored specifically how families cope with the stress and strain of racism in their lives, although the influence and effects of MEES emerge in any ecologically based research study (e.g., McAdoo, 1978, 1980; Peters, 1976; Shimkin et al., 1978; Stack, 1974). Peters (1976) examined coping strategies and attitudes of Black parents concerning racial identity and racially motivated incidents. Parents were asked to respond to hypothetical stories of situations involving children and race. Then parents were asked what they thought about how a parent or teacher handled a situation when, for example, a child asked a question about racial differences or when a child was the recipient of a racist slur or racist act. Interesting answers were obtained which indicated that children are aware of racial identity at an early age—often, by age four or five. The parents in Peters' study (1976) fully expected their children to encounter racial discrimination or prejudice "some day," but most wanted to avoid this "brutal awakening" as long as possible. Some felt that it was impossible to prepare a child for the future rebuffs or rejections he/she would experience. Others felt that there was danger in overpreparing a child because a child might become unnecessarily self-conscious about race.

This exploratory research suggests the richness of this area of family dynamics and indicates the potential for better understanding of the ecology of Black life and the growth and development of children.

FAMILY SOCIALIZATION AND THE YOUNG BLACK CHILD: TIES

Preliminary data from an ongoing longitudinal study of Black children and their families, called the Toddler Infant Experiences Study—TIES (Peters & Massey, 1981), allows for analysis of Black family processes and child socialization under conditions of MEES. This research is a descriptive, developmental study of Black children during the years of one to three; the childrearing behaviors, attitudes, and values of their parents; and their family environments.

The data consist of observational records, interviews, questionnaires, test results, and videotapes of parent-child interaction which provide a rich picture of how Black children develop socially, intellectually, emotionally, and physically as they interact with their parents or other caregivers. The data provide many examples of parental behaviors or attitudes which are examples of the cultural values described in the literature as characteristic of Black families. These values and behaviors, summarized in Tables 1 and 2, are

Table 1

CULTURAL SPECIFIC VALUES SHARED BY AFRO-AMERICAN FAMILIES

AREA	CULTURAL SPECIFIC VALUES	REFERENCE
DISCIPLINE	Strict discipline appreciated; Situation-specific discipline considered appropriate.	Peters (1976); Young (1970)
PERCEPTION OF CHILDREN	Value child, essentially for who he/she is; i.e., child of this family; Encouragement of "individualistic" personality within the primary group	Bossard and Boll (1960); Young (1970)
EXPECTATIONS RE AGE/SEX APPROPRIATE CHORES AND RESPONSIBILITIES	Responsibility training (self-care, help with housework) required earlier. Less distinction made in assigning tasks to boys and girls.	Lewis (1975); Peters (1976)
FAMILY ROLES	Role flexibility within family; Sharing both income-producing and household, child care and financial mangagement responsibilities	Hill (1972); Peters (1976); Willie (1976)
EXTENDED FAMILY	Preference for Black community; Preference for extensive and active kin/friend support system	Nobles (1976); Stack (1974)
RACE/ RACISM	Awareness of dual identity; i.e., both American and Black American; Awareness of the routine, pervasive nature of racism as well as of its potential for producing major, unpredictable crises disrupting the lives of the family, community or the larger society.	Knowles and Prewitt (1969); Pierce (1975)

viewed as functional, survival strategies which can serve either as a vehicle for stress reduction or which can be seen as examples of the cultural heritage of Black families.

In this section, we would like to highlight three of these cultural values, using findings from the TIES data, which are characteristic of how Black parents manage MEES in their lives. The selected values are: (a) approaches to discipline; (b) extended family network systems; and, (c) the impact of racial identity. These three areas are closely related and recent research has suggested that discipline techniques and extended family support systems have developed, in part at least, as a Black family's coping strategy for handling the stresses and strains of racism and discrimination (Gay, 1975; Nobles, 1976; Peters, 1976; Pierce, 1975; Young, 1970).

Table 2

SPECIAL QUALITIES/BEHAVIORS TOWARD WHICH BLACK
CHILDREN ARE SOCIALIZED

EMPHASIS ON:

1. Allowing both males and females to express emotions such as affection, anger, jealousy, hate, love, fear, happiness, unhappiness
(Gay, 1975; Nobles, 1974; Peters, 1976)

2. Importance of sharing
Importance of working on chore or task collaboratively with others
Expecting help from others
(Gay, 1975; Nobles, 1974)

3. Humanistic orientation:
   solving human problems
   working with/for people
   jobs involving people preferred to technical jobs
   high value on getting along with others
(Abrahams, 1970; Gay, 1975; Nobles, 1974)

4. Respect for authority figures
Importance of following orders
(Gay, 1975; Kohn, 1977; Peters, 1976)

5. High value placed on variety of responses, abilities and talents:
   physical/motoric/rhythmic/
   musical/athletic/body movement/
   verbal/social
(Abrahams, 1970; Gay, 1975; Gay and Abrahams, 1972; Peters, 1976)

6. High development of skills for oral transmission of information
(Abrahams and Gay, 1972)

7. Open receptivity to multiple environmental stimuli:
   dual attention ability
(Gay, 1974; Pierce, 1975)

Approaches to Discipline

Past studies have found Black parents to be very discipline-oriented (Brophy, 1970; Clarke-Stewart, 1973; Hess & Shipman, 1965; Peters, 1976). Too often, descriptors such as harsh, overcontrolled, punitive, etc., have been used to categorize Black parents and caregivers without a basic understanding of what discipline means and why strict discipline is valued in these families. In general, parents in TIES appear to vary widely in their use of discipline. Some are quite strict with the infant or toddler and much of the conversation between a parent and a one year-old may consist of a series of very firm orders. Other parents prefer to discipline or control behavior by distracting the child or by removing him/her from too inquisitive investigations. Some parents do teach their young children how to handle expensive or valuable objects in the home, such as stereo or recording equipment, whereas other parents prefer to remove valuable, breakable objects.

Findings regarding control and discipline issues as seen in parent-child interactions during a child's second year of life generally support a hypothesis that obedience and respect are highly valued. Discipline and respect can be viewed in many ways. It may represent a strong sense of respect for elders which can be traced to a basic African tradition. It may represent a desire to maintain control in one's home environment where there is little control of the external environment. It may even be an avenue of stress reduction for the parent. What is important to note, however, is that discipline cannot be viewed in isolation and vacuous comparison to White family styles of discipline is problematic and misleading.

Extended Family (Kin/Friend) Network

The study families, although nuclear, are nevertheless found to be embedded within a larger family system. Kinship bonds appear to be very strong and stable.

Day-to-day management of the household and care of children is made easier, these families say, by having relatives nearby who can and do help out once in a while. Many mothers indicated that when they have a problem, whether financial or personal, they can and do talk to a family member about it. Having relatives near gives them a place to visit where they know their children are welcome and where there are other children they can play with. The extended family/friend support network appears to provide stability and a necessary resource and support for families whose needs are constantly changing. However, the network has its price, as well as its disadvantages. This is seen in the relationships demanded by the support network. For example, some parents in our study still were expected to assume responsibility for their younger siblings, or were still treated as dependent children by their mothers.

Since many of these families live in the same community as their own parents, grandparents are a babysitting resource they use. Children are often cared for by grandmothers, either in the child's own home or in the home of the grandparent. The flexibility necessitated by split shifts, and ever changing circumstances (such as temporary scheduling changes on a job, lay-offs, overtime demands, and the need to take a job whenever one becomes available) is maintained by the parents in this study because of the back-up support of their own parents or other kin.

Single parents especially benefit from the accessibility of the extended family. Mothers have, when necessary, moved into their parents' home with their children in emergency situations, such as during a temporary or permanent rift between spouses, or a change in residence.

Racial Awareness

A third major area of interest is the impact of racial identity on parents and children. TIES families are very aware that they are Black and the significance of this is of deep concern to many of the parents.

There seems to be a strong desire on the part of some of the parents to teach their children that they are Black and that being Black is a positive attribute, something of which to be proud. For example, in many homes, Black dolls or picture books showing Black people were very much in evidence.

The knowledge that in America there is a pervasive negative stigma attached to being Black motivates some parents to emphasize Black identity, to teach children to respect, understand, and accept themselves as Black. These parents felt that they have a dual task: to give their children a positive Black identity and to teach children how to cope in an outside hostile environment.

At the same time, many of these parents discussed how they had suffered racial discrimination in their lives and how they thought racism would affect (or not affect) their children. A number of parents felt it necessary to prepare a child to deal with a racist system, to deal with both individual racism and institutional racism. Many viewed their children as victims or potential victims of racism (e.g., being called a "nigger"), especially when the child starts school.

A parent summed it up by saying:

> Being Black causes problems and kids will be subject to discrimination. It hurts them because they can't see a way out. They don't think they're ever going to get a decent job when

they get out of school—you know, a decent paying job. And it just makes them put themselves down. It makes them turn to drugs and other criminal activities. And then that way they keep institutionalized!''

Some parents felt that being Black did not bring an added stress into the lives of their children. Their reasons gave us insightful glimpses into the kind of preparation Black parents, consciously or unconsciously, give their young children for handling the negative consequences of being Black. For example, one mother in explaining why she felt that being Black was not stressful said:

It all depends on how you bring up the child, really. If you show your children how to handle someone calling her a nigger, for instance—she's not a nigger so why should anyone call her that? So, if a parent does that and lets the child handle the situation, then there's no special stress. You know, children take care of these things better than you can, sometimes, so there's no point worrying about it.

This example illustrates how the stress of racism is such a normal part of the everyday life of Black people that some do not view discrimination, prejudice, or institutionalized racism as a special or added stress, but as a normal part of everyday living and not worth worrying about. Most mainstream Americans are not faced with this kind of problem.

APPLYING THE ABCDYX MODEL: A CASE EXAMPLE

In this concluding section, analysis of Black family stress and coping, using Hill's augmented formula (Figure 3), will be applied to a specific case situation drawn from the TIES sample. Identifying details have been altered to protect the anonymity of the respondents.

A. The Events(s)

1. Job hassles and major and minor intrigues caused Ms. Stevenson to come to dislike her promotion, to realize that the deep-rooted general resentments of her co-workers at having a Black female supervisor could not be ameliorated, and finally, she have her notice

[in spite of the anticipated financial hardships since this occurred at a time when she and her male partner (the father of her two children and co-habitant) had separated again].

2. Although she was now experienced in her work and also possessed a favorable recommendation from her superior, and although comparable jobs were available in her city, Ms. Stevenson found her unemployment checks running out with no viable job prospects in sight for her.

B. Crises-Meeting Resources

1. Partner: Ms. Stevenson, her partner, and their two children, a boy and a girl, have lived together intermittently for the past five years. When sharing an apartment, the parents, both of whom have been usually employed, pool their incomes. When the father moves away, as he has done several times, he keeps in close touch with the children, ages 2 and 4, often keeps them overnight, on weekends, or comes to visit. He now provides financial support on a "request" basis.

2. Mother: Ms. Stevenson's mother is widowed and lives in a two-story home with her four younger children, ages 6 to 16. Ms. Stevenson is close to her younger siblings, whom she helped raise, and to her mother who has always worked. In times of past financial crises, Ms. Stevenson has easily moved into her mother's house where she is welcomed, in spite of the overcrowding, because her mother strongly dislikes her daughter's partner and his family. Moving back to mother allows Ms. Stevenson to save on food, rent, and also provides babysitting resources as she seeks or goes to work on a job. Ms. Stevenson has moved back home several times in the past and she understands the value of this support and the flexibility allowed her. She has also experienced the consequences of this arrangement: decreased autonomy and privacy, some conflict between her and her mother in discipline of her children, and most importantly, as an upwardly mobile, intelligent, and ambitious young woman attempting to provide her own children wider opportunities and experiences than she has had, the move back home is viewed as a necessary but unwanted backward step.

3. Work/Family Roles: Ms. Stevenson has been in and out of the job market throughout high school, through two pregnancies and the infancy of two children. At various times she has worked part-time, full-time, nights, days, and on variable schedules. Although em-

ployed, she has maintained a home for her male partner and their children, arranged for baby-sitting services, and with her children and partner has been actively involved, socially, with her partner's parents and his adult siblings and their children. Responsibilities and patterns of living have changed, but in the past, role flexibility has allowed her, she believes, to maintain a stable life for her children.

C. Definition of the Event

1. Ms. Stevenson considers her current unemployed status and inability to obtain advertised jobs for which she has experience and training to be caused by racial prejudice and discrimination in the employment market, both against Blacks and against women.

2. Ms. Stevenson's family and friends share her opinions, offer her support and encouragement, and share with her their own similar job-related experiences and survival strategies. "It's the name of the game," they say.

D. Mundane Extreme Environmental Stress

1. The experiences of Ms. Stevenson are the realities of the job world for Black people. Racial oppression and real or potential job discrimination are factors which must be recognized as inherent in the economic sector of American society (Ogbu, 1977; Pierce, 1969; Williams, 1979). This means that coping strategies appropriate for Ms. Stevenson's situation are developed within this perspective.

Produces X. (The Crisis)

1. Loss of breadwinner's job
2. Family forced to move from own apartment into child's maternal grandmother's home

And Y. (The Reaction)

1. Ms. Stevenson's response to (a) being out of a job and (b) to moving in with her mother involved both No Action and Action.

No Action response: The unfair racist undertones which resulted in Ms. Stevenson's resigning from her job were not challenged by her in any way. She did not take her complaints to higher authorities within the business in which she worked, nor did she ask for help from a community action group or other organization which monitors unfair, racially motivated situations.

Action response: At the same time, Ms. Stevenson (a) complained to her estranged partner and to her family and friends (and to us) about the many subtle personal detractions and non-cooperative acts of her associates on her job, thus releasing some of her anger and frustrations and (b) began to remedy her situation. The latter involved, as described above, her giving up her apartment to save on expenses and moving in with her mother. While job hunting (she has finally obtained a job), she contacted a government agency which assists low-income families in obtaining mortgages to buy inner-city homes, located a small house, livable, but in some need of repair, bought it and has subsequently with her two children moved into her own home.

This example illustrates the relevance of inserting the factors of real or potential institutional racism and MEES into Hill's formula for analysis of stress and crisis situations in Black families. This enables us to better understand the underlying dynamics of the situation: (a) job expectations are muted, thus tempering the effect of job performance on an individual's self-esteem; (b) the combination of family/friend understanding and support through a difficult time fortifies a parent's coping strategies; and (c) the acceptance of the realities of MEES and the support systems maintained by the Black family and community.

This example also illustrates how American society is in reality a caste-class system with a ceiling on upward mobility which only a relatively few fortunate Blacks are able to penetrate (Billingsley, 1968; Ogbu, 1977; Williams, 1979). Ogbu's research graphically demonstrates how families through their own experiences and in their socialization and childrearing behaviors and attitudes are subtly forced to cooperate with our oppressive caste-class system in order to survive. Data from the parent interviews of the TIES study appear to support Ogbu's findings.

These kinds of observational and interview data of family behavior and interaction allow us to analyze and refine our concepts of stress and coping in the context of mundane environmental stress. While much more research and theoretical discussion are needed, this is the kind of information that will prove useful for developing social policies and programs for families in this minority group.

NOTES

1. Chester Pierce, a psychiatrist and professor, Medical School, Harvard University and Harvard University Graduate School of Education, has written and lectured widely on the mundane, extreme environment and its effect on learning. According to Pierce, the characteristics of an extreme environment include the following: forced socializing, spatial isolation, time elasticity, biological dysrythmia, sociological dysrythmia, increased free time, noise/silence extremes, loneliness, fears of abandonment, anxiety panic, and inability to escape. He emphasized the need for research which would provide careful descriptions of Black populations—their behaviors, attitudes, and coping strategies.

2. It is such factors as traditional employment practices of business and industry, sales practices of real estate agencies, and "red-lining" practices of banks that have influenced the segregated residential school systems, which in turn result in Blacks being disadvantaged in the job market.

3. In 1979, California Federal District Court Judge Robert Peckham handed down a long-awaited decision, *Larry P. vs. Riles,* which stated that IQ tests "are racially and culturally biased, have a discriminating impact on Black children and have not been validated for the purpose of (consigning) Black children into educationally dead-end isolated and stigmatizing classes." This case resulted in a permanent moratorium on using IQ testing in California for placement of "educable mentally retarded" students.

REFERENCES

Abrahams, R. D. *Deep down in the jungle.* Chicago, IL: Aldine, 1970.

Abrahams, T. D., & Gay, G. Talking Black in the classroom. In R. D. Abrahams & C. Troike (Eds.), *Language and cultural diversity in American education.* Englewood Cliffs, NJ: Prentice Hall, 1972.

Aschenbrenner, S. *Lifelines: Black families in Chicago.* New York: Holt, Rinehart & Winston, 1972.

Barnes, E. J. The Black community as the source of positive self-concept for Black children: A theoretical perspective. In R. L. Jones (Ed.) *Black psychology.* New York: Harper & Row, 1972.

Bernard, J. *Marriage and family among Negroes.* Englewood Cliffs, NJ: Prentice-Hall, 1966.

Billingsley, A. *Black families in White America.* Englewood Cliffs, NJ: Prentice-Hall, 1968.

Blauner, T. Internal colonialism and ghetto revolt. In M. Westheimer (Ed.), *Confrontation.* Glenview, IL: Scott, Foresman & Company, 1970.

Blauner, R. *Racial oppression in America.* New York: Harper & Row, 1972.

Boss, P., McCubbin, H. I., & Lester, G. The corporate wife's coping patterns in response to routine husband-father absence: Implications for family stress theory. *Family Process,* 1979, *18,* 79-86.

Bossard, J., & Boll, E. *The sociology of child development* (3rd edition). New York: Harper Bros., 1960.

Boykin, A. W. Black psychology and the research process: Keeping the baby but throwing out the bath water. In A. W. Boykin, A. J. Franklin, & J. F. Yates (Eds.), *Research directions of Black psychologists.* New York: Russell Sage Foundation, 1979.

Brophy, J. E. Mothers as teachers of their own preschool children: The influence of socioeconomic status and task structure on teaching specificity. *Child Development,* 1970, *41,* 79-94.

Carew, J. The care of young children: Some problems with research assumptions, methods and findings. In Stevens, Joseph & Mathews, (Eds.), *Mother/child father/child relation-*

ships. Washington, DC: National Association for the education of young children, 1978.
Carnoy, M. (ed), *Schooling in a corporate society: The political economy of education in America.* New York: David McKay Company, 1972.
Carmichael, S., & Hamilton, C. *Black power.* New York: Vintage Books, 1967.
Clark, K. B. (Ed.). *Racism and American education: A dialogue and agenda for action.* New York: Harper & Row, 1970.
Clarke-Stewart, K. A. Interactions between mothers and their young children: Characteristics and consequences. *Monographs of the society for research in child development,* 1972, *38,* 6-7.
Cruse, H. *Rebellion or revolution.* New York: William Morrow & Company, 1968.
Daniel, J. *A definition of fatherhood as expressed by Black fathers.* Ann Arbor, MI: Xerox University Microfilms, 1975.
Davison, J. *National day care home study: Parent study component—Preliminary report.* Washington, DC: Department of Health, Education & Welfare, 1978. (Contract Number 105-77-1051.)
Drews, E., & Teahan, J. Parental attitudes and academic achievement. *Journal of clinical psychology,* 1957, *13,* 328-332.
Gay, G. Cultural difference important in the education of Black children. *Momentum,* October, 1972, 30-33.
Gay, G., & Abrahams, R. D. Black culture in the classroom. In R. D. Abrahams & R. C. Troike, (Eds.), *Language and cultural diversity in American education.* Englewood Cliffs, NJ: Prentice-Hall, 1972.
Geiger, K. Deprivation and solidarity in the Soviet urban family. *American Sociological Review,* 1955, *XX,* 57-68.
Gibson, F., & Yeager, S. Trends in the federal employment of Blacks. *Public Personnel Management,* 1975, *4,* 189-195.
Hale, J. *Black children: Their roots, culture and learning styles.* Paper presented at annual conference of the National Association for the Education of Young Children, Atlanta, Georgia, 1979.
Harrisson, R. P., & Wyden, B. *The Black child.* New York: Columbia University Press, 1973.
Heiss, J. *The case of the Black family.* New York: Columbia University Press, 1975.
Hess, R., & Shipman, V. Early experience and the cognitive modes in children. *Child Development,* 1965, *36,* 869-886.
Hill, R. Social stresses on the family. In M. B. Sussman (Ed.), *Sourcebook on marriage and the family.* Boston: Houghton, Mifflin, 1963.
Hill, R. B. *The strengths of Black families.* New York: Emerson Hall Publishers, 1972.
Katz, M. B. *Class bureaucracy and the schools: The illusion of educational change.* New York: Praeger, 1972.
Knowles, L. L., & Prewitt, K. *Institutional racism in America.* Englewood Cliffs, NJ: Prentice-Hall, 1969.
Kohn, M. *Class and conformity* (2nd edition). Chicago: University of Chicago Press, 1977.
Koos, G. L. Class differences in family reactions to crises. *Marriage and Family Living,* 1950, *XII,* 77-78.
Lewis, D. The Black family: Socialization and sex roles. *Phylon,* 1975, *36,* 221-237.
Longfellow, C. *Social support and mother-child interactions.* Unpublished doctoral dissertation. Harvard University, Graduate School of Education, 1979.
Martin, E., & Martin, J. *The Black extended family.* Chicago: University of Chicago Press, 1978.
Mathis, A. *Social and psychological characteristics of the Black liberation movement: A colonial analogy.* Unpublished doctoral dissertation. University of Michigan, 1971.
Mathis, A. Contrasting approaches to the study of Black families. *Journal of Marriage and the Family,* 1978, *40,* 667-676.

Massey, G., Scott, M., & Dornbusch, S. Racism without racists: Institutional racism in urban schools. *The Black Scholar*, 1975, *7*, 3.

McAdoo, H. P. Factors related to upward mobility in Black families. *Journal of Marriage and the Family*, 1978, *40*, 761-768.

McAdoo, H. P. *Stress absorbing systems in Black families.* Paper presented at 1980 Groves Conference on Marriage and the Family, 1980.

McCubbin, H. I., Dahl, B., Lester, G., Benson, D., & Robertson, M. Coping repertories of families adapting to prolonged war-induced separations. *Journal of Marriage and the Family*, 1976, *38*, 461-471.

Moynihan, D. P. *The negro family: A case for national action.* Washington, DC: U.S. Government Printing Office, 1965.

Myers, H. F. *Cognitive appraisal, stress, coping and Black health: The politics of options and contingencies.* Los Angeles, CA: Fanon R and D Center, Charles R. Drew Postgraduate Medical School, 1977.

National Black Child Development Institute (NBCDI). *The status of Black children in 1980.* Washington, DC: National Black Child Development Institute, 1980.

Nobles, W. W. Africanity: Its role in Black families. *The Black Scholar*, 1974, *5*, 10-17.

Nobles, W. W. *A formulative and empirical study of Black families.* Report submitted to United States Department of Health, Education, and Welfare, Office of Child Development (Contract 90-C-255), December 1976.

Nobles, W. W., & Goddard, L. Consciousness, adaptability, and coping strategies: Socioeconomic characteristics and ecological issues in Black families. *Western Journal of Black Studies*, 1977, *1*, 105-113.

Ogbu, J. U. *The next generation.* New York: Academic Press, 1974.

Ogbu, J. U. Racial stratification and education. *IRCD Bulletin*, 1977, *XII*, 3.

Peters, M. F. *Nine Black families: A study of household management and childrearing in Black families with working mothers.* Ann Arbor, MI: University Microfilms, 1976.

Peters, M. F. Notes from a guest editor. *Journal of Marriage and the Family*, 1978, *40*, 655-658.

Pierce, C. *The effects of racism.* Paper presented at AMA 15th Annual Conference of State Mental Health Representatives, Chicago, Illinois, 1969.

Pierce, C. The mundane extreme environment and its effect on learning. In S. G. Brainard (Ed.), *Learning disabilities: Issues and recommendations for research.* Washington, DC: National Institute of Education, 1975.

Powell, G. *Black Monday's children: A study of the effects of school desegregation on self-concepts of southern children.* New York: Appleton-Century-Crofts, 1973.

Reiss, D., & Olivieri, M. E. Family paradigm and family coping: A proposal for linking the family's intrinsic adaptive capacities to its responses to stress. *Family Relations*, 1980, *29*, 443.

Renne, K. Correlation of dissatisfaction in marriage. *Journal of Marriage and the Family*, 1970, *32*, 54-67.

Scanzoni, J. *The Black family in modern society.* Boston, MA: Allyn & Bacon, 1971.

Shelsky, H. *Wandlunger in der deutschen Familien in der Gegenwart.* Stuttgart: Enke-Verlag, 1954.

Shimkin, D., Shimkin, E., & Frate, D. (Eds.), *The extended family in Black societies.* The Hague: Mouton Publishers, 1978.

Stack, C. B. *All our kin: Strategies for survival in a Black community.* New York: Harper & Row, 1974.

Staples, R. *Introduction to Black sociology.* New York: McGraw-Hill, 1976.

Taylor, R. Black youth and psychological development. Journal of Black Studies, 1976, *6*, 353-372.

U.S. Bureau of the Census. *The social and economic status of the Black population of the United States.* Current Population Reports. Special Studies. Series P-23, Number 80, 1978.

Williams, J. D. (Ed.), *The state of Black America 1979*. Washington, DC: National Urban League, 1979.
Willie, C. V. *A new look at Black families*. Bayside, NY: General Hall, Inc., 1976.
Woodson, C. G. *The miseducation of the negro*. Washington, DC: Associated Publishers, 1969.
Young, V. Family and childhood in a southern negro community. *American Anthropologist,* 1970, *72,* 269-288.

Chapter 10

Analytic Essay: Family Stress and Bereavement

Kris Jeter

Stress and death are connected through the processes of bereavement, grief, and mourning. This essay focuses on books which explain the stress survivors experience when a family member dies. First, definitions and derivations of common terms are provided. Then, eight recently published books on bereavement are discussed and interrelated into a family stress framework suggested by McCubbin, Cauble, and Patterson (1982).

The word bereavement is derived from the French word *reafian,* meaning rob (Barnhart, 1964). The bereaved are deprived ruthlessly and violently of hope. Bereavement behavior is the total physiological and psychological response displayed by a person facing a loss. The word grief is derived from the Latin word *gravare,* which means to weigh down (Barnhart, 1964). Grief is a collection of biologically derived physiological reactions to loss. The phrases of death grief are shock; disorganization; denial which may be searching behavior; desolate pining; despair; guilt; anxiety; jealousy; shame; protest; aggression; letting go; resolution and acceptance; and reintegration (Ramsay & Noorbergen, 1981, p. 66). The word mourning is derived from the Latin word *memor,* meaning mindful (Neilson, 1953). Mourning is a socially dictated, psychologically healthy, conventional behavior to express grief. As the ancients, people today surviving the death of a family member do feel robbed, weighted down, and are mindful of the past, knowing that life will never be the same.

Dutch behavioral psychologist Ronald W. Ramsay and professional writer Rene Noorbergen discuss survivors' stress in their

1981 book *Living with Loss.* Death, especially a sudden one, precipitates bereavement and motivates the body's defense system to respond. Ramsay and Noorbergen relate data compiled by Beverly Raphael. The occurrence of death for a surviving spouse in the year following the bereavement may be ten times the normal rate and for a close relative five times the normal rate. If the death does not occur at home, the survivor's risk for death increases two to five times (Ramsay & Noorbergen, 1981, p. 35).

Ramsay and Noorbergen then present a description and a transcription of Guided Confrontation Therapy. Ramsay has used Guided Confrontation Therapy to work with a woman severely grieved about the deaths of her mother, father, and daughter. Excerpts from the initial interview and six therapy sessions featured on CBS's "60 Minutes" in 1976 are provided. Guided Confrontation Therapy clients enter a therapy contract; share their feelings about the death; disclose hidden negative memories; admit that the death has occurred; converse with an image of the dead person; accept without pain reminders of that person; say "goodbye" to that person; and then start a new life. Guided Confrontation Therapy has been used with clients facing losses other than death, such as accidents, bankruptcy, divorce, loss of home country, rape, and surgery (Ramsay & Noorbergen, 1981).

Ellen B. Berlinsky, as a psychotherapist, has studied a clientele whose parents died during childhood. Psychologist Henry B. Biller personally experienced the loss of his father and grandfather as a child and his mother as a young adult. Their highly motivated professional concerns are voiced in the volume *Parental Death and Psychological Development.* In 1978, 1.4 percent of the population under eighteen years of age had lost a mother through death and 3.5 percent a father (Berlinsky & Biller, 1982, p. 1). The authors organize 193 pieces of literature into a multidimensional framework and conceptual model to determine the existence, nature, and source of immediate and long-term differences between individuals who experience the death of a parent during childhood and individuals who do not lose a parent through death while a child.

Oversimplification appears to be the primary criticism of research on this topic to date. Such work could be strengthened by addressing behavioral correlates, developmental stages, potential benefits, and time variables and by adhering to scientific procedures. The ideal research would be a longitudinal study with a large sample assessing children before and after a parent's death.

Literature on intervention tends to propose treatment approaches rather than documenting treatment outcomes.

Berlinsky and Biller recommend that the child needs accurate cognitive information regarding dying and death and permission to discuss feelings about her or his self and the deceased and surviving parents. Emotions expressed range from anger for abandonment, desire to please the remaining parent, guilt, inability to control life, personal vulnerability (especially from genetically linked illness), regrets, and responsibility for the death. Preventive therapy would be death education with the intention to lessen anxiety and reduce the mystery about death (Berlinsky & Biller, 1982).

Education professor Joanne E. Bernstein provides a valuable resource for death education. In *Books to Help Children Cope with Separation and Loss,* Bernstein discusses the concepts of separation, loss, and bibliotherapy. She recommends references for adults teaching children about losses ranging from adoption to death, divorce, foster care, illness, newness, and stepparents. Bernstein's guide consists of 438 children's books about loss—some classic and most published between 1970 and 1976. Entries contain basic findings, ordering, and bibliographic data; a critical annotation; interest area; and reading grade range. These books are cross indexed according to author, interest area, reading level, subject, and title (Bernstein, 1977).

Ramsay and other therapists suggest the need to disclose feelings in order to work through bereavement. Personal storytelling is one form of disclosure and is lauded in Bernstein's critical annotations. Alice Bloch, professional writer, provides a narrative which transcends facts and favors emotional sharing. She chronicles in diary, memory, and poetry form her life from 1972 to 1980 in *Lifetime Guarantee: A Journey Through Loss and Survival.* During the time her aunt, father, and sister, Barbara, died of chronic diseases, Bloch broke up with her first lover and moved across the United States and began a second relationship. Bloch during this period told others in black humor that she would take the longevity record for her family. She writes: "Each separation makes my life riskier, more precarious, more adventurous. With each loss, I gain some freedom. I don't want to lose everything. I don't want total freedom" (Bloch, 1981, p. 126).

Bloch was the oldest of three brothers and one sister. When she was nine and Barbara was three, their mother died. Within her family, she felt responsible for the death. Bloch became half child, half parent to her sister. Her mother's death brought drama to the lives of her classmates. Without a mother, she was stigmatized by other children and experienced shame. While writing this book at the age of 33, the actual event of her mother's death, in 1956, lies hidden under associations, emotions, and lies.

With relatives fighting to live, Bloch becomes the "maiden aunt"— available to be with the family during crises (Bloch, 1981, p. 18). Bloch represses feelings, experiences incessant body aches, and creates and shatters visions. Every night she dreams of saving Barbara from death.

Bloch writes that Barbara left "a collection of seashells, several pads of drawings and notes, a jack-in-the-box for my dresser, an elephant teapot with elephant-foot cups, some of her imagination and spunk, a huge wad of grief, a hole in my life where she had been, and an unfinished project: an article we had planned to write together, describing our experiences during her illness" (Bloch, 1981, p. ix). Writing, accepting, and incorporating her sister's creative spirit has kept Bloch alive. The precise vividness of the memories fade. Bloch relaxes into strength and endures. "The only guarantees—and I learned this from Barbara—are that we can be alive until we die, and that something of our bond with each other can endure. We are guaranteed a whole lifetime, whatever its length" (Bloch, 1981, p. 131).

Two stories with believable quality and telling of the enduring bond are written especially for bereaving young children. Leo Buscaglia, who has authored popular personal insight books, has written, in 1982, *The Fall of Freddie the Leaf.* He extends his concept of love to envelop the entire life span including death. Freddie and other leaves on the tree experience the four seasons, falling to rest on the winter snow. The life cycle of the leaf affects the life cycle of the tree and the forest. Likewise, the life cycle of a human affects the course of history (Buscaglia, 1982).

Buscaglia's Freddie the Leaf follows in the steps of Judith Viorst's Barney the Cat. Her 1971 volume, *The Tenth Good Thing about Barney,* has remained a popular book for over a decade for children facing the loss of a friend, relative, or pet. The story is told in first person by a child whose cat has died. The child's mother suggests that the child think of ten good things about Barney. The tenth item thought of is Barney's, like Freddie's, ability to compost and enrich the earth (Viorst, 1971).

This concept of death influencing future life is explored by professional author Helen Epstein, who questions the effect of a historical event on the generation living at that time and on succeeding generations. Epstein's book is entitled *Children of the Holocaust: Conversations with Sons and Daughters of Survivors.* Epstein, herself a daughter of parents who survived Nazi concentration camps, writes in an intimate style of her bearing "slippery, combustible things more secret than sex and more dangerous than a shadow or ghost . . . Whatever lived inside me was so potent that words crumbled before they could describe" (Epstein, 1979, p. 9).

Interwoven into her family's life experience are case studies and observations gleaned from over two hundred interviews with children of other Holocaust survivors. Survivors tended to marry quickly after release from concentration camps and to birth children whom they named after relatives who had not survived. The social circle included other Holocaust survivors and children intermarried within this group. The unspoken past highly affected children born to these marriages. Children expressed having anxious feelings, resentment, and a need to correct history's injustice. Epstein recommends that research be conducted on the relationship of history to successive generations of different family groups—Blacks, immigrants, and POWs, as well as survivors of disasters, such as Hiroshima (Epstein, 1979).

Rabbi Harold S. Kushner, father of a child who died of progeria (rapid aging) at age 14, analyzes the process occurring *When Bad Things Happen to Good People* and presents practical suggestions for grievers from his experience as a griever and a pastoral counselor. His sincerity in writing to people no matter their religious stance and in verbalizing with talk show hosts and audiences have made him and his book popular.

Kushner discusses the findings of Emile Durkheim, the French sociologist, who studied religion of the South Sea island natives. Durkheim was interested in the original purpose of religion before it was bureaucratized, formalized, and professionalized. He found that the primary purpose of early religion was to develop relationships between people themselves, rather than between people and God. Through religion, people could share joyous moments of birth, harvesting, marriage, planting, winter solstice, and the vernal equinox. Frightening periods of time, such as bereavement, would not be faced alone (Kushner, 1981, p. 119).

Using a Socratic teaching style, Kushner concludes that God does not cause or prevent tragedies, kill or cure people. God summons friends to lessen burdens and to fill voids. God inspires people to assist other people. Prayer lets people know that they are not alone and that they have hope, patience, and strength to renew themselves.

Response to grieving should be active presence, compassion, empathy, listening, and physical comforting rather than scolding and theological explanations. Grievers often feel guilt because of a personal and scientific belief in cause and effect. Children can be told that childhood death is unusual and not a punishment and be allowed to express their feelings. Upon examination, common sayings may be nonsensical. For instance, "God needs your friend more than you" and "God took your friend away" leads grievers to believe that the death is their fault and to direct resentment toward God. "In the final analysis, the question of why bad things happen to good people translates itself into some very different questions, no longer asking why something happened, but asking how we will respond, what we intend to do now that it has happened" (Kushner, 1981, p. 147). The "ability to forgive and the ability to love are the weapons God has given us to enable us to live fully, bravely, and meaningfully in this less-than-perfect world" (Kushner, 1981, p. 148).

In *Family Stress, Coping, and Social Support,* Editors Hamilton I. McCubbin, A. Elizabeth Cauble, and Joan M. Patterson present classic theory and research efforts and studies on normative and non-normative stress. Normative stress is caused by predictable developmental changes over the individual and family life cycle (McCubbin, Cauble, & Patterson, 1982; McCubbin & Figley, 1983). Non-normative stress is caused by unanticipated situational family experiences (McCubbin, Cauble, & Patterson, 1982; Figley & McCubbin, 1983). The four major areas of family stress research are the relationship between stress and illness, the stress caused by a dysfunctional family, the lack of stress experienced by some individuals and families, and the positive benefits of social support networks on stressed families (McCubbin, Cauble, & Patterson, 1982). Recent literature on bereavement, grief, and mourning tends to address directly or indirectly these family stress research areas.

REFERENCES

Barnhart, C. L., Editor. *The American college dictionary.* New York: Random House, 1964.
Berlinsky, E. B., and Biller, H. B. *Parental death and psychological development.* Lexington, Massachusetts: Lexington Books, 1982.

Bernstein, J. E. *Books to help children cope with separation and loss.* New York: R. R. Bowker Company, 1977.
Bloch, A. *Lifetime guarantee: A journey through loss and survival.* Watertown, Massachusetts: Persephone Press, Inc., 1981.
Buscaglia, L. F. *The fall of Freddie the leaf: A story of life for all ages.* Thorofare, New Jersey: Charles B. Slack, Inc., 1982.
Epstein, H. *Children of the Holocaust: Conversations with sons and daughters of survivors.* New York: G. P. Putnam's Sons, 1979.
Figley, C., and McCubbin, H. I. *Family and stress: Volume II—Catastrophic stress.* New York: Brunner Mazel, 1983.
Kushner, H. S. *When bad things happen to good people.* New York: Schocken Books, 1981.
McCubbin, H. I., Cauble, A. E., & Patterson, J. M., Editors. *Family Stress, Coping, and Social Support.* Springfield, Illinois: Charles C. Thomas, 1982.
McCubbin, H. I., & Figley, C. *Family and stress: Volume I—Normative transitions.* New York: Brunner Mazel: 1983.
Neilson, W. A., Editor. *Webster's new international dictionary of the English language.* Second Edition, Unabridged. Springfield, Massachusetts: G. and C. Merriam Company, Publishers, 1953.
Ramsay, R. W., & Noorbergen, R. *Living with loss.* New York: William Morrow and Company, Inc., 1981.
Viorst, J. *The tenth good thing about Barney.* New York: Atheneum, 1971.

Chapter 11

Researching Family Stress

Laura A. Shepard

As the sixth in a series of bibliographies, the following is a list of sources which can be consulted for references to research on stress and the family. To do extensive research on this subject one must not only consider the family as a unit, but also the particular family members (parents, children, adolescents), life stages (divorce, death, aging, sex role changes, marital conflict), and the particular problems that are faced by special (ethnic, low-income, single parent) families. Since it is impossible to cover all of the sources that might be helpful, depending on the particular variables of one's research, the emphasis of this review will be only on the narrow topic of stress within the family unit, with the understanding that most of the more specific topics can also be accessed through the same sources.

Indexes and abstracts list mostly periodical articles, although some of them also make reference to books and proceedings of professional meetings, as do the bibliographies. Many of the indexes are also available as databases, which can be especially helpful with researching a narrow topic. For more details on this service, see "Information Search Strategies: Cults and the Family," by Jonathan and Patricia Jeffrey (*Marriage and Family Review,* Volume 4, Number 4, Fall/Winter).

Encyclopedia articles are useful for definitions and classic literature in the field, whereas books can be used as an overview of the subject. The ones listed here were chosen for the reasons given, although there are others which are also significant—for a more comprehensive literature review, see "Family Stress and Coping: A

Laura A. Shepard is Associate Librarian, Reference Department, University of Delaware Library, Newark, DE.

Decade Review," by Hamilton I. McCubbin et al. (*Journal of Marriage and the Family,* Volume 42, Number 4, November 1980, pp. 855-871). The lists of tests and measurements will help to identify pertinent tools for measuring numerous aspects of family stress.

Suggested subject headings have been included as initial steps for doing research. When researching the more specific subjects, especially in the indexes that use keyword or title access, be sure to use as many synonyms as possible, i.e., stress, coping, crisis.

1. Indexes and Abstracts

Comprehensive Dissertation Index. Ann Arbor, MI: Xerox University Microfilms, 1973. Has annual supplements.
> Indexes *Dissertation Abstracts International.* See appropriate synonyms under the major headings "Health Sciences, General," "Psychology," "Social Work," and "Sociology."

Current Index to Journals in Education (CIJE). Publisher and frequency vary. 1969- .
> "Stress Variables"

Dissertation Abstracts International. Ann Arbor, MI: University Microfilms, 1938- . Published monthly.
> See appropriate synonyms.

Education Index. New York: Wilson, 1929- . Published monthly with annual cumulations.
> Good for the influence of stress on children. "Stress (Psychology)" is the best heading, although most of the citations deal with teacher burnout.

International Bibliography of Research in Marriage and the Family, 1900-1974. Minneapolis: Minnesota Family Study Center and the Institute of Life Insurance, 1967.
> Indexed by keywords from the titles of the articles. See appropriate synonyms.

Inventory of Marriage and Family Literature. Minneapolis: Minnesota Family Study Center and the Institute of Life Insurance, 1973- . Published annually.
> Supplements *International Bibliography of Research in Marriage and Family, 1900-1974.*

Psychological Abstracts. Lancaster, PA: American Psychological Association, 1927- . Published monthly.
> "Family Crises"

Readers' Guide to Periodical Literature. New York: Wilson, 1905– .
"Family," "Stress"

Resources in Education (formerly *Research in Education*). Publisher and frequency vary. 1975– .
"Stress Variables"

Sage Family Studies Abstracts. Beverly Hills, CA: Sage Publications, 1979– .
"Stress" includes citations that aren't specifically on the family as a group, but that are related to particular members, i.e., adolescents, parents, women.

Social Sciences Citation Index. Philadelphia: Institute for Scientific Information, 1966– . Published 4 times a year, with annual and quinquennial cumulations.
Pairs the significant words in the title of an article together with all other significant words in a title. See appropriate synonyms.

Social Sciences Index (formerly *Social Sciences and Humanities Index*). New York: Wilson, 1974– . Published quarterly, with annual cumulations.
"Stress (Psychology)" is the best heading, although it includes all types of psychological stress.

Sociological Abstracts. New York: Sociological Abstracts, 1952– . Published 6 times a year.
"Stress"

Social Work Research & Abstracts (formerly *Abstracts for Social Workers*). New York: National Association of Social Workers, 1977– . Published quarterly.
"Crisis," "Crisis Intervention," "Families (Family)," "Stress"

2. Bibliographies

Bibliographic Index; a cumulative bibliography of bibliographies. New York: Wilson, 1937– . Published monthly, with annual cumulations.
"Family"

International Bibliography of the Social Sciences: International Bibliography of Sociology. London: Tavistock Publications, 1952– . Published annually.
"Family"

3. Encyclopedias

Encyclopedia of Social Work. Washington, DC: National Association of Social Workers, 17th, 1977.
"Crisis Intervention," "Family," "Family Services"
International Encyclopedia of Psychiatry, Psychology, Psychoanalysis and Neurology. New York: Van Nostrand Reinhold, 1977.
"Coping Behavior," "Crisis," "Families," "Stress"
International Encyclopedia of the Social Sciences. David L. Sills, ed. New York: Macmillan and the Free Press, 1968.
There are several headings under "Family" which are appropriate. "Family Disorganization & Dissolution" has a section entitled "Methods & Research—Family Crisis."

4. Books

Glick, Ira D. et al. *Family Therapy and Research: An Annotated Bibliography of Articles, Books, Videotapes, and Films Published 1950-1979.* Second edition. New York: Grune & Stratton, 1982.
See Section 4.4, "Family Crisis Studies"
Mogey, John M. *Sociology of Marriage and Family Behavior, 1957-1968.* The Hague: Mouton, 1971.
International in scope, this bibliography includes several sections pertaining to family stress. See Section 500, "Special Problems," which is subdivided into such things as "Family Disorganization," "Family and Economic Stress," and "Family and Geographic Mobility."
Umana, Roseann F., Steven Jay Gross, and Marcia Turner McConville. *Crisis in the Family: Three Approaches.* New York: Gardner Press, 1980.
Written as a text, "this book examines the relationships among three major, popular movements in mental health: family crisis intervention, family therapy, and crisis intervention." Is good for an overview of the area. Includes a bibliography.
Wakefield, Rowan A., Catherine Allen, and Gail Washchuck, eds. *Family Research: A Source Book, Analysis and Guide to Federal Funding.* Westport, Connecticut: Greenwood Press, 1979.
The results from a survey "of family research supported extramurally by all the federal agencies" of the government are reported here. Eleven hundred abstracts of research being

funded during the 1976 government fiscal year are published in their entirety. See "Coping Behavior," "Crisis Intervention," and "Stress."

5. Tests and Measurements

Buros, Oscar Krisen, ed. *Mental Measurements Yearbook.* Highland Park, NJ: Gryphon, 8th, 1978.
Title and publisher varies.
──────. *Personality Tests and Reviews; Including an Index to the Mental Measurements Yearbooks.* Highland Park, NJ: Gryphon, 1970.
──────. *Tests in Print; a Comprehensive Bibliography of Tests For Use in Education, Psychology and Industry.* Highland Park, NJ: Gryphon, 1961.
Goldman, Bert A., and John L. Saunders. *Directory of Unpublished Experimental Mental Measures.* New York: Behavioral Publications, 1974– .
Supplements *Mental Measurements Yearbooks,* by including tests "not available commercially, using as sources those journals that carry studies and reports employing experimental instruments. The present volume is offered as the first in a series, this one based on the 1970 issues of 29 journals."